OASIS IDENTITIES

OASIS IDENTITIES

Uyghur Nationalism Along China's Silk Road

Justin Jon Rudelson

Columbia University Press   *New York*

Columbia University Press
Publishers Since 1893
New York   Chichester, West Sussex
Copyright © 1997 Columbia University Press
All rights reserved

Library of Congress Cataloging-in-Publication Data
Rudelson, Justin Jon.
    Oasis identities : Uyghur nationalism along China's Silk Road /
    Justin Jon Rudelson.
        p. cm.
    Includes bibliographical references and index.
    ISBN 0-231-10786-2. — ISBN 0-231-10787-0 (pbk.)
    1. Uighur (Turkic people)—History. 2. Sinkiang Uighur Autonomous
    Region (China)—Ethnic relations. I. Title.
    DS731.U4R84 1997
    305.8'009516—dc21   97-11066
                                                              CIP

Casebound editions of Columbia University Press books are printed
on permanent and durable acid-free paper.
Printed in the United States of America
c 10 9 8 7 6 5 4 3 2
p 10 9 8 7 6 5 4 3

*In memory of my father, Jerry Rudelson (1929–1971),
God's gift of love and laughter*

*Dedicated to my mother, Jody Rudelson,
who sweetens up life's lemon tree*

Contents

Illustrations

Photographs

Figures

Tables

Acknowledgments

And on that day you will know that
I, Uyghur, was right.
—"Uyghur," "Awaken! (*Oyghan*)"

My research on the Uyghurs of Xinjiang began in 1982 with the dream of connecting my own desert-dwelling people in Israel with the desert dwellers of Xinjiang, China. The ensuing struggle was guided by numerous mentors, teachers, and friends.

My deepest gratitude goes to Swedish anthropologist Ingvar Svanberg, who has been a rock of support as a mentor, friend, and model of what it means to be a scholar.

At Harvard University, my greatest debt goes to my principal adviser, Thomas Jefferson Barfield III, whose example in providing intellectual guidance, immediate comments, and massive amounts of time is an inspiration in my career. My other advisers, Kwang-chi Chang and Nur Yalman, enriched my understanding of the Uyghurs in a global context. I owe special thanks to James L. Watson for comments that provided the impetus for this book's organization.

Before recognizing the other colleagues whose contributions to this book are without number, I must acknowledge the teachers who in the Confucian tradition of great learning have given me wings and taught me how to be human: Hua-Yuan Li Mowry, Wayne Broehl, Robert Hendricks, Herbert T. Schmidt, Jr., and Louis L'Amour.

Many colleagues in the United States have graced this work with their input and advice, especially Kalman Applbaum, Ingrid Jordt, Lawrence

Cohen, Linda Hunt, Yan Yunxiang, Jonathan Lipman, Patrick O'Neill, Ilana Wistenetzki, James Millward, Michael Lambert, Linda Benson, Jun Jing, Jay Levi, Jay Dautcher, Gulamettin Pahta, Kahar Barat, Edward Allworth, and Morris Rossabi. Nancy Mullenax offered crucial editing assistance on the initial draft. William Jankowiak provided extensive, perceptive comments and helped shape the book's final form. Susan Spitler created and adapted the maps appearing in the text.

Several foreign colleagues have provided direction and insights: Andrew Forbes (Britain), Thomas Hoppe (Germany), Shirin Akiner (Britain), Chaya Haesner (India), Chi Cheng (Taiwan), Gervais Lavoie (Canada), Reuven Merhav (Israel), and Ambassador Gunnar Jarring (Sweden).

In Xinjiang, Zhao Songqiao, Liu Zhixiao, Xiong Jianhong, Zhang Xuezu, Mao Dehua, Ji Dachun, Mao Baodi, and Xu Jixing have been of great help to me. My Xinjiang adviser, Xia Xuncheng, kept me going during miserable and frightening times with his humor and tact. In Turpan and throughout Xinjiang, various Turkic colleagues, both Uyghur and Kazak, have provided tremendous help, inspiration, and warmth. They are Abbas Borhan, Mohtar Mahammed, Ablet Semet, Roza Rymbaeva, Sattar Haji, Zordun Sabir, Mohammät Shah Niyaz, Tohti Ayup, Turghun Almas, Litip Tohti, Ibrahim Mutii, Jamilikhan, Imin Hasil, Mamet Imin, Mohammed Haji, Abdurehim Ötkür, and Nizamdin Yüsüyün. Most were not aware that my work would come to interpret "Uyghur land use" and "oasis culture" in the way it has, but my arguments and conclusions were guided by their multiple "truths" about the Uyghurs.

A few months before my fieldwork was to begin, research funding to China was suspended because of the Tiananmen Massacre. Several organizations graciously provided material support to help keep the project going, including Patagonia, Fuji Film, and Adventure 16. My late grandmother, Hilda Feinblum, provided initial funding to get me to the field.

To other family, friends, and colleagues who have eluded mention, my appreciation is enormous and my love eternal. This gratitude is extended to the numerous foreign "families" that have adopted me as their own throughout my studies, to those that must go unmentioned to protect their safety, and to those who are so much a part of me that separate mention would be an offense to my spirit—my brother Jordan, for example.

The photographs in this book were made possible by camera and film support from *National Geographic* magazine. I am indebted to William Graves and Barry Bishop for taking a chance on me, and to Bruce McElfresh, who trained my eye and culled gems from my work. My gratitude goes also to *Newsweek International* and photographer Michelle Litvin for permission to use their magazine cover, to the Owen Lattimore Foundation for permission to use Owen Lattimore's photo of Urumchi, and to Linda Benson for permission to quote portions of her book.

I am grateful to John Michel, Executive Editor at Columbia University Press, for his gracious and determined shepherding of this book; to my manuscript editor, Leslie Kriesel, for turning my California speed-bump grammar into fluid glide; to editorial assistant Alexander Thorp for keeping my train on schedule; and to designer María Giuliani for incorporating images that provide flesh for Uyghur traces and desiccated bones.

This research has been supported by various scholarship organizations: Reynolds Scholarship (Dartmouth College), Foreign Language and Area Fellowship (FLAS), Mellon Dissertation Completion Fellowship, National Science Foundation Fellowship, and Committee on Scholarly Conduct with the People's Republic of China. While I gratefully acknowledge all of the above support and guidance, I am solely responsible for the contents and arguments of this book. May *Oasis Identities* be of service to other Central Asian scholars who follow the road of silk, and a guide to Uyghurs seeking their identity to build a future of peace. *Yol bolsun* (May there be a road).

> Fort Addo, Trinidad
> August, 1997
> Av, 5757

OASIS IDENTITIES

Introduction

My heart breaks for you my Uyghur people.
—Abdukhaliq ("Uyghur"), "Awaken! (*Oyghan*)," 1932

In April of 1990 the reports of violence in China's northwesternmost province of Xinjiang sounded ominous. Turkic Muslims in the far west near the Afghanistan border had rioted, and as many as sixty people were killed. Apparently this violence broke out after local officials in Akto, a small town near the oasis of Kashgar, barred the construction of a mosque. Whatever the cause, the rioting was severe enough that the Chinese crushed the rebellion with troops and sealed the province from outside contact. This was the bloodiest confrontation since the Tiananmen turmoil in June of 1989.

Soon, the newspapers in the United States were ablaze with wild headlines and sensational articles declaring that the Turkic Muslim Uyghurs (pronounced WEE-gurs), the majority nationality in Xinjiang, "the Children of Tamerlane and Attila the Hun," were on a rampage. The media speculated that cracks were beginning to appear in China's empire. The *Chicago Tribune* went so far as to proclaim that "China's Ethnic Turks May Wage Holy War" (Schmetzer 1990). Who are these people known as the Uyghurs? What led them to this violence? What is their relationship with the Chinese state, and what will their future be like?

I had returned to the United States from field research among the Uyghurs only one week before. Day after day I read reports in the press about the "Uyghur rebellion against the Chinese state." Several days after the first reports of violence near Kashgar, I received a call from the Beijing correspondent for *Newsweek* magazine. The Uyghurs were to be featured in the cover story for *Newsweek*'s international edition, and she asked me to assist in writing the article.

It is fortunate for a social anthropologist to have the ethnic group or people he or she studies on the cover of *Newsweek* or *Time*, if not to bring attention to this group then to validate years of research. Such is especially true if the group is not widely known. I appreciated the opportunity to shed light on the situation in Xinjiang, which I had been trying to understand for the previous nine years, and I described it in great detail. The article made the cover of the international edition of *Newsweek* on April 23, 1990, emblazoned with the heading "The Other China" (see figure In.1). Unfortunately, little of my opinion appeared in the article. Complex analysis by social anthropologists does not make for sensational copy.

My interest in Xinjiang began in 1981 when I was a sophomore in college. After three years of Chinese language study, including one year at Tunghai University in Taiwan, I spent the summer at Beijing University. I visited an exhibit of desiccated human mummies, some of which still had blonde hair on their scalps, found in the Täklimakan desert of Xinjiang, home of the Uyghurs. Later, I viewed a movie about a Han Chinese who was sent to Xinjiang to work among the Uyghurs. The Uyghurs in that film looked European. When I returned to Dartmouth College to complete my undergraduate studies, I continued to research Xinjiang and studied Japanese, Cantonese, Hebrew, and Russian. I developed a project, funded by Dartmouth, to study arid land research and technologies in China and Israel. My interests met in Xinjiang and centered on the Uyghurs and oasis agriculture.

I traveled to Israel and developed a plan to introduce Israeli desert technologies to Xinjiang and the Uyghurs. In my idealism, I thought this might lead to the establishment of diplomatic relations between China and Israel, nations that did not in fact establish formal relations until 1991. The mentor who guided my research was the writer Louis L'Amour, who had traveled through Xinjiang in the 1930s and whose first novel, about the area, was never completed. I also received significant training, film, and camera support from the National Geographic Society.

My project began in September 1984 with four months of Uyghur language study at the Central Institute for Nationalities, now the Central University for Nationalities, in Beijing. Conditions at the school were severe. I was taught in my room by a Uyghur teacher. I was not allowed

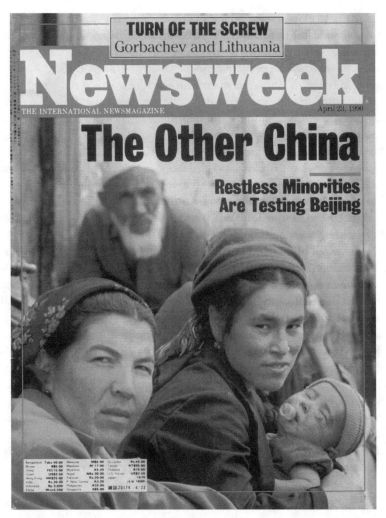

FIGURE IN.1   Uyghurs on the Cover of *Newsweek* (international edition), April 23, 1990. Photo by Michelle Litvin © 1990. Cover © 1990 Newsweek, Inc. All rights reserved. Reprinted by permission.

to eat with students or teachers at the campus dining hall, nor was I permitted to audit classes or use the library. I could not have friends visit me in my room, though I was permitted to visit students and teachers in theirs. In December, the famous Chinese geographer Zhao Songqiao suggested that I go to Xinjiang to help organize the first international conference ever held there. This conference, sponsored by the Institute of Biology, Soil, and Desert Research and the Institute of Geography, both part of the Xinjiang branch of the Chinese Academy of Sciences, was to focus on the development of arid lands. In January 1985, I went to Xinjiang's capital, Urumchi, where I worked for the next nine months.

Conditions in Urumchi were even more severe than in Beijing. On the day of my arrival in January the temperature was -30°F. I lived in the Academy's guest house and was the sole guest for four months. During this time I met many Uyghur intellectuals, writers, poets, and scientists, as well as peasants and merchants. I also traveled through the major Uyghur oases of Xinjiang for two months, and was able to establish contacts useful in introducing various advanced irrigation technologies from Israel and the United States. After one year in Xinjiang, I decided to pursue a Ph.D. in the Social Anthropology of Central Asia at Harvard University.

This book is the result of the first prolonged anthropological fieldwork ever conducted in Xinjiang—the first to provide an analysis of ethnic undercurrents there. It explores the interethnic tensions that foster or undermine ethnic nationalism and demonstrates how geographical and social boundaries shape competing ethnic identities at the local oasis and regional levels (see figure In. 2). Some competing identities parallel the Chinese government's highly promoted "pan-People's Republic" Chinese identity, while others define a nationalistic Uyghur identity that rejects Chinese authority. Uyghur intellectuals, who are most influential in the creation of a pan-Uyghur identity, compete with one another because their conceptions of identity tend to be sentimentally tied to the oases of their birth. Ironically, intellectuals are often frustrated at the home oasis level, for peasants and merchants maintain notions of Uyghurness that undercut intellectuals' formulations of Uyghur ethnic identity.

UYGHUR IDENTITY

While in Xinjiang in 1985, I heard numerous legends about the great past of the Uyghurs. Stories are told about Uyghur history and the origin of the people, but no one could provide me with an accurate and comprehensive account of Uyghur ethnic development. Uyghurs told me that their founding ancestors arrived in Xinjiang 6,000 years ago; intellectuals told of the relationship between the Uyghurs and the Huns, Genghis Khan, and even Adolf Hitler. However, by piecing together Uyghur his-

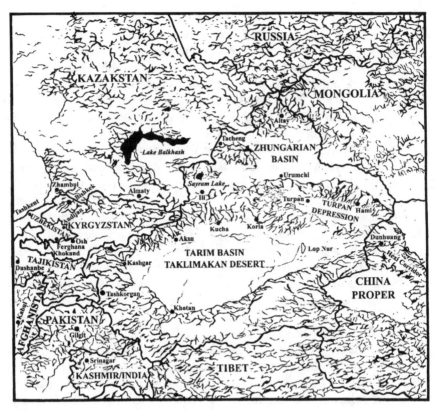

FIGURE IN.2   Bordering Countries and Regions Influencing Uyghur Ethnic Identity

tory, I learned something startling: as they are presently defined, the modern Uyghurs have existed only since 1935.

Scholars consistently trace the ethnic origin of the Uyghurs to the Uyghur Empire (744–840 C.E.) located in northwestern Mongolia.[1] However, it was not until the mid-1930s that the Chinese government defined the modern Uyghurs as oasis-dwelling Muslims of Xinjiang's Tarim Basin. Prior to 1935, the name *Uyghur* was not associated with Islam. Moreover, during the nearly 500 years between 1450 and 1935, the name ceased to be used as an ethnic label. I thought that this falling out of use might pose a problem for present-day Uyghurs, and decided to trace the shifts in Uyghur identity over its 1,200-year existence.

The term *Uyghur* has had vastly differing meanings throughout its history. It was first (744–840 C.E.) used to refer to a Turkic, steppe, nomadic, shamanistic, and Manichaean society in Mongolia.[2] Later (844–932), it became the name for a sedentary, oasis, Buddhist, Manichaean, and Nestorian Christian society centered in Turpan.[3] Finally (932–1450), it became the referent for an elite, primarily Buddhist, Turkic society centered in the Turpan oasis, which during this period was known as "Uyghuristan."[4] In this case, the term was used to distinguish this society from the Islamic Turks living to the west. The term fell into disuse for 500 years after the Buddhist Uyghurs converted to Islam in the fifteenth century. However, the Uyghurs did not cease to exist during this period. The identity became an historical undercurrent, part of a symbolic repertoire that could be tapped into or redefined when the occasion demanded.

That occasion presented itself in 1931 when Chinese government officials attempted to manipulate the hereditary leadership in the eastern Xinjiang oasis of Hami, plunging the region into ethnic turmoil. The violence set the local Turkic population, today defined as Uyghur, in opposition to the Han Chinese and to the Tungans (also known as Chinese Muslims or Hui), a non-Turkic people. More bloody battles ensued. Tungan armies from the neighboring Gansu province invaded to take advantage of the unrest in Xinjiang. In February of 1933, the rebellion against the Chinese government spread to the southern rim of the Tarim Basin. There, Turkic Muslims established an independent government called the Turkish Islamic Republic of East Turkestan (TIRET).[5] By the end of 1933, Chinese authority in the region had virtually collapsed. TIRET, however, was crushed by Xinjiang's Chinese military leader, Sheng Shicai, who defeated the Turkic rebels with Soviet and Tungan assistance and set himself up as the leader of Xinjiang.[6]

Although the Tungans were also Muslim, there was a long history of animosity between them and the Uyghurs, heightened by the fact that the Chinese utilized Tungan troops and officials to maintain their rule in the region. The Uyghurs viewed the non-Turkic Tungans as allies of the Han Chinese administration and thus as the enemies of the Turkic Muslim peoples (Forbes 1986:67). It was this enmity and opposition that helped Turkic Muslims envision themselves as a single group.

The ethnic violence set the stage for a revitalization of Uyghur identity by the Chinese government. Han Chinese government officials, with the aid of Soviet advisers, defused the tense interethnic climate by applying the kind of Soviet ethnic policy and classification system used in Soviet Central Asia. This policy gave each group particular political rights that accompanied their minority nationality status; it seemed to have met with some favor among the Soviet Central Asians. Under this process, the Chinese defined the oasis dwellers of Xinjiang as Uyghurs.

But the ethnic term *Uyghur* was already used by exiles from Xinjiang in Soviet Central Asia by 1924, a decade earlier, and it seems likely that Sheng Shicai's Soviet adviser, Garagin Apresoff, suggested this term to Sheng. Scholars debate how the term *Uyghur* first began to be used in its modern ethnic context.[7] Gunnar Jarring (1991) contends that it was introduced into the Eastern Turki vocabulary (modern Uyghur dialect) in only 1921 and that it was not used in southern Xinjiang until the revolution of the 1930s. Another scholar, Omeljan Pritsak (1959:525), believes that the term *Uyghur* appeared in connection with the increasing Soviet influence in southern Xinjiang in 1934.[8]

The label *Uyghur* recognized a common culture that was already in place and also allowed for multiple relationships: the Turkic Muslim oasis dwellers were defined as Uyghurs, while the other significant ethnic groups were defined as Kazaks, Tungans, and Hans. The Uyghurs could therefore more easily accept the label because it excluded all groups that were not culturally and linguistically similar to them. However, the use of the term *Uyghur* covered over a whole host of internal differences among the oases of the Tarim Basin, and the Chinese government's classification of the Uyghurs shaped their ethnic identity to a large extent. Whether the Chinese government and their Soviet advisers knew it or not, by uniting all the sedentary Turkic Muslim oasis dwellers under a single identity, they effectively drew a map within which the Uyghurs already saw themselves living.

An important aspect of this new Uyghur ethnic identity was that it allowed the oasis dwellers to compete with the Hans, the Tungans, and the Kazaks as a nationality. In fact, the Uyghurs became the largest of the nationalities in Xinjiang. This was a powerful incentive for them to accept their classification, even though Uyghur identity had previously been associated with Buddhism and never with Islam. But it is clear that the newly defined Uyghurs never considered this aspect of Uyghur history. Instead, all of the Turkic history of the Xinjiang region, including that of Kashgar, was interpreted as Uyghur. The new definition provided a clear differentiation among the majority sedentary Turks (now Uyghurs), the Tungan Muslims, and the Han Chinese.

NATIONALIST IDEOLOGIES AND OASIS IDENTITIES

I arrived in Xinjiang in 1985, a watershed year in the development of Uyghur nationalist ideology. Not only were new freedoms extended to Uyghur intellectual elites to construct their own versions of Uyghur his-

tory, but international borders were reopened, permitting the reestablishment of transborder contacts and international trade networks. The next
four years, during which I conducted fieldwork in Xinjiang, was thus a
crucial time of experimentation and change for the Uyghur oasis dwellers.

My main purpose was to understand how nationalist ideologies fil-
tered down to create a Uyghur identity in the local oases of Xinjiang. I
also examined how such local understanding of Uyghur identity affected
the generation and propagation of contending intellectual views in the
provincial capital, Urumchi. It became clear that Uyghur identity was
more fragmented by social group (intellectuals, peasants, and merchants)
and occupation than by family type, descent, or ethnicity. Intellectuals'
conceptions of the Uyghur nationalist ideology often contrasted dramatically with those held by peasants and merchants, and there were wide
gulfs separating all three social groups from one another. Similarly, em-
bedded oasis identities undermined the efforts of intellectuals to shape a
uniform Uyghur nationalist ideology. If Uyghur intellectual versions of
their own historiography and identity were to succeed, they had to resonate among Uyghur peasants and merchants at the local level.

The concepts of identity, consciousness, ethnicity, and nationalism are
often ill-defined. I have adopted Richard Fox's concept of "nationalist
ideology" defined as "the production of conceptions of peoplehood."
This definition emphasizes what is shared by "the social beliefs and
practices labeled as ethnicity, racial identity, and nationalism: they are all
cultural productions of public identity" (1990:3–4). Such ideologies
shape consciousness and produce "contests in which alternative conceptions of the world enter into conflict" (Verdery 1991:9).

However useful this definition, it must be modified to fit the Uyghur
case because "nationalist ideology" cannot be applied to local notions of
Uyghur identity, whether peasant, merchant, or intellectual, for these
fail to encompass a "peoplehood." Intellectuals, even those actively
involved in the production of a Uyghur national culture, rarely transcend their own parochial oasis identity, which they tend rather to project broadly as "Uyghur." This local identity is rooted in a tripartite
social division—intellectuals belong to the most prestigious social category, which follows an Islamic intellectual tradition—and combines
with local ties of kinship that bind Uyghur intellectuals to their natal
oases. "Nationalist ideology" is therefore the body of historic symbols
that contributes to notions of an overarching "identity" of the whole
group but, in this case, is not identical to individual and group beliefs
held in each oasis.

The Turpan oasis, where I conducted fieldwork in 1989 and 1990, demonstrates this problem. A variety of factors have contributed to the development of a unique oasis world view and strong Turpan identity. Turpan has stronger ties historically with China than do other oases, and religious reforms and the wealth gained from raisin cultivation have fostered positive views about recent Communist government development of the region and about the Chinese government in general. Furthermore, the Uyghur practice of oasis endogamy has resulted in an intense localization of identity that is normally unchallenged. This localization includes Uyghur naming practices that are also often oasis specific and mark natal oasis. For the most part, two people meeting are able to place each other in a local oasis context and act accordingly. In addition, notions of oasis identity have been strengthened by transborder contacts and trade networks, as each oasis has a distinct set of networks.

Within the oases, identity also varies by social group. In the eastern Xinjiang oasis of Turpan, middle-income and poor peasants, who for the most part do not travel outside of the Turpan region, identify strongly with Islam and maintain strong Turpan (*Turpanlik*) oasis identities. Turpan merchants who trade in China proper with cities including Beijing and Shanghai, and wealthy peasants such as grape growers who benefit from China's development policies, see themselves as citizens of the Chinese state. These identities stand in marked contrast to the prescriptive views held by Uyghur intellectuals who attempt to speak for all Uyghurs. Intellectuals are highly nationalistic, supportive of a pan-Turkic ideology that would unify all the Turks of the world, and are against Chinese control of Xinjiang.

The interests of Uyghur intellectuals and peasant oasis dwellers are fragmented and crosscutting. It is the self-identification of peasants and merchants that poses the greatest challenge to the acceptance of the nationalist ideologies created by Uyghur intellectuals. Ironically, while the name *Uyghur* is considered by Central Asian scholars to mean "confederacy" or "unity," intellectuals are finding it difficult to guide the disparate oasis dwellers, subsumed under the same ethnic identity, to a unified vision that might fuel a nationalist movement.

Fieldwork in Xinjiang

Politically my fieldwork research on Uyghur identity in Xinjiang began at an inauspicious time. I arrived in September of 1989, three months after the dramatic events in Tiananmen Square had crushed the student-led democracy movement. My scholarship from the Committee on Scholarly Conduct with the People's Republic of China had been suspended because of Beijing's violent crackdown. In the United States, scholars were calling on their colleagues to refrain from working in China. While sympathetic to such calls, I also realized that this was a period of ferment and therefore of great scholarly interest—and that the opportunity to conduct research in Xinjiang, a highly "sensitive" region, was hardly likely to produce results the regime would be proud of. I decided to go to Xinjiang on my own funds.

My host in China was the Chinese Academy of Sciences in Xinjiang, where I had worked four years previously, helping to successfully put on the first international conference ever held in Xinjiang, a symbolic opening of the region to the world. My plan was to spend at least eight months in the Turpan oasis, located 120 miles southeast of Urumchi. The Academy of Sciences had a desert research center in Turpan, so I could maintain contact with it throughout my research. Initially the political atmosphere in Urumchi was extremely tense. The government had sought to bolster support for its crackdown on students by posting signs proclaiming the greatness of Maoism and the Chinese Communist party, reminiscent of the propaganda I had seen in China in 1981 during the early days of reform. I remained in the city for two weeks and reestablished contacts with the Uyghur intellectuals I had known in 1985.

My adviser, Xia Xuncheng, the director of the Academy's Institute of Biology, Soil, and Desert Research, drove with me to Turpan by Jeep. Unable to grant my request to live with a Uyghur family due to the political situation, Professor Xia arranged for me to live in an ornate building resembling a mosque at the Turpan Hotel. The hotel was in the center of town and convenient to the seven Turpan villages I regularly visited. After Xia returned to Urumchi, I was left alone and unsupervised for my entire stay except during several short visits from scientists at the desert research station. However, I was closely watched by government officials, public security, and police, something I invited in order to allay suspicion. I taught English to a public security officer and was often visited by a Uyghur policeman, the relative of some friends I had made in Urumchi. In January, I returned to Urumchi to do further research among intellectuals and then returned to Turpan.

In Turpan I concentrated on a small village, Subeshi, located in the Kyzyl Tagh (Red Mountains). There I met with officials and interviewed merchants, *molla*s (religious leaders), and healers. Given my inability to live in a village and the political difficulty of conducting systematic interviewing, I wandered the streets and stopped anywhere I found social interaction, met friendly people, or was approached by curious children. Many Uyghurs invited me in for tea, cookies, and candy— always prepared in advance for any visitors who might drop by. On weekend mornings, when I heard the thumping of wedding drums outside my hotel room, I ran over and asked to join the celebration, bringing my cameras. In the bazaar I asked merchants about their wares and their trade networks. I challenged Uyghurs to play pool at the scores of tables found throughout Turpan, interviewing them during the game and asking questions about Uyghur history, authors, and nationalism. I met young doctors when I was treated for various minor stomach ailments at the Uyghur hospital and was invited to their homes. I was also assisted in my research by Uyghur scholars I had met in 1985 and by employees at the Turpan Hotel. Some of the hotel workers brought me home to meet their families and to attend funerals and weddings, an important means of learning about kinship, trade networks, and village concerns. Although I focused primarily on Uyghurs, I also interviewed Hans and Tungans (Chinese Muslims or Huis), who speak Mandarin.

As part of the research, I began with a series of handwritten questions about conceptions of Uyghur identity. I discovered that people had difficulty answering triad and other comparative tests that asked, for example, "Which two of the following three oases are most alike?" Uyghur peasants refused to compare oases that they had never visited. Thus, it was difficult to obtain data that might indicate rivalries among the oases. Through trial and error, however, I discovered the most successful question: "Rank the following five words to describe yourself in order of importance: 1) Muslim, 2) Turpanlik, 3) Uyghur, 4) Turk, 5) Chinese." The answers revealed the tremendous differences among peasant, merchant, and intellectual notions of Uyghur identity.

Another successful way of obtaining cultural information about oasis identity was to use still photos in open-ended interviews designed to elicit self-reflective responses. I distributed Quicksnap disposable cameras, donated for this research by Fuji Photo Film, expecting that the Uyghurs themselves would document aspects of their lives and culture that they deemed important. I planned to select the most representative photos to use for further interviews about perceived differences in the oases. However, the resulting twenty-five rolls of developed film consisted mainly of pictures of Uyghur feet: Quicksnap cameras do not have viewfinders, and Uyghurs frequently jerked the camera down when shooting, even after being instructed otherwise. So I abandoned this approach, eventually using photos I had taken in the various oases during 1985 and asking several informants to select ten out of one hundred photos that best represented differences among the oases and with Urumchi. These photos were crucial in eliciting information about inter-oasis rivalries. Four others, taken in the 1930s and part of the Owen Lattimore collection at Harvard University, were an index of the economic development of Xinjiang since 1930 and were useful in eliciting evaluations of the changes the Chinese government had brought to the region.

This book is a Turpan-centric study of Uyghur ethnicity because my historical research indicated that the original Uyghur elite settled in Turpan after they were driven from Mongolia in the ninth century. Thus Turpan is considered the center of ancient Uyghur culture. Also, over the previous forty years it had been the least volatile of the oases. It was therefore considered the least politically sensitive by the Chinese gov-

IN.1   Red Hill (Hong Shan) in Urumchi, c. 1930, taken by Owen Lattimore. Today Urumchi is a city of 1.5 million. Uyghur intellectuals who claimed that China had done little for Xinjiang's development were stunned silent when viewing this picture. Photo courtesy of the Owen Lattimore Foundation.

ernment, which might have forbidden similar research in oases that had long histories of resistance to Chinese rule.

During my seven months of fieldwork during 1989 and 1990, I was accorded almost unlimited freedom. I was given a work unit card from the Academy of Sciences identifying me in Mandarin as "Yusupu Lu Desheng," and I had Uyghur business cards made using the name Yüsüp, the Uyghur equivalent for Joseph, a biblical name popular among Uyghurs that is also the Hebrew name I received at birth. Lu Desheng is a direct Mandarin translation of my surname, Rudelson, with the meaning "mainland moral life" (see figure In.3). The Chinese government also gave me letters permitting access to the villages and requesting that village officials assist my research to the best of their abilities. In short, I was able to go wherever I wanted.

I am certain this freedom was granted in the spirit of cooperation and good feelings that my contributions to the Academy of Sciences had engendered in the past. But it was also inspired by my arrival in the aftermath of the events at Tiananmen. The Chinese officials were eager

使　用　规　则

一、此证由本人妥为保存与使
　　用，不得涂改与转借，如
　　有遗失应即报告发证机关
　　登记作废。
二、此证按学期注册后有效。
三、休学、退学或毕业等离院
　　时，应将此证交回。

In.3   Academy of Sciences work unit card.

to show that scientific work could continue after troops were mobilized against student protesters, even if only at the low level of a graduate student who had no significant rank or position in his home country. While I was forced to stay at the Turpan Hotel, I was able to visit overnight at Uyghur homes on at least twenty occasions. Many of these stays were unplanned because I found it difficult to return home at night when visiting villages located twenty or more miles from downtown Turpan, and because frequent power blackouts in villages at night prevented my safe return to the hotel.

My work proceeded smoothly until the Berlin Wall fell, along with most of communist Eastern Europe. China was not pleased with the images on the evening news of its most significant communist ally, Nicolae Ceauşescu, lying dead with a bullet through his head. And to the rest of the world, China appeared as one of the last reactionary holdouts that might itself collapse. Uyghur peasants joked that in the past the government said only socialism could save China, but now the government believed only China could save socialism. Blows to China's prestige came when the Dalai Lama received the Nobel Peace Prize in recognition of his defense of Tibet throughout China's occupation of the region and when Fang Lizhi, a Chinese advocate for democracy and human rights, was given protection by the American embassy in Beijing, where he remained for a year. The Chinese believed these gestures were clearly intended to castigate them, and relations with the United States steadily deteriorated. In February 1990 a military officer from Xinjiang appeared on television, warning that hoodlum elements had downed power lines near Kashgar, an indication of building tensions in that frequently volatile oasis. I wrote in my notes: "Things seem to be getting hot. I may have to move out of here in a hurry."

And indeed, my fortunes started to dim. My Uyghur friends began to be questioned about my activities, and many said my work and friendship with them was causing difficulties. By the end of March 1990, I thought it best to return to Urumchi while things cooled down, and planned to use the time to travel to other oases for comparative research. Several days after I informed the Foreign Affairs and Public Security offices of my intention to return to Urumchi—in fact, only a few hours before my return—a Foreign Affairs officer summoned me to his office. There, two scholars from the Historical Collections Department sat with their heads bowed—reminding me uneasily of Chinese films I had seen of the Cultural Revolution. These scholars had helped me find printed information on the history of the *karez* irrigation system in Turpan, which

I was using to write an article requested by my adviser, Xia Xuncheng, for an upcoming conference sponsored by the province's own Academy of Sciences. I had borrowed the materials and photocopied them at a technical institute down the street. The Foreign Affairs Head, a Uyghur, informed me that these documents were secret and I could not leave without turning them over to him. It did not seem to matter that the scholars from the Historical Collections Department had shown me the documents because of the letter of introduction I had from the Turpan government, or that the documents I copied were published in a book, or that they were historical records from 250 years ago. I was informed that my research had gone beyond permitted bounds, although the Head could not tell me what those bounds were—presumably they were secret too. When I asked to call Professor Xia and the Academy of Sciences, he yelled at me, "Do you think they do not know what we are doing here today?" The interrogation continued for six hours. All my bags were searched and I was forced to give up all photocopied materials. Fortunately the books, articles, and poetry I collected, materials used in the Uyghurs' ideological confrontation with the Chinese state, were not seized. Some of these materials have subsequently been banned and will perhaps never be published again.

When I returned to Urumchi, Professor Xia apologized and said that the official in Turpan had been out of line and that my studies were not in jeopardy. Soon, however, he informed me that the government insisted I could continue my work in Uyghur areas only with an official guide, and that my time in any one place would be restricted to ten days. The government also insisted on developing my film and watching the videos I had taped. Much worse, it was clear that my presence was causing my hosts at the Academy of Sciences considerable political trouble. I learned from a friend in the government that before my interrogation, officials from the Academy had met for a week with Xinjiang government officials about my research. I decided to return home. Six days later, Kyrgyz and Uyghurs clashed in a town near Kashgar. At home in the United States, I learned from newspaper headlines that "Xinjiang's Muslims May Wage a Holy War." The Chinese government closed the province of Xinjiang to foreigners. My fieldwork had officially ended.[9]

Who Are the Uyghurs? 1

We have a world renowned name, Uyghur.
—"Uyghur," "Unsettled (*Ich Pushush*)"

While a geographical description of a region often accompanies an ethnography, rarely is such a description connected to the theoretical argument of the text. In this case, however, it is central to my argument, for insufficient understanding of Xinjiang geography has clouded modern studies. For the most part, scholars have viewed the region as a single entity. I argue that Xinjiang is composed of four distinct geographic regions, each influenced by a different bordering culture. On the map it appears that Xinjiang abuts a cul-de-sac on its western edge, enclosed by four mountain ranges: the Pamirs, the Karakoram, the Hindu Kush, and the Tianshan. These mountains seemingly block access to the region by the peoples of India, Pakistan, Afghanistan, Uzbekistan, Kyrgyzstan, Tajikistan, Kazakstan, and Russia. In contrast, the flat desert wastes between the individual oases of Xinjiang appear to present no obstacle to movement.

Xinjiang's geography, however, has had the opposite effect: historically, contacts across the borders have been much more frequent and important than those among the oases. In the past, people covered the distances between oases so slowly that the oasis populations remained isolated from one another.

Xinjiang is the size of Germany, France, and Italy combined, and it consists of three major subregions: the Zhungarian Basin in the north, which

FIGURE 1.1   The Physiography of Xinjiang

is divided from the Tarim Basin in the south by the Tianshan Mountains, and the Turpan Depression in the east (see figure 1.1). The Tarim Basin is the most striking physical feature of the area, containing the Täklimakan Desert, one of the largest moving deserts in the world, second only to the Sahara. In Western and Chinese lore, *Täklimakan* is said to mean "once you go in you cannot come out," but most Central Asian experts, such as Swedish scholar Gunnar Jarring, reject this translation as unfounded and simply untrue (personal communication, 1994). The Russian geographer Marzaev insists that it means "abandoned or forsaken place" (Benson and Svanberg 1988:13). Uyghur scholars maintain that the word comes from *Täklimak-Maqan*, which means "buried civilization," or *Tärkli-maqan*, meaning "ruined town." According to them, somewhere in this desert, perhaps under more than 200 meters of sand, lies a city of gold.

Most of the Uyghurs live in the Tarim Basin of Xinjiang. This oval-shaped area is 600 miles long, east to west, and 250 miles wide, north to south. The region can be visualized as a series of concentric belts, beginning with the outer mountains and moving inward past the foothills and into the alluvial fans. The several oases that lie in a string along the perimeter of the Täklimakan are irrigated by snow and glacier melt from high mountains—the Pamirs, the Karakoram, the Kunlun, and the Tianshan—that border the region on three sides and divide Xinjiang in half. In between the oases are long stretches of barren gravel and sand. Xinjiang is one of the most desolate and remote places in the world.

The oases of Xinjiang dot the ancient Silk Road and provide access to the surrounding peoples and cultures. These oases do not fit the popular image of a tiny patch of land with a well and three palm trees. Rather, they range from 20,000 inhabitants in Guma, a region in the south near Khotan; to over 450,000 in the Turpan region, which encompasses three smaller oasis districts: the city of Turpan, Pichan (Shanshan), and Tohsun; and reach their maximum in the Kashgar region, with a population of over 750,000. The total area of the Turpan Region, where I conducted most of my fieldwork, is 73,000 km². The Turpan Basin is traversed by the Qyzyl Tagh or "Flaming Mountains" that stretch 100 kilometers east to west and are ten kilometers wide. From the city of Turpan the basin slopes down southward to the lake basin of Ayding Köl. The lowest area is 161 meters below sea level.[1]

An oasis region may be composed of several villages. Similarly, an oasis county region may be made up of several oasis towns. Several of the oasis towns, such as Urumchi, the capital of Xinjiang, are not desert oases, for in northern Xinjiang the major towns are steppe oases located in relatively well-watered lands.

Both climate and geography have been barriers to development of this region. The presence of the huge mountains and deserts and the isolation from any body of water result in an extremely arid environment with wide temperature variations. In the early part of this century, a German explorer, Albert von Le Coq, discovered that Turpanliks called their oasis "the India of Turkestan" because of its heat (1985 [1928]:51). Turpan has recorded a maximum temperature of 47.8°C (128°F), but the average winter temperature in northern Xinjiang ranges from -13 to -30°C. Precipitation also varies widely. There is much rainfall in the Ili Valley, located in the northwest of the region, but some villages in the Turpan region get less than fifteen millimeters annually. In Turpan, local farmers have developed underground canals (*karez* in Uyghur; *qanat* in Persian) that tap the groundwater supply and enable luxuriant crops to grow. Xinjiang produces valuable fruits prized by the Chinese, such as grapes, and its Hami muskmelons are world renowned. It also supplies China's best-quality cotton.

NATIONALITY AND GEOGRAPHY

The oases populated by the Uyghurs lie primarily in the south of Xinjiang, in the Tarim Basin. The region is known as *Altä-shähär*, "the six cities," named for the six historically major oases (Khotan, Yarkand, Kashgar, Uch-Turpan, Yangi-Hissar, and Aksu). This area has also been called Huijiang, the "Muslim Territories" (Haneda 1978:7). The Zhungarian Basin in northern Xinjiang was named for the nomadic Zhungar Mongols, a confederation of Oirat Mongols (known by the various names of Eleuth, Ölööd, and Western Mongols), who inhabited this region until their expulsion in the mid-eighteenth century by armies of the Qing, the Manchu-ruled final dynasty of China before the modern period.[2] After destroying the Zhungars, the Qing dynasty developed new agricultural areas in the region. Initially, it was this northern region that was called Xinjiang, "the New Territories," by the Qing dynasty; the name was later applied to the whole region.

The Qing did not conquer a blank slate. A number of diverse ethnic groups inhabited Xinjiang, and the Qing needed to develop policies to negotiate with them. Besides the Zhungars and their component tribes, including the Khoshuud, Khoit, and Dorbet—who had been for the most part annihilated during the conquest—other Mongol groups included the Chachar, Torghuud, Kalmuk, and Khalkha (Fletcher 1978:62). In northern Zhungaria there were also Kazaks who moved south to fill the void after the Qing elimination of the Zhungars; however, they never truly became Qing subjects. The other Turkic nomads, the Kyrgyz (formerly called Burut and Kirghiz-Kazakh by the Russians), resided in the western Tianshan and Pamir mountains. The oases of the Täklimakan Desert (Tarim Basin) south of the Tianshan were home to eastern Turkestanis, divided between those in the east in Hami (Qomul) and Turpan and those to the west in the Altä-shähär (six cities) region. Some of the eastern Turkestanis had been sent by the Zhungars to the Ili region in western Zhungaria to develop agricultural lands. These groups became known as Taranchis, "tillers of the soil." There were also merchant communities from Badakhshan, Kashmir, Leh, and other Himalayan areas settled in the southern rim of the Täklimakan, and western Turkestanis from towns such as Khokand, Andijan, and Bukhara in the Kashgar region. Immediately after the Qing conquest, there was an influx of other groups, including Manchus, Tungans (Chinese Muslims), and some Hans.

As a pluralistic empire, the Qing tolerated the diverse ethnic groups in Xinjiang and developed ethnic categories to control them.[3] Although Dru Gladney correctly argues that to understand ethnic identity in Communist China we must recognize the importance of the state in ethnic identity construction (1991), the Chinese Communists did not begin this project from scratch. State definition of Xinjiang's ethnic groups began in the eighteenth century, so the time line must be extended farther back. In fact, historian James Millward argues that Communist China's ethnic policies probably owe as much or more to Qing Emperor Qianlong (r. 1736–1795) as to Josef Stalin, the architect of Soviet ethnic policy (1995, personal communication). Historian Jonathan Lipman recognizes that the conceptual foundation for Communist China's ethnic policies was also greatly influenced by General Zuo Zongtang, the imperial commissioner in charge of Xinjiang military affairs who reconquered Xinjiang for the Qing in 1877–1878 after the Yaqub Beg uprising (1997, personal communication). The years of revolts and riots against Qing rule continued until the Qing collapse in 1911; this shows that the dynasty's policies were not sufficiently sensitive to Xinjiang's ethnic complexity.

Today, the Uyghurs are one of the thirteen officially recognized nationalities of Xinjiang (see table 1.1). Most members of these nationalities are speakers of Turkic dialects that are closely related. Indeed, the Turkic peoples of Xinjiang often wonder why Turkic dialects that are mutually intelligible are considered separate languages, when mutually unintelligible Chinese dialects like Mandarin and Cantonese or Fukienese are considered a single language.[4]

The Kazaks are the other major Turkic nationality wielding significant political power in Xinjiang. They number over 1.1 million and have their own independent nation just across the border in Kazakstan. The Xinjiang Kazak population arrived in northern Xinjiang in the mid-1800s, when they were pushed eastward by the expanding Tsarist empire. They are nomadic pastoralists who historically lived in *yurts* (round felt tents), raising horses, sheep, goats, cows, and camels. Almost all the Kazaks in Xinjiang live in the northern part of the region—in Ili, Barkol, and Mori—where three Kazak autonomous areas have been established. This area contains Xinjiang's best pasture land. During the Communist period, China euphemistically declared these pastures "waste lands" and targeted the region for agricultural and industrial development, pushing the Kazaks into smaller areas within the region.

The other major nationalities of Xinjiang, besides the Han Chinese, who today number over six million, are relatively small (see table 1.1 and figure 1.2). But the interethnic character of the region has had a great influence on the social and political development of Xinjiang. Besides the Uyghurs and the Hans, the largest of the other nationalities is the Tungans, or Hui Muslims, who numbered 682,912 in Xinjiang according to the 1990 census. At 8.6 million throughout the country, they are China's largest Muslim nationality; Tungans are found in every county in all of China's provinces. Tungans have moved into Xinjiang in large numbers since the nineteenth century and have taken an intermediary position between the Hans and the Uyghurs. In Xinjiang, many Tungans are bilingual and live in close proximity to the Uyghurs.

The Kyrgyz are pastoral nomads who live on the border between the independent nations of Kyrgyzstan and Afghanistan. The Kyrgyz numbered 141,840 in Xinjiang in the 1990 census. Like the Uyghurs and the Kazaks, they are Sunni Muslims, and their language and culture are very close to those of the Kazaks. Only 14,715 Uzbeks live in Xinjiang, but they are growing in economic power as trade links between their homeland, Uzbekistan, and Xinjiang develop. Among the Turkic groups, the Uzbeks are most culturally and linguistically similar to the Uyghurs, as they are sedentary agriculturists who are heavily involved in trade. Most of the Uzbeks live in Ili in the northwest.

In China there are 4.8 million Mongols; those that live in Xinjiang are concentrated mainly in the north. In 1990 there were 138,021 Mongols living in Xinjiang. Their language is distinct from the Turkic languages. Other minor ethnic groups include the Tatar, Salar, Tajik, Manchu, Xibo,

TABLE 1.1

The Largest Nationalities in Xinjiang and Total in China According to 1990 Census

	Xinjiang	China
Uyghur	7,191,845	7,214,431
Han	5,695,409	1,042,482,187
Kazak	1,106,271	1,111,718
Tungan (Hui)	682,912	8,602,978
Kyrgyz	141,840	143,537
Mongol	138,021	4,806,849
Uzbek	14,715	14,763
Russian	8,065	13,504

SOURCES: Guojia Tongjiju Renkou Tongjici (1993); Renmin Ribao (1990); Zhongguo Minzu Renkou Ziliao: Renkou Pucha Shujiao (1990).

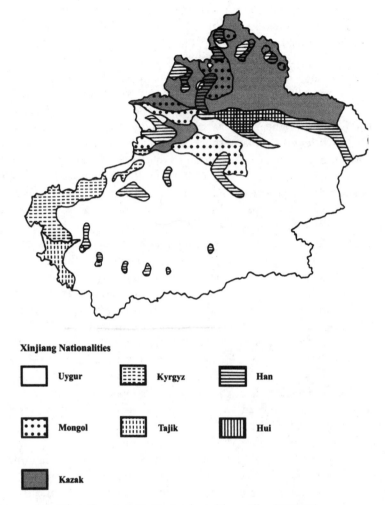

FIGURE 1.2   Ethnic Groups in Xinjiang. Adapted from Allen (1996a:14).

Daur, Russians, Zhuang, Dongxiang, and Tibetans (Benson and Svanberg 1988:23–28)[5].

Xinjiang has been defined by the flux and flow in its ethnic populations, with refugees and political exiles forming some groups (Kazaks, Xibo) and a history of internal geopolitical struggle bringing about imposed classifications of its peoples. Xinjiang is on the whole characterized by unclear divisions and an unparalleled ethnic and cultural diversity.

According to Nizamdin Yüsüyün, a Uyghur folklorist, there are seven divisions among today's Uyghurs. These include the Dolans, Lopliks, Abdals, Keriyaliks, Kashgarliks, Eastern Uyghurs (Turpan and Hami), and the Kuldjaliks or Taranchis (Ili).[6] The Dolans live in the Merkit area near Kashgar. Because it is their social custom to walk barefoot, the Uyghurs view them as being both poor and primitive even though they are no less poor than many other oasis dwellers in the south of Xinjiang.[7] The Lopliks live near Lop Nor in a fishing community. Today, some Uyghurs view the Dolans and Lopliks as separate nationalities. The German explorer Le Coq encountered this same perception, and noted, "It is remarkable that both the Dolans and the dwellers of Lop Nor are looked upon as people of another race by the Turks" (1985 [1928]:109). Today the Dolans and Lopliks are generally considered to be Uyghurs, but are still thought of as "different."[8] Soviet ethnologists regard groups like the Dolans and Lopliks as "ethnographic groups," or subgroups of an ethnic group.[9] The Abdals are a peripatetic group living in southern Xinjiang who are Alevi- or Shia-influenced heterodox Muslims. They are often called on to perform circumcisions. Most Abdals are quite poor, and because they beg for alms, many Uyghurs refer to all beggars as "Abdals." Keriyaliks, who live in the southern rim of the Täklimakan east of Khotan, appear to have been greatly influenced by northern Indian culture. Uyghurs perceive them to have the most Caucasian features. Only in Keriya do women veil in white head-scarves with small teacup-sized hats pinned to the scarves, a feature of unknown origin but also attributed to Indian influence. Kashgarliks have been most influenced by Islamic civilization from the west, making the oasis the Xinjiang "Mecca" for devout Muslims. The Eastern Uyghurs in Turpan and Hami are most closely related to the Uyghur Empire of the eighth and ninth centuries C.E. However, many Uyghurs consider them the least Uyghur, since they historically have maintained close relations with China and appear to have the most Chinese features of all of the seven Uyghur subgroups. The Taranchis, "tillers of the soil," were oasis Turks who were moved from the Tarim Basin into the Ili area after the Qing conquest of the Zhungars in 1759; they were considered a separate ethnic group until 1949, but are now considered Uyghurs.

DIVERSITY AND GEOGRAPHY

"Diversity," Fernand Braudel writes, "is the eldest daughter of distance" (1988 [1986]:119). In Xinjiang, this diversity was fostered throughout

FIGURE 1.3   The Three Regional Divisions Used by the Local Population—East, North, South

history by the great distances separating the oases from one another (see figure 1.3). Thus, geography is key to understanding the tremendous cultural diversity of Xinjiang, which exists not only among the various Muslim nationalities, such as the Kazaks, Uyghurs, and Tungans, but also within the Uyghur nationality itself. For example, in Kashgar, women veil in thick brown cloth and Islam is strictly followed, while in Ili women wear Western-style clothing and no veils.

The most significant oases and towns in Xinjiang today are Kashgar, Khotan, Turpan, Hami, Ili, and Urumchi, the capital. Their significance is directly related to their oasis locations, allowing their populations access to particular social, cultural, economic, and religious influences from across borders. Furthermore, large distances separating the individual oases effectively isolated them from one another. During the modern period, since Communist control, China's incorporation of

Xinjiang and its closure of cross-border ties have masked the causes of the region's diversity. The desert oases that dot the Täklimakan Desert in the south of Xinjiang are often described by scholars as pearls on a necklace, but this gives the mistaken impression that each oasis is similar to its neighbor. Instead, they should be viewed as individually set jewels: these oases have maintained separate and strong local identities despite their common religion, language, and culture.

Kashgar Region

Kashgar throughout its history has been the most violent and volatile of the Xinjiang oases, under the influence of civilizations and cultures lying to the west. C. P. Skrine commented, "Kashgar is . . . the most Musulman of the Six Cities (Alte-shahr). Culturally it belongs to the Transcaspian Khanates, Khoqand, Bokhara, Samarqand and Khiva, strongholds of Islam" (1926:205). Islam arrived in Kashgar from these khanates by 950 C.E. The subsequent turbulent and often violent nature of Kashgar came directly from its strong ties with these Islamic centers, which manipulated religion in competition for the loyalty of the Kashgar inhabitants. Today, Kashgar remains the Islamic heartland of Xinjiang.

The Ferghana Valley, the heartland of the Khanate of Khokand, was one of the major centers of Turkic rule in Central Asia; prior to the arrival of Islam, both Manichaeanism and Zoroastrianism came to Kashgar from the Ferghana Valley and areas to the west. Over several centuries, beginning in the 1500s, there were constant hostilities between the Khokand Khanate and Kashgar. In 1831, a treaty was signed allowing the Khan of Khokand to impose duties on all foreign goods imported into Aksu, Uch-Turfan, Kashgar, Yangi-Hissar, Yarkand, and Khotan (Altä-shähär). In this way Khokand acquired great influence over Kashgar (Schuyler 1966 [1877]:343).[10] Khokand influence also increased as a result of the rivalry between two Naqshbandi Sufi orders of Islam that exerted strong religious influence in Kashgar and Yarkand.

The Khokand Emirate manipulated Kashgar through Andijani religious and commercial groups that exerted a strong influence there. The Qing had made concessions to the Khokand Emirate allowing thousands of merchants from Khokand and from the towns of Osh, Samarkand, and Bukhara, all collectively known in Xinjiang as Andijanis, to reside and conduct business in Kashgar. In the last quarter of the nineteenth century, the Andijanis comprised one quarter of the total population of Kashgar (Fletcher 1978a:393–94). These Andijanis kept open communication lines among the people of the six major Tarim oases (Altä-shähär) and their previous rulers, the Khojas of the Naqshbandi Sufi brotherhoods (Fletcher 1978:87).[11]

After a series of revolts, the oases erupted in a massive uprising against Qing rule in 1862, expelling China and establishing an independent Kashgar Emirate led by Yaqub Beg, who ruled the region from 1864–1877. It was perhaps the greatest Turkic threat ever to the Chinese leadership.[12] Yaqub Beg, who has become a nationalistic symbol for the Uyghurs, took control of southern Xinjiang after leading his forces from his home town of Andijan in today's Uzbekistan to take advantage of religious strife. When the Qing dynasty armies finally gained control of Xinjiang, they resorted to the old Chinese practice of buying peace and quiet on the border, but did so in a manner that gave Khokand too much control of Kashgar affairs and allowed for a continued Andijani presence. During the period of Yaqub Beg's rule, pan-Turkic sentiment was strong. The Ottoman flag was raised over Kashgar from 1873–1877, and coins were minted depicting the Ottoman sultans (Forbes 1986:67). Older Uyghurs still speak of the great Andijani presence that continued up until the early part of this century. A Chinese expeditionary force restored Qing control after Yaqub Beg's death in 1877.

Yaqub Beg's rule showed that Qing power in Xinjiang was fairly weak, and led two European powers to believe that they could exert a great influence in Xinjiang or take it over outright. Kashgar became the nexus of the so-called "Great Game," in which European rivals and China contended with one another for control of Eastern Turkestan. The major European players in the game, Britain and Russia, whose colonial expansion met on the borders of Kashgar, both believed that someday they would gain possession of Xinjiang.[13] China sought to preserve its Qing dynasty conquests against both European rivals and local revolts. Both the British and the Russians built consulates in Kashgar. The British consulate, called the *Chinä Bagh* (Chinese Garden), was located outside of the main bazaar in Kashgar; ironically, today it serves as a hotel to huge numbers of Pakistani traders, former British subjects, who come to Kashgar using the Karakoram Highway.[14]

Khotan Region

Khotan was a major cultural center in Central Asia, not only because of its key position on the southern branch of the Silk Road, but also because of its links to South Asia and Tibet. It lies near the base of a mountain road through the lofty Karakorum Mountains into Kashmir and India, roughly the same route now taken by the modern Karakorum Highway linking China and Pakistan. Before the modern highway was built the trek took seven weeks and was considered very hazardous (Skrine 1926:2). It was via this route that Buddhism penetrated Xinjiang. Buddhism thrived in Khotan as it made its way to China.

Khotan, which lies in the south of the Tarim Basin, east of Kashgar, was historically one of the most isolated areas of the Xinjiang region and was beyond Kashgar control. "The great oasis of Khotan . . . is in many ways the most interesting of all, for it is the part of the Tarim Basin which has been least affected by outside influences, including Islam" (Skrine 1926:205). Given this isolation from Islam throughout its history, it is ironic that the most memorable event occurring in Khotan this century is the establishment of a short-lived Islamic republic.

In 1931 one of the largest Uyghur rebellions against the Nationalist Chinese broke out in Xinjiang and culminated in the establishment of an Islamic republic in Khotan. The revolt, which resulted in the near collapse of Chinese control in Xinjiang, began in the Hami oasis (Qomul) in eastern Xinjiang and spread south, ending in the establishment of the Turkish Islamic Republic of East Turkestan (TIRET) with its capital in Khotan. TIRET attempted to obtain recognition from the Soviet Union, Britain, and even the Nazis in Germany, all to no avail. Although TIRET lasted only one year (1933–1934), it led the Chinese government to begin a program of redefining the modern Uyghur identity so as to place this minority firmly under control. TIRET was crushed by Tungan forces who set up their own independent short-lived country, known as Tunganistan. Today, as then, Khotan remains a backwater as the routes eastward are blocked by windblown sands that bury the fragile roads.

Ili (Kuldja) Region

Ili has always been considered the richest area in Xinjiang and perhaps all of Central Asia. In the last century, the American diplomat Eugene Schuyler observed that Ili "seems to be the only part of Central Asia that will ever repay the expenses bestowed upon it" (1966 [1877]:198). Traditionally this was the agriculture, livestock, and trading center of much of northern Xinjiang (McMillen 1979:13). Ili, also called Kuldja (pronounced Ghulja), lies on the western edge of the Tianshan range where it meets the Kazakstan, once Russian, border; it is geographically isolated from southern Xinjiang and physically oriented toward

Kazakstan. From Kashgar the shortest route to Ili was over the Muzart (Ice) Pass (elevation 11,450 feet) in the Tianshan Mountains, which took a week to cross by caravan.

During the post-Zhungar war period, after the Qing recovery of Central Asia in 1759 and as part of the Manchu resettlement policy, the Qing encouraged 10,000 Muslim families to move from the Altä-shähär region to the Ili region in order to recover land devastated and depopulated by the Zhungar wars. Those who settled in Ili were known as Taranchis, or "tillers of soil." Though the Taranchi settlers were heavily taxed and not allowed to return to their native districts (Saguchi 1978:70), they maintained strong cultural ties to the regions west of the border. Later, both the Soviet Union and China viewed the Taranchis as a distinct ethnic group, separate from the Uyghurs. In 1949, however, the Chinese reclassified the over 80,000 Taranchis as Uyghurs.

A series of strategic passes and low-lying gaps in the mountains on the western frontier of Xinjiang, along the Ili River Valley, afforded relatively easy access to western Central Asia and contributed to the geographical orientation of Ili toward the west.[15] This was one factor leading the Russians to briefly take over the Ili region during the Yaqub Beg revolt that engulfed Xinjiang from 1864–1877; they feared the violence would cross over into their province of Semirechia, a fertile territory populated by many thousands of Russian colonists (Schuyler 1966 [1877]:327).

Ili has posed the greatest Turkic political threat to the Chinese government in this century. From 1944 to 1949, the Ili region revolted against Chinese rule and established the Eastern Turkestan Republic with support from the Soviet Union. It was the most significant indigenous independence movement in this century. The leaders were sophisticated and highly intellectual, wrapping themselves in the cloak of democracy and antifascism. The rhetoric of their pamphlets connected the Uyghurs to the struggle of all Central Asian Turks, language today echoed by Uyghurs in private conversations. One good example is a pamphlet signed by the National Freedom Group entitled "Why Are We Fighting":

Who are we? Who and where are our near and far relations? Where are the burial grounds—so dear to us—of our beloved and renowned ancestors?

In answer to these questions, any man who seeks the truth and whose heart is right cannot fail to say that the root of our nation and soul is not in China, but in Central Asia, in Kazakstan, Kirghizstan, and Tatarstan. Our native place is East Turkestan; we are the east-

ern branch and part of that race—bound to us by blood relationship—the other parts of which lie within the Soviet Union; we are
the part that is fighting.   (Benson 1990a:200)

Other writing demonstrates the nationalistic tenor and passion with
which the Ili leadership fought for their independence:

> In the same way that fascism counts as its enemies all people who
> love peace and freedom, thus did Sheng [Shicai] Tupan [warlord
> governor] and the savage Chinese who surrounded him count us,
> the native people of East Turkestan, as their enemies and as an
> inferior race. They oppressed us with every kind of cruelty . . .
> arrested over four thousand others of the vanguard, of those who
> were most liked, of those who knew the most, of those who were
> most clever, of those who were outstanding for leadership. Can we
> forget them?   (Benson 1990a:201)

plane crash
conspiracy

Stalin-
mao

Just before the establishment of the People's Republic of China, the central leaders of the East Turkestan Republic died in a plane crash on their
way to meet with the Chinese Communist leaders. The independent
republic was then taken over by the People's Republic. Many Uyghurs
believe that the crash was a conspiracy between Mao and Stalin, both of
whom would have wanted to topple the Ili threat.

The tension in this region has continued to the present, but reached its
height in 1962 as Chinese-Soviet relations fell apart. As millions of
Chinese faced famine and starvation as a result of the failure of the Great
Leap Forward, the Soviets helped an estimated 60,000–120,000 Uyghurs
and Kazaks to flee from Ili and other northern Xinjiang border regions to
the Soviet Union. Many Uyghur intellectuals fled with them, further
draining the indigenous Turkic leadership.

Some Uyghur intellectuals today still speak of the Chinese as fascist
colonizers who have destroyed the best and brightest Uyghurs, leaving
only unthinking stooges as Uyghur Communist leaders. In effect, they
bemoan the fact that the Communist Chinese have prevented the development of an effective vanguard.

Turpan Region

It was in Turpan that the elite of the Uyghur empire settled after 840 C.E.,
maintaining a separate "Uyghur" identity until the mid-fifteenth century.

Thus the Turpan oasis is the historic center of Uyghur culture. The Uyghur Empire was non-Islamic, powerful, and highly developed. The symbolic image of the non-Islamic and thus "pure" Turkic Uyghur Empire played a significant role in Kemal Atatürk's establishment of a modern Turkish identity based on roots that existed prior to Uyghur contact with Islamic and Persian culture. The Modern Turkish language of today reflects the association of Uyghur with high culture: the Turkish word *uygar* in fact means "civilized."

The period of greatest Uyghur prominence was during the thirteenth century, when the Uyghurs of the Turpan region, then known as Uyghuristan, were granted a special place in the Mongol Empire. Allsen writes that "Uyghuristan functioned as a reservoir of trained administrative personnel, which the Mongol khans drew upon extensively" (1983:267). The Uyghurs served as scholars, scribes, administrators, and advisers to Genghis Khan and were the ideal intermediaries between the nomad Mongols and other peoples encountered in Central Asia.[16]

The strategic importance of Turpan is often overlooked because the oasis sits in a deep depression and the heat and narrow passes leading to it made it an unpopular target for military campaigns.[17] Chinese and Tungan armies stayed north, in the steppe, and bypassed Turpan, moving on to Urumchi and from there south toward Kashgar. Only after securing the south would they return to capture Turpan. This gave Turpan more autonomy. It has always remained outside the influence of the six major oases of the Tarim Basin, the "Six Cities." However, when Yaqub Beg finally captured Turpan, he renamed the "Six Cities" the "Seven Cities" (*Yättä-shähär*), including Turpan in his domain (Hamada 1978:79).

The geographic legacy of Turpan kept the region focused east toward China. This influenced Qing Dynasty policy in both Turpan and Hami, which differed substantially from policy applied to the Altä-shähär oases west of Turpan. While in the rest of the Tarim oases an official (*beg*) system was created in which local Muslims were appointed to administrative posts, in Turpan and Hami the princes were made autonomous hereditary rulers (Saguchi 1978:64). The Qing government had more confidence in the political dependability of Turpan and Hami because both oases had a longer history of interaction with China and "Qing control was deeply rooted there" (Fletcher 1978:78).

In the mid-1930s, the Uyghurs used the historical symbol of the Uyghur Empire (744–840 C.E.) in the definition of the modern Uyghur people. The Uyghurs' reference to an early period of flourishing Turkic culture parallels the use of the ethnic label *Han*—harking back to the

Han Dynasty (third century B.C.E. to third century C.E.), considered a pinnacle of Chinese culture—for the majority Chinese population in the People's Republic.

Turpan is a truly beautiful and fascinating place.[18] In *The Gobi Desert* Mildred Cable wrote:

> There is no more interesting oasis on the Asian highways than Turfan, which lies on the trade-route between Hami and Kashgar, and is always called "Turpan" by its own inhabitants. . . . Turpan lies like a green island in a sandy wilderness, its shores lapped by grit and gravel instead of ocean water, for the division between arid desert and fertile land is as definite as that between shore and ocean. Its fertility is amazing, and the effect on the traveller, when he steps from sterility and desiccation into the luxuriance of Turfan, is overwhelming.   (1987 [1942]:183)

Today, once again, the Uyghurs have the possibility of reestablishing their intermediary role in Central Asia. Uyghur merchants and intellectuals speak Mandarin and are relatively comfortable interacting with Han Chinese. Most Hans, on the other hand, feel awkward dealing with Central Asian Turks. Therefore, Uyghurs can serve as negotiators and liaisons for Han trade and political negotiations with the former Soviet Central Asian states and companies.

OASES AND INTELLECTUALS

In 1985, Uyghur intellectuals were allowed, for the first time under Communist rule, to somewhat openly pursue their agendas to better the position of the Uyghur people. The timing coincided with China's opening of Xinjiang to international tourism and trade, from which it had been sealed off since the Sino-Soviet split in 1962. While intellectuals were able to be more open about their work, their endeavors have been made difficult by continuing Chinese government censorship, which forces Uyghur debates to include multiple levels of meaning to avoid censorship or an outright ban from writing. For this reason, in Uyghur writings the surface historical events and personages may seem to represent one thing, but contain below the surface other discernible elements that send quite a different message. For example, in the late 1920s, Abduhaliq, known as "Uyghur," a nationalist poet from Turpan, called on the Uyghurs to "cut the heads off of the enemy." But who was the enemy? Did he mean the Han Chinese, as some Uyghurs hold today, or the Chinese Nationalists (Kuomintang-KMT), as the Communists claim? Would the publication of poetry of this nature be dangerous to the Communist government?

Intellectuals must consider the reaction of the Chinese government to their publications and select histories and heroes that do not threaten the Chinese state by stirring overtly nationalist sentiments. In this process Uyghur intellectuals sometimes come into conflict with the state over symbolic reinterpretation. Sometimes these conflicts are introduced by outside forces. For example, in 1985, when Chinese television quoted Turkish Prime Minister Torgut Ozal as stating that Xinjiang was the homeland of the Turkic peoples, it was interpreted by radical Uyghurs as support for pan-Turkism: all Turkic peoples united in one nation-state. These Uyghurs had long maintained that Turks in Turkey called the Uyghur people "Ata-Turk," the father of the Turkish peoples, and the Prime Minister seemed to confirm this belief.[19] Such statements led the Chinese government to crack down on any expressions of Uyghur separatism.

China greatly fears the development of pan-Turkism in Xinjiang and throughout the Turkic world, for it could threaten Xinjiang stability. For many years China opposed the work of Isa Yusup Alptekin, a Uyghur who fled political persecution in Xinjiang in 1951 and was the leader of the Uyghur exiles until his death in 1995. From his base in Turkey he headed the Eastern Turkestan Refugees Association, *Doğu Türkistan Gocmenler Derneği*, established in 1960. The organization's emblem and flag—a white star and crescent on a blue background—use the same design as the failed Turkish Islamic Republic of East Turkestan (TIRET). Alptekin was both pan-Turkist and pro-Muslim; he sought to attract Muslim support from the Arab world for a pan-Turkic nation but met with little success.[20] As the Chinese have been vigilant against pan-Turkist activities, Alptekin's influence is rarely perceptible among Uyghur intellectuals: anyone whose writing is deemed by the government to touch on Uyghur separatist or pan-Turkic themes could face imprisonment, house arrest, or a lifetime ban from writing.

Uyghur intellectuals are key figures who evaluate and appropriate historical symbols, salient historical events and individuals, that can be manipulated to produce contending nationalist ideologies. Passed on by word of mouth and through historical studies written by the Uyghurs themselves, these symbols have become politically significant and powerful because they challenge Chinese versions of Uyghur history and mobilize national sentiment.

Uyghur nationalist ideology is concerned with the intentions and agendas of Uyghur intellectuals because they believe their versions of history will lead the Uyghur people in new directions. By selecting heroes and histories, these intellectuals attempt to reshape the future by manipulating the past. They produce alternative images of a Uyghur nationalist ideology that are intimately connected with their own political choices and strategies. Katherine Verdery speaks of the struggle over such strategies as a "drama of alternatives" (1990:85). These alternatives not only define Uyghur identity vis-a-vis the Han Chinese, but also are a means of influencing local politics. Challenges are made to other intellectuals from other oases, not necessarily to deny their local histories' importance but to make them less salient in a new "national" history.

It may be questioned whether the intellectuals themselves understand they are in fact contending with one another over versions of Uyghur history and the respect and honor that each believes should be accorded a particular Uyghur figure. In a similar case, of Romanian intellectuals, Verdery found that although the participants might not experience their activity as a "struggle" or "competition," this did not mean that their alternative values were not in a competitive relation (1991:19). In Xinjiang, however, competitions over history are so intense and explicit that local oasis presses often refuse to publish materials written either about or by Uyghurs from rival oases.

Usurping Oasis Legacies

Communist China's incorporation of Xinjiang was an attempt to override historical and geographical divisions there within a short time span, and to turn the region into an internal colony. Until 1949, Xinjiang had been relatively independent from the central authorities in China and was influenced instead by the civilizations on its western border. Its inadequate transportation and communications, compounded by its harsh terrain and great distance from China proper, were the greatest barriers to the integration of this frontier region with China's core.[21] Xinjiang's physical isolation from China led to a great amount of penetration by the outside, principally Russia, which had the advantage of proximity. Much of Xinjiang's trade was directed westward; a significant quantity of its cotton, raisins, apricots, and silk was exported to the Soviet Union. The Soviets had signed treaties early on with the Nationalist Chinese government and later with the Chinese warlords in Xinjiang, which gave them wide-ranging rights to exploit Xinjiang's natural resources. The Chinese Communist government soon realized that they must radically alter this geographically determined situation.

When the Communists took control of Xinjiang, they had to consider two historical legacies. First, both the Kashgar and Ili regions were politically volatile. Kashgar remained an Islamic stronghold, and Russia still exerted powerful influence in the Ili region. Second, a distinct territorial division existed between the nomadic Kazaks and the sedentary Uyghur oasis agriculturists. The Kazaks, less numerous than the Uyghurs, lived in Zhungaria, to the north, and the Uyghurs inhabited southern and eastern Xinjiang. The Chinese took advantage of this situation by playing the Kazaks against the Uyghurs. When they pushed the Kazaks into smaller pastures and took their land for agricultural and industrial development, the Chinese compensated them by increasing their political leadership of Xinjiang.[22]

The Communist Chinese government sought to fully incorporate Xinjiang into its core political economy for several strategic reasons. The geopolitical borders of Xinjiang were of major importance to Chinese security interests vis-a-vis the Soviet Union. Furthermore, China needed the region's oil, coal, and other mineral wealth. Its goals therefore included shifting Xinjiang's economic and geographic focus away from the west to diminish its trade with the Soviet Union and toward Urumchi and the east. Urumchi was made the transportation hub toward which all roads of Xinjiang were oriented. This new highway network was of immense strategic value for the Chinese. However, it was the westward extension of the railroad in 1962, from China proper to Urumchi, that had the greatest effect on Xinjiang (see figure 1.4).[23] Once the center of Xinjiang shifted to Urumchi, the importance of the cities of Kashgar and Ili diminished.[24]

The railroad system spurred industrial and agricultural growth. As part of this wide-scale development, large irrigation projects were set in motion to further industrial and agricultural development requiring the exploitation of limited fresh water and fertile soil resources that otherwise would have been utilized by indigenous Uyghurs and Kazaks. The importance of this developed infrastructure was summarized by McMillen, who writes,

> The transportation network, especially the railroad, was to provide a means for strengthening the security of Xinjiang and its valuable natural resources by giving the Chinese an easier and more efficient way to ship goods, equipment, Han settlers, and troops into the

FIGURE 1.4   Geographic Reorientation and Incorporation of Xinjiang into China Proper

region from the East. It would also provide an outlet for Xinjiang's raw materials and products to China proper.   (1979:173)

But the most dramatic changes to take place in Xinjiang were demographic ones.

UYGHUR/HAN SOCIAL BORDERS AND STATE POLICY

The migration and settlement of huge numbers of Han Chinese after the region came under Communist control profoundly affected the population distribution in Xinjiang. Redistribution followed the general geographic shift of the region away from the western towns of Ili and Kashgar and toward Urumchi.[25] The urban population in northern Xinjiang increased drastically because changes in the transportation networks allowed increasing numbers of Han immigrants to enter Xinjiang more easily. Han Chinese migration to Xinjiang to help with industrialization caused a dramatic population increase in the northern cities that lie on the east-west belt along the Tianshan Mountains, including Urumchi, Changji, Shihezi, Karamay, and Boertala.[26] In order to speed the growth of industry centered around Urumchi and provide food for the predominantly Han Chinese migrant workers, agriculture in northern Xinjiang was given priority in the areas along the rail line (McMillen 1979:175).[27]

Large numbers of Han Chinese built paramilitary state farms to meet China's mandate for agricultural development of the region. These Han Chinese were primarily demobilized Communist troops and Nationalist (Kuomintang) forces who had been under the command of Chiang Kai-shek and were then ordered to take up positions on the fringe of "wasteland" areas—the areas north and south of the Tianshan Mountains, the steppe lands of Zhungaria, and locations along the main transportation routes linking Urumchi with China proper. In 1954, these farmers were reorganized into the Production and Construction Corps (PCC).[28] The PCC served as an effective sponge for the Chinese government, absorbing Han Chinese who left or were forced out of China proper. These included Han with stigmatized family backgrounds, youths sent to the countryside in the wake of the Cultural Revolution, retired and demobilized servicemen, excess urban labor, and political prisoners and criminals.[29] The PCC, with a population of over 2.2 million in 1992, has been a major political force in maintaining Chinese control of Xinjiang. By mid-1982, it had established over 170 state farms and had built 691 medium-large factories (McMillen 1984:587). By 1984, the PCC accounted for a quarter of the value of Xinjiang's total production, but with Xinjiang's great expansion of production and trade beginning in 1985, the PCC contribution dropped to 15 percent by 1992 (Xinjiang Shengchan Jianshe Bingtuan and Tongji Nianjian Bianji Weiyuanhui 1993).

Before the People's Republic of China conquest, southern Xinjiang (south of the Tianshan range) had historically been the center of economic activity. Until 1949, over 70 percent of the 4.3 million people in Xinjiang lived in the south (Korla, Aksu, Khotan, Kashgar). A mere 4 percent lived in the east (Hami and Turpan), and only 25 percent lived in the north (Urumchi, Shihezi, Ili, Altay). Today, however, due to the migratory influx and development of the north in the 1960s and 1970s, this region now possesses the majority of the population, having overtaken the south in 1980. By the end of 1984, inmigration also caused the urban population to skyrocket to 3.5 million, 26 percent of Xinjiang's total population (Yuan 1990:65, 68).

The Chinese government had a policy of settling Han immigrants in new lands not occupied by Uyghurs or in new towns adjacent to older Uyghur communities. Hans claim this settlement pattern allowed the Uyghurs to continue their way of life without Han interference. To many Uyghurs, however, it was perceived as an encirclement. Uyghurs increasingly saw the Han Chinese as their opponents, and no longer focused on their rivalries with Uyghurs in other oases.[30] This change obscured the historical ethnic divisions that existed in Xinjiang prior to Communist arrival.

2

Oasis Identities and Cross-Border Influence

They call us "turban heads (*chantou*)."
—"Uyghur," "Unsettled (*Ich Pushush*)"

The modern definition of the Uyghur people as encompassing all the oasis Turks of Xinjiang hides two traditional divisions of Uyghur society that have existed since 840 C.E.: the strong local oasis identities and the different strategies that each oasis employs in response to political, social, economic, and geographical forces. Historically, contacts across borders with other countries were much more frequent and important than those among the oases themselves; people covered the distances between oases so slowly that the oasis populations remained isolated from one another. Prior to the arrival of motorized transport, a camel caravan took forty-five days to travel from the Kashgar oasis in the west to Turpan in the east. In contrast, the Ferghana Valley in today's Uzbekistan was less than a week's journey from Kashgar. These geographical relationships have had profound effects on local identity: Kashgar was strongly influenced by the Islamic civilizations to its west, while Turpan was more affected by Han Chinese culture and Khotan had close connections with India.

This pattern is of long standing. According to archaeological evidence, the oases in the west and along the northern Tarim rim were populated by Iranian Sakas. The southern frontier, from the Yarkand region to Lop Nor, was occupied by Indians who had come from northwest India over the mountains. The region that extended eastward through Turpan was ruled by another Indo-European people known as the Tokharians. The Zhungarian region was populated by western Mongolian and Turkic nomadic tribes (Samolin 1957–1958:48). The pattern forms a geographic template that has determined where and to what extent outside civilizations influenced the region throughout its history.

In the modern period, the Chinese government weakened the relations between individual oases and the peoples and cultures outside today's borders by radically turning Xinjiang's focus inward. Motorized transport shrank the temporal distances between oases. Furthermore, and most important, after 1949 Communist China attempted to cut Xinjiang's cross-border ties and linked Xinjiang's economic development with China. For the first time in their history, the inhabitants of the Xinjiang oases were completely isolated from their historical, religious, kin, and economic ties; the imposed internal focus became a crucial factor in the development of modern Uyghur identity.

The historical legacy of oasis division carries over into contemporary local conceptions of Uyghur identity. Uyghurs still identify themselves according to the oasis in which they live, and perceived differences among the oases are extremely significant. They influence how Uyghur intellectual elites select local heroes and manipulate Uyghur historiography and, through this definition process, create contesting versions of Uyghur national identity that peasants at the local oasis level either internalize and use, or reject and abandon.

The opening of the borders in the 1980s strongly affected the focus of the oases, once again turning their economic, political, social, and cultural attention from Urumchi and China to their neighbors across the borders. For example, during this period Pakistani merchants were frequent visitors to Kashgar and other southern oases, but not to Ili or Urumchi. Japanese tourists were more prominent in Turpan than in any other oasis because its Buddhist historical sites are significant to a Japanese sect. Uyghurs from Soviet Central Asia who fled Ili in 1962 began returning there to visit relatives. These travelers from various countries are profoundly influencing the Uyghur worldview within each oasis location.

When I returned to conduct fieldwork in 1989, I suspected that the opening of Xinjiang's borders to neighboring countries was leading to radical changes in Uyghur worldviews and notions of ethnic identity—to a breakdown in the modern, unified Uyghur identity and a reestablishment of traditional trade and cultural ties with other countries. This would cause rivalries among the oases to resurface, which would lead to further fragmentation of Uyghur identity along traditional lines.

Xinjiang's geographic template produced axes of outside cultural influence that penetrated the region (see figure 2.1).[1] These can be delineated as follows. The region in the southern Tarim Basin, from Yarkand past Khotan to Keriya, was most strongly influenced by Indian culture. The region west and north of the Tarim Basin, from Kashgar toward Kucha, was influenced by the western Turkestan region, particularly by the peoples of the Ferghana Valley, including the Andijan, Khokand, and Osh areas. The northwestern Zhungarian Basin was oriented to the Semiretchia ("Seven Rivers") region of what is today Kazakstan and parts of western Central Asia, and it included nomadic Mongolian and Turkic tribes. Finally, the eastern part of Xinjiang, including Turpan and Hami (and Urumchi), was tied closely to China.[2]

FIGURE 2.1   The Four Geographic Template Divisions of Xinjiang

Almost a century ago, C. P. Skrine, a British diplomat, observed that "In considering the manners, customs, folklore, etc. of the Tarim Basin, it must be remembered that considerable differences exist between the four or five chief oases, corresponding roughly to their geographical positions" (1926:12). These differences were caused by the great distances between the oases, which impeded frequent interaction. Distances based on camel and horse caravan travel time, as reported by Skrine in the 1920s, further clarify why some cross-border trade routes proved more effective, leading oases to be influenced by particular border areas (see table 2.1 and figure 2.2).

The oases are the essential lines along which outside cultural influences were and are transmitted, each line forming the axis of a sector of civilization. It must be stressed that the historical focus of the Xinjiang oases was not inward, toward each other, but outward, across borders. Because the various outside civilizations affected each oasis quite differently, one may say that there are many Xinjiangs.

Turpan is best known for its grapes, and since 1985 the government has encouraged its specialization in grape production. Turpan headgear reflects the "grape consciousness" of the oasis dwellers: their round caps, called *doppa*, are almost always decorated with the grape-flower motif. Each oasis, Kashgar, Khotan, and others, has its own *doppa* design;[3] throughout Xinjiang, the *doppas* worn by Uyghur men indicate which oasis they are from.[4]

TABLE 2.1

Xinjiang Temporal Distance (Horse, Donkey, and Camel Transport)

Kashgar to Ili (via Muzart pass)	7 days
Kashgar to Osh (Ferghana Valley)	5 days
Khotan to Kashmir	49 days
Khotan to Keriya	4 days
Tacheng (Chuguchak) to Urumchi	16 days
Turpan to Beijing	115 days
Turpan to Tunhuang	17 days
Qarashähär to Kashgar	31 days
Lop Nor to Tunhuang	20–25 days
Kashgar to Beijing (telegram)	7 days
Kashgar to St. Petersburg (telegram)	7 days
Kashgar to Andijan	5–7 days
Kashgar to Beijing	5 months (with rail)
Kashgar to Urumchi	25–30 days

SOURCE: Skrine (1926).

FIGURE 2.2   Xinjiang Temporal Distance Before Motorized Transport

Hami (Qomul), like Turpan to the west, is closely linked to the classical Uyghur Empire and Uyghuristan culture (744–1450). Mokhtar Moham-med, a Uyghur folklorist, claims that the music and songs from both Hami and Turpan closely resemble those of classical Uyghur culture. Since the center of this culture was in Turpan and not Kashgar, his argument is jus-tified. Most Kashgar Uyghurs are shocked by such findings, since they consider Turpan and Hami Uyghurs to have been strongly influenced by Han China and thus less Uyghur than themselves. Mokhtar Mohammed, himself from the Merkit region (near Yarkand and Kashgar), concludes that the Turkicness or classical Uyghurness of the songs and music seems to be better maintained where Chinese influence is stronger than Islamic cultural pressures.

Khotan's connection with India is still reflected in Uyghur medicine, which is related to both Greek and Indian medicine. The sole modern Uyghur medical college is located in Khotan. Some Uyghurs also believe that because of intermarriage with northern Indians over centuries, Khotanliks have lighter skin and look more Caucasian, more Indo-

2.1   Veiled Kashgarlik women selling *doppas* of various designs (1985).

European. An even more distinctive characteristic of Khotan is the large number of people with goiters. This striking feature was noted by Marco Polo when he went through the region in the thirteenth century. Today the ailment persists because Khotanliks do not have a source of seafood and prefer *tash tuz* (rock salt), mined in the desert and boiled with water, over iodized salt sold in stores.

The differences brought about by location and distance helped maintain the distinct oasis identities and engender strong oasis loyalties in spite of general similarities. This point has not been stressed adequately in most studies of the modern Uyghurs (Benson 1990a, Forbes 1986, Gladney 1990). These geographical features and oasis loyalties favored decentralization and impeded unification under a single political system.

CROSS-BORDER CONTACTS

By 1990, it was clear that cross-border contacts were affecting aspects of Uyghur religion, politics, education, economics, and ethnicity as they had for generations before Communist China's attempt to incorporate Xinjiang. Understanding the relation between contemporary and historical international contacts requires examining how these aspects of Uyghur society and culture have been variously affected by interactions with outside bordering cultures over the past century.[5]

Religion

The history of Islam in Xinjiang has not been harmonious. Violent raids and warfare by two rival Sufi sects wreaked havoc in Xinjiang from the seventeenth to the twentieth centuries.[6] Before 1949, mosque property, *vaqf (wahpi)*, consisted of agricultural land. In Turpan it included grapevines, which provided considerable income. People also gave their mosques water from *karez* canals, and landlords (*pomishik*) gave mosques substantial economic support. When Xinjiang came under Communist control, the party's political and economic administrative structure excluded Islamic clerics, known as *mollas*, thereby weakening their power and prestige. Since the religious reforms of 1978, however, mosques have been rebuilt and new ones constructed at a rapid pace. Their growing wealth has paralleled that of Uyghur peasants, who give a percentage of their income to the mosques. Although Islam separates the Uyghurs and Hans, both religiously and ideologically, Chinese lib-

2.2   Bus stop along the northern Tarim route of the ancient Silk Road (1985).

eralization policies related to religion have fostered positive sentiments toward the Chinese government among Turpan Uyghurs.

This reaction contrasts markedly with that of Uyghurs in Kashgar, who over time have tenaciously held to anti-Chinese sentiments. Kashgar has less land for grape and cotton cultivation and therefore has not experienced the same economic growth as Turpan. In general, Islamic life in the south, particularly in Kashgar, is more conservative. For example, women are completely veiled in brown cloth, while women in Turpan wear only head-scarves.[7] In addition, precisely because of the strong anti-Chinese sentiment in Kashgar, the Chinese government has regulated religious education and mosque construction there more strictly.

Although the Chinese government plays up the Islamic threat in Xinjiang, Kashgar is the only volatile Islamic center that historically incited many rebellions against Chinese rule. Even today, anti-Han sentiment is still stronger in Kashgar than in any other Uyghur oasis, mainly because of its religious tradition. The Islamic culture of Kashgar came from the ancient cities of the Ferghana Valley, which before motorized transportation was only five days away by pony caravan across the mountains (Skrine 1926:2). Since a journey to Beijing took five months, a great deal more contacts and trade were developed between Kashgar and the Ferghana Valley than between Kashgar and Beijing.

The practice of Islam can be a strongly symbolic means of confronting the Chinese state. By embracing Islam, Uyghurs reject the atheism of Chinese Communism as well as its goals of modernization and social liberation. In Xinjiang, Islam permeates all realms of Uyghur life—political, social, and economic. In fact, the term Muslim (*Musulman*) is not only a reference for a religious person, but is used to refer to all native Central Asians. Thus, to call oneself a Uyghur is also to accept Islam. Even Uyghur intellectuals who are against Islamic traditionalism and its resurgence consider themselves *Musulman* and take part in Islamic cultural practices. Here there is a clear symbiosis between national identity and religious identity.[8]

In general, the Chinese view Turpan citizens as more trustworthy than those of oases to the south. Chinese officials appear to believe that the growth of Islam in Turpan, a historically quiet region, is less likely to produce anti-Chinese disturbances than in the western oases. Hence there are discrepancies in China's religious policies toward various regions. The special relationship Turpan Uyghurs have with the Chinese has given them more influence within the Xinjiang government in recent years. For example, Xinjiang's former Uyghur leader, Tömür Dawamät, long-term chairman of the Xinjiang Uyghur Autonomous Region, is from the Turpan region, as is Yüsüp Äsa, vice chairman of Xinjiang and former mayor of Urumchi.

The growth of Islamic tradition at the local level is extremely significant because it encourages a variety of responses to Chinese attempts at acculturation, ranging from overt resistance to outright indifference.

Uyghur reactions to Islam also vary greatly according to oasis. But in the oases where Islamic culture tends to deepen the sense of separation many Uyghurs feel from Chinese society and cultural influence, Islam is reinforced. It is this relationship that the Chinese seem not to understand in their attempts to limit or control Islam.[9] Government religious reforms were intended to quell Uyghur disaffection with Chinese rule and cause Uyghurs to develop more harmonious sentiments for the Han Chinese. However, the Chinese are caught in a dilemma: when they suppress Islam, most Uyghurs feel oppressed and oppose the government; when they allow or encourage it, Uyghurs become more content with the government but their strengthened Islamic practice leads them to feel more separate from and apathetic toward Chinese society. Kashgar and Khotan, two major southern oases, have shown the most resistance, if not outright violence, toward government restrictions on Islamic practice, while Turpan, Ili, and Hami have reacted less forcefully, sometimes with seeming indifference.

Muslim rituals influence all realms of Uyghur life. The most meaningful one for Uyghur males is circumcision, which most often takes place at the age of seven, when children are old enough to understand at least some of the religious significance of the ritual. Abdals, members of a Shia-influenced heterodox sect who are a pariah group within Sunni Muslim Turkic territory and are considered Uyghur for census purposes (Benson and Svanberg 1988:22), perform the circumcisions. Many Abdals are beggars, musicians, makers of small handicrafts, and peripatetic mystics (Svanberg 1989a:41). Most Uyghurs do not know that the Abdals are of a different Muslim sect.[10]

Mannerheim wrote about Abdals in Xinjiang:

> They are pursued by the curse of the Imam Hussein and are forced to go in for begging as their occupation. . . . You meet them everywhere, carrying a beggar's staff, some in rags, others well dressed and wearing ornaments of some value, rings, necklets, brooches, etc. The sight of Abdals as beggars is so common that many people make the mistake of calling beggars Abdals. They seldom admit that they belong to this tribe and seem to consider the name Abdal an insult.   (1969 [1942]:92)

There are few beggars in Xinjiang, but many Uyghurs do not treat them well. Children throw rocks at them and merchants chase them away. In fact, Tungans tend to treat Uyghur beggars better than the

Uyghurs themselves do. This is because Tungans consider all Uyghur beggars to be religious mystics, where Uyghurs see this possibility only in terms of the beggars' separate function of performing circumcisions.

The Islamic ritual calendar also reinforces a strong Islamic identity at the local level.[11] By and large, the older Uyghur generation is more devout, observing all the events and requirements of the Islamic ritual calendar. In contrast, a number of younger Uyghurs, those under forty, do not observe the month-long fast during Ramadan. But their numbers are diminishing as Islam gains in popularity. As a result of Islam's growth, the influence of the more conservative elders at the village level has also grown.

During the Qurban Festival, when Muslims complete their *hajj* to Mecca to honor Allah's intervention in Abraham's attempted sacrifice of his son Ishmail, some Uyghurs from Turpan make a pilgrimage to Kashgar, the Islamic center of Xinjiang. Historically, Kashgar came under the greatest influence from the Islamic centers of Bukhara and Samarkand. In Turpan, families purchase sheep to slaughter for feasts eaten at home. Musicians sing religious ballads and storytellers recount the Abraham and Ishmail story (Islam maintains that since Ishmail is Abraham's firstborn son and not Isaac, Ishmail was the son nearly sacrificed). Increasingly, Uyghurs decorate their homes and restaurants with posters depicting such religious themes rather than political ones. The posters reinforce Uyghur consciousness of the Muslim patriarchs and spur their mission to multiply the followers of the faith. Religious posters are sold only in Urumchi and Kashgar, since Urumchi is central to all Muslim minorities in Xinjiang and Kashgar is the Uyghur religious Mecca.

Pakistan and Saudi Arabia are the focal countries for Islam. Pakistan is the major transit point for Uyghurs on their way to Mecca for the *hajj*, traveling first by bus and later by boat or plane.[12] Many Uyghurs asked me to translate affidavits from Pakistani relatives attesting to their ability to host a relative hoping to visit Pakistan. The affidavits are invitations to Uyghur peasants to go to Pakistan and then to the *hajj*,[13] and are required by the Chinese government for permission to leave the country. Due to the great number of applications to leave, however, there was a three-year wait in 1990. Though the people sending the invitations from Pakistan are supposed to be relatives, they are often friends of friends, or simply people Uyghurs meet on the road to Saudi Arabia and from whom they ask the favor.

Saudi influence has developed because of the Uyghur *hajj* to Mecca. The pilgrimage is a major aspiration for Uyghurs, and posters and car-

2.3   During the Qurban Festival, a storyteller outside Kashgar's Id Kah Mosque describes Abraham's attempted sacrifice of Ishmael (1985).

pets with images of Mecca are found in many Uyghur homes and restaurants. The *hajj* takes about three months and cost US $1,850 in 1990. It was then also possible to pay for the trip in Chinese currency: 10,000 *yuan* (US $1 = 3.7–4.7 *yuan*). In 1987, about 180 people from Turpan and a total of 1,600 from China made their way to Mecca. One Uyghur writer

2.4   Pakistani merchants bringing goods to Xinjiang along the Karakoram
Highway (1986).

who had made the *hajj*, Zordun Sabir, related a rumor about a squadron
in the Saudi Air Force made up solely of Uyghur pilots. He also stated
that there are about 30,000 Uyghurs in Saudi Arabia, living in Medina,
but Uyghur exiles in the United States suggest that the number is closer
to 10,000 Uyghurs living in various Saudi localities.

Political Cross-Border Contacts

In 1985 cross-border contacts linking Ili and Kashgar with Kazakstan and the Soviet Central Asian republics were rare.[14] But by 1989 and 1990, numerous trade, technical, and cultural exchanges between Central Asian republics and Ili and Urumchi were taking place. Like the "Ping-Pong diplomacy" between the United States and China in 1972, these exchanges have warmed cross-border relations considerably. The famous Kazakstani singer, Roza Rymbaeva, performed in Urumchi during the Chinese National Day festivities in 1989, and a well-known Soviet Uyghur author, Turghun Tohtomov, came to Urumchi on a cultural exchange later that year.

In 1989, all indications pointed to a major rapprochement between the Soviet Union and China with Gorbechev's visit to Beijing. Later, in 1992, the railroad from Urumchi to the Kazakstan border, called the "Iron Silk Road" by Chinese officials, was completed and trains went into operation. The rail link to Western Europe is projected to be a boon to Xinjiang's economy. Xinjiang's fruit and coal will be able to reach Europe in less than a week, and the foreign currency received in exchange will be a tremendous help for Xinjiang. However, it is not expected that Xinjiang province will be able to keep all the money, since traditionally most is returned to the central government in Beijing.[15]

.   By 1989, cross-border travel had increased so much that an Aeroflot desk was opened at the Overseas Chinese Hotel in Urumchi. Over the past several years, many Uyghurs have begun to receive letters from family members in Central Asia for the first time since 1962. At the Turpan post office I was often asked to help people write letters in Russian to Uyghurs or help post office personnel read packages addressed in Russian to Turpanliks. Until 1985, Uyghurs had to travel to Beijing to obtain permission to travel to Soviet Central Asia to visit their relatives, the majority of whom left Xinjiang in 1962; Uyghurs now obtain permission in Urumchi. At the Public Security Bureau there, a great number of people, many with relatives from Central Asia accompanying them, were always trying to get permission to go to Central Asia. Because of these increased contacts, Uyghurs in Urumchi began to study Russian intensively, hoping to take advantage of better relations between Russia and the Central Asian republics to develop further ties to the West. Han Chinese, on the other hand, think it best to study English because they see little hope for Russia and hope to go directly to the West instead.

2.5   In Ili, a Uyghur man and his sister reunite in 1985 for the first time since his flight to Kazakstan in 1962.

Relations with other nations developed rapidly in 1989 and 1990. Several trade delegations from Ankara, Turkey visited Xinjiang. The Uyghur leader at the time, Tömür Dawamät, was shown on television speaking to the Turkish representatives without interpreters, linguistic evidence of the Uyghurs' close ethnic ties with Turkic peoples throughout the world. The Uyghurs, especially those in Kashgar, looked to Turkey for pan-Turkist inspiration and believed that Turkey supported their pan-Turkist aspirations as well as the growing Islamic movement in Xinjiang.[16]

Education

There were few educational opportunities in Xinjiang until the 1930s. Writing in the 1920s, Claremont P. Skrine explained that there were

no schools except those attached to mosques, at which nothing is taught by the mullas but reading, writing and the Qur'an. By means of a strict censorship not only are books and all written or printed matter dealing with current events kept from the hands of Chinese and Muhammadans alike, but the dissemination in writing of news or of any ideas whatever among the inhabitants is effectually prevented.   (1926:61)

This rather hopeless educational situation began in 1911, when the revolution against the Manchu government brought an end to the Qing Dynasty and established the Republic of China. In the same year, a Yunnanese Han Chinese named Yang Zengxin, commander of a military force in Gansu, became the first warlord governor of Xinjiang during the Republican period. He prohibited newspaper circulation and the importation of books to eliminate foreign influence in the region.

Even before the arrival of Yang, and well prior to Soviet takeover, reformist efforts such as the Jadid Movement in the first years of the twentieth century began to influence the Muslims of Central Asia (Allworth 1990:121). During Tsarist times and up until 1924, a small number of Jadid reformists established numerous secular schools promulgating "scientific" (*päni*) education that stressed Western concepts of nationalism, including the notions of independence and autonomy for ethnic peoples. Xinjiang governor Yang Zengxin, who straddled Tsarist and Soviet regimes and was alarmed by both Russian and later Soviet intentions, feared a Turkic uprising inspired by the Russians and thus banned all Turkic-language publications, prohibited political discussions, and installed a strict system of surveillance that included a repressive security force and Turkic informants (Forbes 1986:14). The numerous tortures and murders carried out by Yang's security force caused fear throughout Xinjiang. Yang restricted Sufi Islamic teachings, already strong in the region, and blocked contact with Russian Muslims by limiting cross-border travel.

Yang did in fact have reason to worry about the events transpiring across the border in Russian (later Soviet) Central Asia. At that time, Central Asia was similar to Xinjiang: both regions had stagnated under social institutions dominated by religious conservatives. Under the Tsars and the Soviets, Central Asian people were caught within a rigid traditionalism. Jadid nationalist reformers in Central Asia had sought to develop secular education to empower the Turkic peoples. Their movement was usurped by the Soviets, who began to replace Jadid schools in 1924 and to "liquidate" Jadid reformers and all others considered Central Asian nationalists in 1930. The Soviets hoped to transform the region through various social, cultural, and religious reforms including changing the script, making Western clothing available, promoting secular schools and general awareness of world events, and raising the status of women. The changes introduced by the Jadids and the Soviets to Central Asia provided a model for Uyghur reformists in Xinjiang decades later. The similarity between the regions helps to explain the subsequent swift rise of nationalism throughout Xinjiang in the 1930s and '40s.

Soviet secular reforms dovetailed with earlier Jadid strategies that used secular education, historiography, literature, religion, theater, presses, and publishing to accomplish their purposes (Allworth 1990:121). Prior to Soviet control, the secular education promulgated by Jadid reformers had the most profound impact on the population of Central Asia and was both the earliest and the most long-lasting of the programs. Histories were written in an effort to educate the populace about their collective past. Historiography was integral to the secular reforms, and the Central Asian educated elite viewed it as a way to stimulate the revitalization of Turkic society (Allworth 1990:121). However, secular education was hampered by efforts of the conservative rulers (Amirs) of Bukhara and Khiva, who created an anti-intellectual climate that resembled Xinjiang's. Numerous Muslim clerics were opposed to the study and teaching of history, considering it a sin (Allworth 1990:124).

Despite governor Yang Zengxin's draconian measures, which were meant to seal off the province of Xinjiang from Tsarist and then Soviet influence, wealthy merchants and ambitious young Xinjiang residents traveled and worked in Central Asia, where wages were higher. Influenced by their new way of life and the comparative stagnation of their homeland, some of the more wealthy merchants opened schools and libraries in Xinjiang and sent Xinjiang students abroad for study.

Given Yang's extreme measures to keep the indigenous population from information and education, the extent to which secular education developed in Turpan under the guidance of one wealthy merchant, Mäkhsut Muhiti, is remarkable. Just before and in the early years of Yang's rule, 1910–1913, Mäkhsut traveled to Russian Central Asia, bringing back Uzbek and Tatar intellectuals to establish secular schools. Courses in geography, history, physical education, writing, arithmetic, and natural science were taught in the Uyghur language. Upon completing their studies, and in the same manner that late-nineteenth-century Jadid educators expanded their influence in Central Asia, students were sent back to their home villages to establish schools and teach an ever-growing number of Uyghurs.

In 1928, Yang Zengxin was assassinated by a Chinese subordinate within his own government, and leadership of the province was seized by Jin Shuren. Less able than Yang, Jin was unable to keep the lid on popular discontent. Although he maintained and expanded Yang's system of surveillance and censorship and prohibited travel outside of the province, increasing numbers of Turkic intellectuals throughout Xinjiang began to establish schools. Newspapers also found their way from Soviet Central Asia and India to Xinjiang, enabling its citizens to keep up with current events in neighboring regions.

This nascent reform movement was seriously curtailed from 1931 to 1934, when rebellion broke out against Jin Shuren's attempt to annex the semiautonomous Hami area and spread throughout Xinjiang. Taking advantage of the turmoil, Tungan (Chinese Muslim) forces invaded Xinjiang from Gansu, in the east. In 1933, government forces under soon-to-be Xinjiang warlord governor Sheng Shicai arrested and executed many of the Uyghur intellectuals involved in reform efforts, in retribution for their allegedly harboring rebel forces.

In the short period of reconciliation that ensued after Sheng's forces quelled the rebellion in 1934, Uyghur reformists again began to influence the region. With Sheng's recapture of Kashgar in 1934, a reformist newspaper, *Yengi Hayat*, began publication. The paper was established by the newly formed Kashgar Uyghur Progress Union, comprised of Uyghurs from various parts of Xinjiang, including Mäkhsut Muhiti from Turpan (Naby 1987:105). The newspaper's articles addressed Uyghur politics, culture, and poetry, as well as international events, especially those taking place in Turkey and the Middle East. Over the next two years, almost 2,500 copies were circulated weekly before publication was terminated by the government. The Kashgar Uyghur Progress Union rapidly built reformist schools resembling the Jadid schools. By 1936, there were seventeen schools serving over 500 students. In the same year, the Union's first director was assassinated by an unidentified assailant, causing a crisis in the Union (Naby 1987:106–7). At this time Xinjiang was still divided into rival Islamic Sufi factions, and some of these attempted to stifle the development of secular education.

Despite the turmoil, Mäkhsut Muhiti remained actively involved in education in Turpan. To increase the number of secular science (*päni*) schools, he organized a six-month teaching course that trained fifty teachers. By the end of 1934, eighteen schools, with a total enrollment of 1,029, were in operation. To end the disturbances in the region, Sheng Shicai relaxed his control of Xinjiang, allowing a brief opening for reform from 1934 to 1936 during which Mäkhsut Muhiti arranged for a large group of students from all regions of Xinjiang to study at the Central Asia University and the Central Asia Military Academy, both in

Tashkent, as well as at other institutions abroad. British sources state that by 1935, 10,000 Uyghurs from throughout the Xinjiang region were studying in the USSR, Turkey, and Egypt, but this number seems highly exaggerated (Anonymous 1935:469).

While Sheng had allied himself with and received support from the Soviets during the two-year reform, he silenced many of the newly Soviet-trained Uyghur intellectuals in 1937, the same year Stalin's "Great Purge" swept across Soviet Central Asia. At this time Sheng increased censorship in the region, expanded his secret police forces, and declared that there was a far-reaching Trotskyist movement in the region. He then arrested 435 Uyghurs, Tungans, Mongols, Tatars, and Hans. Most of these educated activists were executed and many landowners, petty officials, and *molla*s were thrown into prison. This effectively silenced the progressive movements underway among the local population (Forbes 1986:159).

Believing that the Germans would defeat the Soviets, Sheng aligned himself with the anti-Communist Chinese Nationalist government in 1942. In this same year, Communist and progressive individuals, including Mao Zedong's brother, Mao Zemin, and Sheng Shicai's own brother, were arrested and executed in Xinjiang (Forbes 1986:159). Most of those Uyghur students who were studying abroad—in the Soviet Union and elsewhere—were imprisoned or killed upon returning to Xinjiang.

The governments of both Yang Zengxin and Sheng Shicai limited educational and social reform in Xinjiang and nearly precluded the development of Uyghur nationalism. After Sheng was removed from power in September 1944, ethnic revolts broke out, leading to the establishment two months later of the East Turkestan Republic in Ili, which lasted until 1949. By then, in the somewhat relaxed post-Sheng environment, there were twenty-eight Uyghur schools with 102 teachers and 1,638 students in Xinjiang (Gheni Maynam and Keram Tursun 1988:65). But the loss of so many educated Uyghurs was devastating to the development of Uyghur nationalism. In total, during Sheng's rule of Xinjiang about 100,000 people, mostly Uyghurs, were imprisoned; many of these were tortured and killed (Forbes 1986:161).

The stifling of Uyghur nationalism in Xinjiang has continued well into the Communist period. In fact, from 1911, when the Republic of China was established, until the early 1980s, the Han Chinese governing officials kept a strong grip on Xinjiang, greatly limiting the development of a significant intellectual elite among the Uyghurs. Han Chinese culture was the primary influence on educational development as the indigenous population was simply kept in the dark and away from national and global news. This pulled Xinjiang toward the Chinese state and effectively prevented influence from any other regional power except the Soviet Union along the northwestern border in Ili. There were brief periods when the Chinese government's grasp loosened, but when this occurred, nationalistic revolts broke out and engulfed the entire region in turmoil.

After gaining control of Xinjiang in 1949, the Communists launched convulsive social movements such as the Anti-Rightist Movement of 1957, collectivization campaigns during the Great Leap Forward (1958–1961), and the Cultural Revolution (1966–1976), all of which hindered the rise of the Uyghur intellectual elite. These movements attacked Uyghur religious and cultural practitioners, even writers and poets whose work expressed themes that supported the Communist party and its goals. Only after the cultural and religious reforms of 1978 did Uyghur education really begin to develop. Today, with the increase in wealth in oases like Turpan and the ability of villages to fund their own schools, one might expect positive effects on secular school education (*päni mäktäp*) at the local level and greater numbers of students in schools (see table 2.2).

According to teachers in the northeast Turpan village of Subeshi, however, the increase in wealth has caused a decrease in the quality of education. With more money available to each work brigade, many have built their own schools. This has lowered the ratio of students to teachers, but the schools have been staffed by younger, newly trained, less-qualified teachers, which diminishes the overall quality of education. Many of the Uyghur teachers trained in teachers' colleges are taught by Uyghurs who are poorly trained themselves. In addition, many families can now afford television sets, and Uyghur children stay up late to watch television rather than do their homework. Uyghur intellectuals see this as an extremely discouraging trend. While it is only since the opening of Xinjiang to foreign trade and tourism in 1985 that Uyghur intellectuals have been creating

TABLE 2.2
Enrollment in Turpan County Schools, 1982

	Total	Male	Female
Turpan County	116,768	63,345	53,423
Elementary	73,203	38,702	34,501
Middle School	30,495	17,368	13,127
High School	12,517	6,876	5,641

SOURCE: Tulufan Shizhi Bianjishi (Turpan City Historical Collections Department). Internal document.

their own versions of Uyghur nationalist ideology and national culture, they feel that the younger generation may grow up not only uninterested in reading about Uyghur history, but also unable to simply read.

Economics and Tourism

Even prior to its opening in 1985, Xinjiang was influenced by international tourism, especially Japanese tourism inspired by a 1983 Japanese television documentary, with hauntingly beautiful music by the famous composer Kitaro, about the Silk Road, which historically stretched from Xi'an, in central China, through Xinjiang and beyond (see tables 2.3 and 2.4). Since Turpan and Urumchi were considered to be stable areas in Xinjiang, the government allowed limited Japanese and other tourism there. This development continued the historical pattern of Turpan's eastern orientation.

In 1985, Japanese, at times more than 100 tourists per week, flocked to Turpan. This was a very large number by Turpan standards. Japanese tourists to Xinjiang have been so numerous that the Jo En restaurant in Osaka advertised on ashtrays it supplied to the Urumchi Airport. Even though tourism to Turpan fell off dramatically in the wake of the Chinese student democracy movement and the Communists' brutal crackdown at

TABLE 2.3

Number of Tourists in Turpan by Country of Origin, 1989

Japan	1,184
Hong Kong	434
West Germany	329
USA	309
England	258
Taiwan	234
France	206
Austria	138
Australia	137
Switzerland	83
Canada	82
Soviet Union	63
Denmark	62
Sweden	51
Singapore	43
New Zealand	42
Pakistan	25

SOURCE: Turpan Tourist Bureau, 1990.

Tiananmen—from 22,871 visitors in 1988 to 3,680 in 1989—Japanese continued to be the most numerous foreign tourists (see tables 2.3 and 2.4).

Not only is Xinjiang reputed to be the ancient source of grapes for Japan, but it is also the historical center of the Jodo Shinzu, or "Pure Land Sect," of Buddhism, which is very popular in Japan. Count Kozui Otani, the spiritual leader of the sect, sponsored scholarly monks as early as 1902 to dig some of the Tarim archaeological sites that Aurel Stein had explored. It was the Japanese who first discovered the artistic richness of Kyzyl, an oasis lying between Turpan and Kashgar (Hopkirk 1980:191).[17] For these reasons, Xinjiang has captured the imagination of many Japanese. Even the Japanese phone company sells stored-value telephone cards with scenes of Turpan on them.

Japanese tourists in Turpan and other oases have strongly affected Uyghur views about their present condition. For the first time, Uyghurs are in close contact with wealthy Asians and have begun to compare them with the Hans. Chinese sentiments against the Japanese are extreme, but the Japanese are much more respectful of the Uyghurs than Hong Kong Chinese, the other significant Asian tourist group in Xinjiang, who often abuse their welcome with inappropriate behavior. Uyghurs frequently assume that the Japanese must hate the Chinese at least as much as the Chinese hate the Japanese. Likewise, nationalistic Uyghurs often say that they like the Japanese because the Japanese hate the Han Chinese. The Uyghurs were mystified when they learned that the Japanese not only do

TABLE 2.4
Number of Foreign Tourists in Turpan, 1978–1989

Year	Tourists
1978	425
1979	1,698
1980	4,679
1981	5,462
1982	8,075
1983	11,079
1984	10,373
1985	13,012
1986	18,075
1987	18,132
1988	22,871
1989	3,680

SOURCE: Turpan Tourist Bureau, 1990.

not hate the Chinese, but also are largely oblivious to the intense Chinese animosity toward them.

The further influence of the Japanese in Turpan is seen in the desire of Turpan's Uyghur intellectuals to conduct research in Japan, the Turpan Hotel orchestra's performance in Tokyo, and the recent acquisition of the Japanese language by many of the Uyghur hotel staff and some of the teenaged donkey-cart drivers who take Japanese tourists on bumpy rides to historical sites.

From the spring through the autumn, when the high mountain passes are open, large numbers of Pakistani traders come to Kashgar. The trip from Islamabad is an arduous 800 miles over the Khunjerab Pass, which at 17,000 feet is the highest border crossing by road in the world. The journey takes less than a week. In the 1930s, many Uyghurs from Hami, Turpan, and Khotan fled to India and settled in the Rawalpindi area of today's Pakistan. Many Uyghurs are now reestablishing trade relationships with their cross-border kin in Pakistan. The majority of those who conduct trade, however, are Pakistani, and their large numbers in Kashgar have influenced the city. Their dress is distinctive, with flowing long shirts and baggy pants. They import silks and such Western luxury items as Lux soap, and buy bicycles, tea sets, dishes, and electronic

2.6   Japanese tourists and their Japanese-speaking donkey cart driver in Turpan (1990).

goods including radios, televisions, and piano keyboards. For the most part, Uyghurs act negatively toward Pakistanis and accuse them of leering at or making suggestive remarks to Uyghur women. Many Uyghurs consider their skills as merchants to be second to none, especially when compared to the Pakistanis; Uyghurs from Artush near Kashgar, in particular, have a reputation for trading and business, expressed succinctly in a popular Uyghur expression: "When America landed on the moon they found a man from Artush already doing business there."

In 1989 and 1990, many Soviet Uyghurs visited Xinjiang and brought news of the economic troubles in Central Asia.[18] These people perceived Uyghurs in Xinjiang as better off than their relatives in Central Asia—the exact opposite of the views widely held prior to 1985, when the opening of the region had yet to bring about significant changes. Central Asians have begun to regularly travel to Xinjiang to buy consumer goods in its comparatively well-stocked stores, where they stare, wide-mouthed and disbelieving, at the teeming shelves. It is quite clear that Xinjiang and Central Asia will increasingly influence each other in countless ways, though Ili, Kashgar, and Urumchi are sure to reap the major benefits from this renewed relationship, given their proximity to the Russian border. Under new contracts, Xinjiang will also help Central Asian republics build light industries that are in short supply.[19] During 1989 and 1990 there were a series of meetings in Urumchi among officials from the western Central Asian republics.

Stories about the Soviet Union, of a very positive kind, were also popular when I was in Turpan. Some even linked Soviet leaders to Turkic ancestry. An article in the Chinese internal newspaper *Cankao Xiaoxi* reported that Mikhail Gorbechev was actually a Turk whose sister lives in Turkey. It was also later reported that Raisa Gorbechev was a member of the Turkic Tatar nationality.

ETHNIC BORDERS

It is not unusual for Tungans, Hans, and Uyghurs to have difficulty distinguishing themselves from one another. This is especially so whenever Uyghurs encounter Tungans and assume they are Hans. Often when I played basketball with Uyghur children at a school across from my living quarters, the ball would roll into the street and children would call out to a student nearby, "Hey Han, would you get the ball?" Frequently, the child would refuse, saying "I am a Tungan." At a small Turpan restaurant,

I even witnessed the Uyghur proprietor addressing some Uyghurs who somewhat resembled Han Chinese as "Lao Han" (Old Han), not realizing that they were Uyghurs. A Tungan friend from Urumchi was told at a Tungan mosque to go to the Uyghur mosque by a worshipper who mistook him for a Uyghur.

Homes, mosques, and to some extent food establishments are ethnic borders that are rarely crossed by Hans, Uyghurs, and Tungans. These social borders may appear invisible from the outside, but they become salient in structuring interethnic social, religious, and commercial interactions. Hans and Uyghurs rarely mix socially at each other's homes: because Hans eat pork, Uyghurs will not eat in their houses; Hans feel uncomfortable in Uyghur homes, afraid their lack of knowledge of Uyghur social customs may offend their hosts. Furthermore, Hans in general do not like the taste of mutton, which is the staple meat eaten by the Uyghurs.

Hans rarely eat at Uyghur food restaurants, believing that they are not as clean as Tungan ones. While Uyghurs will eat at Tungan restaurants, they never buy meat from a Tungan butcher, for fear it is ritually impure (not *halal*). In fact, this mistrust of Tungan religious observance gave rise to teacher protests in Turpan in 1989. Two Tungans were hired by Han officials to manage the Muslim dining hall at the Turpan Teachers Training Academy, but Uyghur teachers refused to eat, mistrusting the ritual purity of the food.

Tungans

The Tungans have been an integral part of the political map of Xinjiang since the mid-nineteenth century. They have lived in Turpan in large numbers for over seven generations, and have been the central means of fostering positive Uyghur sentiments toward the Hans.[20] This situation is only repeated in the Hami oasis in the east, where Tungans are also numerous. Sharing Islam with the Uyghurs and the Mandarin language with the Hans, the Tungans are the ideal cultural intermediaries between the two. For the most part, relations in Turpan between Tungans and Uyghurs have been good. Tungans show respect for Uyghur customs and society, and also serve as intermediaries for Uyghurs and Hans in Mandarin-language instruction at Uyghur schools. Tungan teachers construct sentences culturally specific to Muslims, and when teaching Mandarin vocabulary give running translations of sentences in Uyghur.[21]

Although the Tungans and the Uyghurs are both Muslim, there is a surprising separation in their religious practices. Tungans pray in separate mosques and maintain separate Islamic schools. Furthermore, they revere different Islamic saints.[22] Clothing worn during mourning is also distinct. Tungans wear on their head a burlap cloth that sticks up like a stovepipe hat, while Uyghurs wear a white turban. Finally, the chief Islamic festival for Tungans is *Roza Heyt*, the end of the Ramadan fast, but the *hajj* pilgrimage festival *Qurban Heyt* remains the chief festival for the Uyghurs.

The intermediate status of Tungans in Han-Uyghur relations affects mutual group perceptions and results in ethnic tensions. Although Hans and Tungans often speak the same language, some Hans feel that Tungans are dishonest and fear that because Tungans are Muslim they might turn on them. Uyghurs express this same view but in reverse: they fear that the Tungans will side with the Hans, with whom they share both language and culture. Uyghurs use the expression *tawuz* (watermelon) to refer to Tungans, because they wobble between siding with the Uyghurs on one issue and with the Hans on another. Some Uyghurs even claim that the Tungans are actually half Han and thus impure in their Muslim observance, as Hans do not practice the Islamic faith.

Both Tungan and Uyghur schoolteachers ameliorate interethnic tensions in their roles as agents of acculturation for the Chinese state. Tungan teachers in Uyghur schools stress the importance of being a good student of the Chinese nationality, emphasizing citizenship of the Chinese state. A Uyghur book commonly used in Uyghur classes is entitled *Män Junggoluq* (*I am a pan-PRC Chinese*) (see figure 2.3). The book stresses the same message that Tungan teachers convey—"we are all citizens of a multiethnic state." In China, a strong distinction is made between the terms *Han* and *Chinese*. All minority groups are members of the Chinese (*Zhonghua*) nation, but none are Hans. In Uyghur, to be a member of the Chinese state (*Zhongguo*) is to be a *Junggoluq*. There is thus no association of Chineseness with Hanness.

Han Chinese

An extremely important new development in Turpan has been the effect of the Han so-called "self-drifters," who have come to Xinjiang on their own, without official government permission, in search of economic opportunity. Traditionally, the Chinese viewed life in Xinjiang as full of hardship and bitterness. However, the Hans from China proper who

FIGURE 2.3   Book Jacket for *Män Junggoluq* (*I am a pan-PRC Chinese*)

have settled in Xinjiang maintain that what they like best there is the weather, even though the extremes are -20°C (-25°F) in winter and 48°C (125°F) in summer. Still, appreciation for Xinjiang's weather is understandable considering winters in China proper, particularly on the southern coast in towns like Guangzhou (Canton) where there is no escape from the cold and no heating: even when it is 4°C (40°F), one has to wear several layers of clothing indoors. In Xinjiang most people have heating in the winter.

Besides appreciating the climate, Hans in China proper perceive Xinjiang as the land of plenty and opportunity. They believe there is much money to be made there and, since 1987, an estimated 250,000 "self-drifter" Hans have poured into Xinjiang each year to look for work. The majority of Hans are taking on menial jobs, often working as hired labor for the Uyghurs. Hans are even working as *karez* irrigation canal diggers, since few Uyghurs are willing to do this arduous and hazardous work. In the northern village of Subeshi, impoverished Hans collect animal bones and old shoes to recycle. Other Hans roam the villages popping rice and corn for Uyghur children for five *mao* (one-half *yuan*) each popping session. The sight of large numbers of Han Chinese doing such menial tasks has profoundly shifted the nature of Uyghur-Han relations in Turpan.

Uyghurs

Grape cultivation in Turpan makes the oasis unique among those of Xinjiang and shapes the identity of the Uyghurs vis-a-vis the Tungans and Hans, who for the most part work as government administrators, merchants, or migrant laborers. In general, everyday life in Turpan revolves around the cultivation and selling of grapes, which requires both collective labor and economic specialization. Uyghurs who cultivate grapes count their wealth in terms of the number and age of their grapevines. Clothing and architecture designs generally involve grape motifs, and young girls all have the suffix "*gül*," which means grape flower, after their first name (e.g. *Ibadet-gül*).[23]

Because of the extremely cold temperatures in the winter, grapevines in Turpan are taken down from their trellises, coiled, and then buried. Once this is done, grape farmers cease agricultural work until March, when the vines are uncovered and put back on trellises. In most areas of Turpan, irrigation water is provided by *karez* systems and pump wells; the vines are irrigated several times during the growing season. Instead of paying for water, the farmers build waterworks for the government for twenty days out of each year. During 1989 and 1990, when there was a massive campaign throughout all of China to build and improve the infrastructure supporting the waterworks, each farmer was required to work for 20 days and pay 15 *yuan* to the government. Television programs showed thousands of farmers out in the barren *gobi* digging ditches and moving earth as part of this campaign.[24]

Each village has at least one team whose job is to clean the *karez* wells throughout the year. These wells comprise a unique irrigation method that channels mountain runoff to the oasis through a system made of shaft wells connected by tunnels. Teams of three to five men clean the silt and clay that builds up and blocks the irrigation tunnels by lowering themselves into the well using a single rope and pulley that is tied to a horse on one end. The horse is moved by a member of the team who remains outside to bring the others up. Team members collect the clay and silt in baskets, and this is pulled out of the *karez* using the same rope that lowered the workers into the wells. At the bottom of the tunnel the men use small cottonseed-oil lamps for illumination.

The cleaning of the *karez* starts in winter and begins with the shafts closest to the fields. The *karez* that waters the fields south of the Turpan central bazaar is approximately five kilometers from the fields, measures twenty-five meters deep, and reaches a depth of sixty meters near the Flaming Mountains, which are about ten kilometers away.[25] Teams consisting of four to six men spend five hours a day, four days a week at this

2.7   *Karez* diggers being lowered into a shaft well by rope and horse (1990).

task. The work is dangerous: rocks falling from the mouth of the shaft have split workers' skulls; other men have developed rheumatism from the damp conditions. Because fewer young Uyghurs are willing to do this difficult and dangerous work, since 1984 some teams have hired Hans from Gansu to help.

The work involved in placing vines on trellises and pulling them down is also labor intensive, and families work together, some cooperating with their neighbors. Families also call on kin from other villages. Uyghurs who work for government organizations or as wage laborers in nonagricultural jobs are given three days off to prepare their agricultural land, bring in the harvest, and put up and put away their vines.

Once the grapes are picked, most are dried to make raisins. The grapes are first placed inside drying rooms (chünje) on bakhalla, cylindrical racks consisting of central poles bisected with sticks extending a foot horizontally in several directions. The mud-brick walls of the chünje are built as lattices so that wind can pass into the chambers but the sun, which causes the golden seedless raisins to discolor, is kept out. Chünje are constructed on raised platforms in family yards, separate from the homes.

Before the vines are twisted and buried for the winter, sheep roam through the vineyards foraging on grape leaves. In the spring, peasant herders of Turpan move about 70 percent of their sheep to graze the pastures on the slopes of the Tianshan Mountains. Thomas Hoppe states that the rhythm of transhumance also corresponds with the nourishment habits of the Uyghurs, who eat more meat in winter than during the hot summer months.[26]

In the south, land not used for grape production is planted with wheat and sorghum one year, and with cotton the next. Cotton can be picked even after the weather gets cold. After the picking is finished, the thick and brittle dead cotton plants are tied together and stored on the roofs of homes for use as kindling.[27] Farmers also grow small crops of vegetables and fruits, especially Hami melons.

The increasing economic opportunities in Turpan have resulted in positive sentiments toward the Chinese government and Han Chinese in general. Uyghur peasants are relatively pleased by the religious, economic, and cultural changes introduced by the government and are optimistic about the future. Uyghur intellectuals, on the other hand, take a wider view and are resentful of the Hans who have entered Xinjiang to become political authorities during the more than four decades of Communist Chinese rule. A Uyghur anecdote about a Han shoemaker who arrives from China proper and is made mayor of the oasis in a week's time and governor by the end of the year is still popular. But the attitudes of Uyghur intellectuals in Turpan toward the Han Chinese began to change markedly in 1989–1990 because of the presence of Han Chinese "self-drifters."

Uyghur perceptions of Han Chinese as the oppressors who are always in dominant positions has changed as Han "self-drifters," temporary laborers, enter the oases to be hired as day workers by Uyghurs. In the villages, I met Hans from Anhui, China who had been in Turpan for four months and were hired as construction workers to build homes and archways. It took them about three days to build an entrance archway to a home, for which they made 100 *yuan*. During 1989 and 1990, there was a major in-migration of Hans from Hangzhou, which, though overcrowded, is considered the most beautiful city in China. The workers explained that their motivation for moving to Xinjiang was simply to make money.

Consequently, Uyghur views of themselves and their position vis-a-vis the Hans have changed. Hans now roam the streets collecting garbage and doing other menial tasks. In general, Uyghur peasants in Turpan do not harbor the strong resentment toward Hans found among Uyghurs in other oases; instead, they see themselves on the same socioeconomic level as, or on even a higher level than, the new Han immigrant "self-drifters." This dramatic change has inspired Uyghur ethnic pride.

2.8   Self-drifting Hans building homes for Uyghurs in Turpan (1990).

Local Identities and Turpan Ideologies

3

It is very close.
Stand up brothers.
—"Uyghur," "It Is Close at Hand (*Yäqin Boldi*)"

There is no other oasis in Xinjiang where the relics of Uyghur history are more vivid than Turpan, where Buddhism flourished alongside Manichaeanism, Nestorian Christianity, Zoroastrianism, and Islam. Yet because Turpan peasants equate Uyghur identity solely with Islam, which Turpan embraced as late as the 1450s, they argue that non-Islamic history is insignificant and unrelated to them; they do not acknowledge the many cultural relics in their oasis, such as the ancient sites of Gaochang and Baziklik, as part of their heritage.[1] Uyghur intellectuals, in stark contrast, glorify Uyghur non-Islamic history in order to claim the history of the people referred to today as Turks. But this historiographical approach presents serious difficulties. When some contend that Uyghur history is 2,000 to 6,000 years old, these historians must downplay their Turkic roots, as Turkic peoples first emerged around the fifth century C.E. and did not arrive in the region until the ninth century C.E.

HISTORY AND IDENTITY

Various historiographies have been generated for this region, and Chinese historical records document Xinjiang's multifaceted legacy and its complex historical permutations. Some of these historiographies have proven to be popular and some have not; they are important, however, as means by which Uyghurs manipulate history to create ethnic identity and unity. In attempts to claim a grand past, they use elements from myths and legends, treating them as historical fact. This has led to bizarre claims, including the linking of Uyghur nationalism to fascist ideologies of the 1930s and 1940s. The most surprising legend associates the Uyghurs with Nazi Germany and Adolf Hitler.

Admiration for Hitler's power and charisma is prevalent throughout all levels of Uyghur society—peasant, merchant, and intellectual. Uyghur intellectuals will often praise a Uyghur cultural hero as a "second Adolf Hitler" (ikkinchi Getlär). I was surprised to hear this expression used to describe Urkesh Döulät, more commonly known by his Chinese name Wuerkaixi, the Uyghur student leader of the 1989 Tiananmen Square protests. In addition, throughout Xinjiang a considerable number of Eastern European movies about Hitler are shown on television and in theaters. Although these films attempt to show the greatness of communism in the struggle against German fascism, most Uyghurs watching the films actually side with the fascists. Uyghurs are impressed by the great power and discipline that the Nazis represent.

The Uyghur peasantry has absorbed the Nazi salute into its cultural repertoire. Uyghurs sometimes greet people dressed in military uniforms, such as police and soldiers, with a smiling "Heil Hitler" and the Nazi salute. Foreigners are also called to in this manner.[2] William Shirer's book *The Rise and Fall of the Third Reich*, translated into Uyghur in 1988 and 1989, was a best seller in the region (see figure 3.1). Even though Shirer's book is not complimentary toward the Nazis, it feeds the Uyghur peasants' dreams of power against China. In addition, popular myths actually link the Uyghurs to Hitler: Uyghurs believe that since they claim descent from the Huns and Hitler likewise related the Germans to the Huns, the Germans are also related to the Uyghurs. Several Uyghur intellectuals told me the story in which two Soviet Uyghur prisoners of war are brought before Hitler, who yells: "Why are you shooting at us? We are your own blood." Uyghurs also claim Hitler said that with an army of Uyghurs he could have taken the entire globe.

This fascination with Hitler does not appear related to anti-Semitism. Many Uyghurs, like most people throughout China, view Jewish people in a positive light and admire such renowned Jews as Albert Einstein, Karl Marx, and Henry Kissinger. Though Uyghurs may express admiration for Jews as the "Sons of Israel" (bäni Isra'il) or disdain them as the

FIGURE 3.1   Jacket for the Uyghur Translation of William Shirer's *The Rise and Fall of the Third Reich*

"enemies' of God" (*Hudaning düshmäni*), few Uyghurs, regardless of social group, are aware of the atrocities the Nazis committed against Jews and other groups, including Gypsies and homosexuals. Uyghur intellectuals were shocked when I told them that Hitler had killed as many Jews as there are Uyghurs.

One German Xinjiang scholar of Jewish ancestry is insistent that the majority of Uyghurs, particularly Uyghur intellectuals, are anti-Jewish and overtly fascist. He argues that since I am very openly Jewish among the Uyghurs, I do not see how anti-Jewish they are. When he worked in Xinjiang in the mid-1980s and early 1990s, he frequently encountered Uyghurs who, when finding out he was German, praised him for the genocide that Germany perpetrated against the Jews. He described the situation as "nauseating and unbearable."

Possible anti-Jewish sentiments aside, there are historical reasons for the Uyghurs' admiration of Hitler. Nazi racist ideology penetrated Central Asia, and German fascists claimed that Uyghur culture was "Indo-Germanic."[3] In the 1930s, Germany sent a mission to Afghanistan hoping to prove, by cranial measurements, that the Afghans were the pure Aryans. The Afghans had previously claimed descent from one of the lost tribes of the Jews, but the German ideology so captured their imagination that they proclaimed Afghanistan the homeland of the Aryans. Today the Afghan airline is called Ariana Afghan Airlines. Another remotely possible means of the spread of Nazi racist ideology to this region was the Swedish scholar Sven Hedin, the first European to show that the Täklimakan Desert could be safely explored. Although Hedin supported the Nazis and their ideology, it is difficult to assess his contribution to spreading Nazi thought or the belief in Central Asians as an Aryan race, since the majority of his expeditions occurred before the 1920s.

Adolf Hitler also supported pan-Turkist factions within the Soviet Union in an attempt to undermine Soviet power in Central Asia, where most of its industry was moved during World War II. The Nazis organized Turkestani troops to liberate Turkestan from the Communist Russians. The Turkestani units, comprised mainly of prisoners of war from various Muslim republics of Central Asia, joined German troops, generally as guerrillas. Many of the Turkestanis hoped for independence or a pan-Turkic union, and viewed Hitler as the *Mahdi*, or messianic leader, as promised in Islamic teachings. Such a view was also held by the Islamic religious leader (*mufti*) of Jerusalem at the time. Turkestani units were continually reorganized and reinforced and eventually numbered several hundred thousand people of Turkic origin (Landau 1981:111). After the war most of them were sent back to the Soviet Union, in accordance with the Yalta agreement, and of these most were killed by government decree. Others were left in camps and were later allowed to go to Turkey or the United States.

While this history helps to explain the preponderance of popular myths about Hitler among the Uyghurs, the fascination with Hitler is best understood as a passive form of resistance and a symbolic means of confrontation. Uyghurs feel powerless in Xinjiang. Though the province is officially called the Xinjiang Uyghur Autonomous Region, its autonomy is questionable. Given the migration of Han Chinese, Uyghurs are quickly becoming a minority nationality within their own province. Although there are periodic riots, infrequent bus bombings, and frequent fistfights between Uyghurs and Hans, resistance against Chinese government control generally is passive, often taking the form of verbal attacks, such as jokes and curses, against the government and Hans. Few other means of protest are viable. Written protest can lead to arrest; marches are broken up and arrests made; riots are swiftly cracked down on and can result in deaths. Perhaps this is why in more recent years some Uyghur dissident groups have bombed public buses and hotels to draw attention to Uyghur disaffection.

One frequently told joke about the train from Beijing to Xinjiang reflects Uyghur views on the Chinese exploitation of Xinjiang's resources. The train is said to enter from China proper speedily into Urumchi making the sound "ach, ach ach" (I'm hungry), and to leave slowly making the sound "toq, toq, toq" (I'm full). The Uyghurs also express their hostility toward China by cheering for any athletic team playing against China when games are televised. When replays of the 1988 Olympic Games were shown on Chinese television in 1989, Uyghurs sided with and cheered for the Soviet Union and the United States teams when they competed against Chinese teams. In World War II movies, however, they cheer for the Nazis, who opposed the Soviets. Hitler is thus a symbol of Uyghur disaffection with Chinese rule. The thought of Urkesh, or any charismatic figure such as Hitler, leading Uyghurs to greater control of their destinies has considerable appeal.

Local Identity and Uyghur/Han Social Borders

Positive interethnic relations have had a strong influence in creating a unique worldview in the Turpan oasis—one that contrasts dramatically with worldviews throughout the rest of Xinjiang. Whereas strong anti-Chinese and anti-Han sentiments are found among the Uyghurs in Kashgar and other areas of southern Xinjiang, in Turpan, as noted, Uyghur attitudes toward the Hans are for the most part positive and constructive. Economic growth and prosperity, coupled with the government's liberalization of cultural and religious policies, has contributed to this positive interethnic environment. Among Uyghur merchants in Turpan, trading relationships with Hans in China proper have also helped to engender positive views of the Hans. This relationship is historically rooted. Turpan has, for most of the past one thousand years, been oriented to the east—economically, culturally, and politically. The Qing government considered Turpan more loyal than other oases to the west because of this historic relationship and the intensive interactions between Turpanliks and Hans. Today, good interethnic relations in Turpan among the Uyghurs, Hans, and Tungans continue.

Hans in Turpan show more sensitivity to minority problems and social customs than do Hans in other areas, and Turpan Uyghurs show less animosity toward Hans. Outside Turpan, the majority of Hans in Xinjiang live in towns where few, if any, Uyghurs live; therefore, the Hans do not become sensitive to cultural differences because they rarely interact with Uyghurs. In contrast, Hans in Turpan come in contact with Uyghurs daily. For example, Hans hold their weddings at Muslim restaurants and invite their Muslim work associates.

The government has made efforts to honor Uyghurs and other minorities throughout the People's Republic of China. In 1985, for example, when Xinjiang was opened to the outside world and foreign tourism, street signs reading "Minority nationalities cannot do without Hans, and the Hans cannot do without minority nationalities" were placed throughout the oases of Xinjiang and Urumchi. Originally, these propaganda messages had been written with Chinese characters above the Uyghur. In the spirit of cultural reform, however, the government reversed the position of the languages, placing the Uyghur lettering above the Chinese.

Hans often comment that life in Xinjiang has distinctly affected their attitudes and lifestyles in comparison to Hans in China proper. They claim that upon visiting their birthplaces in China they realize how much more friendly and open they are in comparison to their friends and family who remained in China proper. Furthermore, unlike Hans in the interior, who are generally uncomfortable interacting with minorities, most Han government officials in Xinjiang have become adept at handling interactions with Uyghurs and Tungans. Uyghurs are employed as interpreters and

3.1   In 1985, in accord with "Uyghur Autonomous Region" status, Uyghur script was placed on top on all bilingual signs. In Urumchi, an old sign hidden behind the tree with Uyghur script on the bottom reads "The Hans cannot do without the Minorities, the Minorities cannot do without the Hans." The new sign exhorts the peoples of Xinjiang to strengthen ethnic unity, better their conditions, and implement the Four Modernizations (1985).

translators in all government offices to aid in cases of village disputes. For example, when disputing Uyghurs from Yar village in Turpan presented their grievances to the director of the Water Management Board, he called in his Uyghur interpreter. Upon hearing the complaints, the director immediately sent another Uyghur employee to inspect the situation, assuring both parties in the dispute that a fair solution would result and that if questions remained after the decision had been made, he would come to inspect the problem himself. He then shook the Yar villagers' hands in the traditional Uyghur manner. Once out of his office, the Uyghurs expressed satisfaction with the director's actions.

Although the two main languages spoken in Xinjiang, Uyghur and Mandarin, are unrelated, they have affected each other, and this has contributed to good relations in the oasis. The Uyghur language has changed the Mandarin dialect spoken by the Hans and Tungans. For example, the Uyghur word *bikar* means "free time," coming from the Persian word meaning "without work" or unemployed. In Uyghur the word *bikar* also means "doing nothing" or worthlessness. Hans have adopted the term, converting it to *bai kar*, and use it to refer to a wasted effort or a worthless, do-nothing person. Many Chinese words for everyday objects have been adopted in Uyghur. These include *bingxiang* (refrigerator), *dianshi* (television), and *zixingche* (bicycle).

In stark contrast to many other oases, where Uyghurs do not speak Mandarin, most Uyghurs in Turpan are bilingual. In many situations, Uyghurs and Hans address one another in their respective languages and are able to communicate. Many Uyghurs feel uncomfortable speaking Mandarin; they are unable to pronunce the tones of Chinese properly, since the Uyghur language does not have tones. The same is true for some Hans who can understand Uyghur but reply in Mandarin.

Turpan has a privileged position in Xinjiang. As mentioned, the former chairman of Xinjiang, Tömür Dawamät, is a Uyghur from Tohsun in the Turpan region who has maintained a position of prominence in the Communist government since the early 1950s. The vice-chairman of Xinjiang and former mayor of the capital Urumchi, Yüsüp Äsa, is also from Turpan. Being a Turpanlik can therefore be an advantage in starting a government career, but in order to advance, Uyghurs must know Mandarin.

Uyghur intellectuals can improve on the Mandarin they learned in primary and secondary schools via the Television University in Turpan, which is beamed by satellite throughout the country to classroom televisions. Government organizations regularly send Uyghur employees to Television University. Village party officials also send Uyghur agriculturists and merchants, but only if they will later be sent to China proper on business. At the Turpan branch of the university, Uyghurs study Mandarin and Hans study English; upon completion of their courses they receive a college diploma. Many Uyghurs resent the fact that Hans are given the opportunity to learn English while they feel forced to raise their competency in Mandarin.

The government has made modest efforts to develop the means by which Hans can learn Uyghur; however, these are superficial and ineffective. For example, in Urumchi one sentence of Uyghur is taught on television each week. There are few programs, or even phrase books, for Hans to use to learn Uyghur, and Hans know very few of the basic Uyghur greetings such as *yakhshi musiz* (are you well?) and *bu nimä* (what is this?).[4] These are inadequate resources for learning the Uyghur language, which Hans do recognize as a member of the globally important Turkic language family and consider very difficult. The sounds are strange and the grammar, with over forty verb declensions, is considered complex, especially by Hans, whose language has no verb conjugation and no plural or gendered noun forms. It is fairly common throughout the world that people prefer to learn the language of the social elite rather than the other way around; thus the Hans' desire to learn English over Uyghur has perhaps more to do with perceived status differences than it does with language difficulty. Like many native English-speaking residents in my own hometown of Los Angeles who employ Spanish-speaking workers but have not learned Spanish, Hans often confessed, with embarrassment, that although they had lived in Xinjiang for thirty years they still could not speak Uyghur.

Uyghur names also pose a problem for Hans. Upon translation into Chinese characters they often become unflattering Chinese puns. For example, the name Ismail, translated as *Si Mayi*, becomes "dead fly" with a change of tone. Similarly, the female name *Kunduz*, "mink," means "empty stomach" (hunger) in Mandarin. During the Cultural Revolution, Uyghur names were twisted in Mandarin to sound patriotic. One woman I met whose name was Ghuncha Khan is still called *Hongqi Khan* (Red Flag Khan).

Uyghurs in Turpan distinguish themselves from other Uyghurs in Xinjiang by their naming practices. All young girls have the word *gül* (flower) added to their names, though in Turpan it specifically means "grape-flower." Common names for women are Hawa-gül, Ibadät-gül, or Pati-gül. Men often refer to unmarried women as *güllar* (flowers), and when women marry, they drop the suffix *gül* and replace it with *khan*, a term of respect derived from the word *khan* (ruler). Recently, however, young women have begun to delay adopting *khan*, feeling that the appellation makes them seem too old. Uyghurs in other oases use *gül* in a few names, but not for all single woman as in Turpan.

Women's names pose the greatest problem for Hans. Often the Hans will use *Gu Li* for a Uyghur girl's name, taken from the suffix *gül*. In Turpan, where all women's names have this suffix, every girl, according to the Hans, has the same name. Thus, many Uyghur women translate their first name into Mandarin without using the *gül* ending, i.e. Pati-gül is translated as *Pa ti*.

A similar naming system is applied to men. Young men use the appellation *jan*, a diminutive name meaning "soul," as in the names Yusup-jan and Qasim-jan. It is changed in boys' early teens to *qari* (i.e., Yusup-qari), a term of respect that literally means "Koranic scholar." When men enter their forties they are called *akhun* (i.e., Yusup-akhun), a reverential term equivalent to *molla*. Finally, after men and women go on the *hajj*, they are referred to as *haji*. For example, if a man whose name is Abliz is also a *haji*, then his son, named Mämät, will be called Mämät Abliz Haji. If the son himself goes on a *hajj*, he will drop his father's name and become Mämät Haji. Government officials often drop their father's name and use their title, often a Mandarin one. Thus someone named Anaytulla Yüsüp, for example, will be addressed as Anaytulla *Xiangzhang* (village head).

In many regions of Xinjiang, Uyghurs use names that are particular to their oasis or region.[5] Names therefore make it possible to determine a person's place of birth. Naming practices are also a key to acculturative trends, political leanings, and oasis differentiation. In Kashgar and Ili, Russian-sounding last names, formed by adding an -ov ending to the father's name, give cultural prestige and reflect the areas' orientations toward the former Soviet Central Asian republics. It is not clear how the collapse of Soviet rule in Central Asia will affect this practice.

LOCAL IDENTITY AND ISLAM

The strong local oasis identities in Xinjiang, so characteristic of the region prior to the 1930s, have puzzled Central Asian scholars. It is clear, however, that the geographic isolation of the oases from one another has caused them to develop their own internal cultures based on unique ways of celebrating different occasions and rituals within Uyghur culture and Islamic and folk religious practice.

In Turpan, there is a resurgence and strengthening of Islam resulting in an increase in power of *mollas*, religious clerics. *Mollas*, in new positions of influence, have taken the opportunity to voice their fervent opposition to certain Uyghur social practices that have gained popularity in the villages, particularly the drinking of alcoholic beverages and mixed-couple dancing to waltzes and fox-trots. One particular tragedy brought this issue into relief: five minutes after I left a wedding party at the groom's home, two drunken guests started to fight, and one of them was stabbed to death. The next day, at the funeral, local *mollas* warned the congregation that if any family served alcohol during a wedding party or permitted mixed-couple dancing the night before the wedding, *mollas* would not allow the groom's parents to be buried in an Islamic fashion and no prayers would be said at their funerals. Besides shyness, this is one reason why men dance in pairs, separate from women, at a disco in the Turpan bazaar.

Of the 365 mosques in Turpan, ninety-one are in the village of Üzüm-chilik (Grape Valley). There is also a fairly large number of Sufis in Turpan, including Naqshbandi and a small number of Khodri.[6] Outside the mosques in the Turpan bazaar, Korans and Islamic books and pamphlets of various complexity are sold. Some of the pamphlets use illustrations to teach people how to wash and pray, others list all the saints and holy people mentioned in the *Tawrät* (Hebrew Bible), the *Anjil* (New Testament), and the Koran. In general, there are materials sufficient to educate and reinforce the understandings of Muslims in Turpan.

Islamic education in Turpan has increased, and consequently so has the prestige of local *mollas*. Before they enter elementary school, many Uyghur children now receive instruction on saying Islamic prayers. Although the government has laws against the Islamic education of minors, which includes those under eighteen years, children between ages thirteen and eighteen attend many of Turpan's small Koranic schools. Uyghur officials look away from these violations, reluctant to be seen negatively by fellow Uyghurs, and Han officials do not want to enforce unpopular laws in a region that has been historically calm and stable. The government also limits the number of students who may be taught in any one location to between six and fifteen; Üzümchilik has seventeen reli-

3.2   A funeral procession in Kashgar (1985).

gious schools with a total of 200 students. Furthermore, the government prohibits study at night. However, if a child is educated for only five years in secular schools, he or she will normally be sent to a school run in the home of a *molla* for an additional three years of Koranic instruction. Many of these students live at this school or frequently stay there overnight.[7]

A large factor influencing the growth of Islamic education is the cost of secular education. Students throughout Xinjiang who attend secular colleges have to pay tuition. A four-year university education cost 10,000 *yuan* (US $2,500) in 1990. Furthermore, since the government no longer places all graduates, students are no longer guaranteed employment. Thus, most Uyghur peasants do not consider secular education—specifically, college education—a viable option for their children. The prevalence of this attitude corresponds with the rise in prestige of Islamic education.

Folk Religious Practice

While traditional Islamic practices differ slightly among the oases of Xinjiang, the degree, type, and frequency of folk religious practice varies tremendously. Folk religious practices are widely conducted among the Uyghurs of Turpan and serve to foster a strong and unique religious identity. These folk practices permeate most Uyghur rituals, except orthodox Islamic rituals; they deal mainly with warding off *jin* (evil spirits). Some ethnographers claim that many of these folk practices are remnants of an ancient practice of shamanism, but this is impossible to prove.[8]

In villages such as Subeshi, it is common to see pouches wrapped in colored thread hanging from branches. They measure about one square inch and are wrapped in colored cloth. Sticks extend from their middles. One that I saw had a five *fen* (.05 *yuan*) note on top; another had a dead bird tied to it. These are called *qonchaq* and are used to ward off *jin*.[9] A 23-year-old Uyghur woman living in Subeshi informed me that *molla*s instruct people who suffer from illness or bodily pain to place *qonchaq*s in trees. Uyghurs believe that misfortune is caused by *jin*, the spirits of people who have died, sometimes at a young age because of a *jin*-caused illness. The most orthodox *molla*s are opposed to *qonchaq* and other amulets, called *tomar* and *köz mönchaq*, that protect against the evil eye. *Tomar*s are triangular leather pouches with Islamic prayers written on paper inside. *Köz mönchaq*s are round black plastic balls the size of cherry pits, with white dots all over them. They are worn by children and sewed in women's garments to ward off the evil eye.

Uyghurs today also use fire to ward off *jin*. Fire is used in childhood rites, wedding ceremonies, and cemeteries. During the *büshük toy*, the swaddling ceremony of a newborn infant, a *molla* waves a flaming stick above the baby to purify it and to ward off *jin*. Some Uyghur families place an unsheathed knife in their baby's crib for the same purpose. During the wedding ceremony, when the bride is brought from her parents' home to the groom's home, a fire is burned in the road and the vehicle carrying her drives over the fire. In some ceremonies, when the bride is transported by a horse-drawn cart, the cart is led around the fire seven times, seven being a religiously significant number in Islam as it is in Judaism and Christianity. A fire is also placed in a ladle inside the entrance to the groom's home, and the bride steps over it upon her arrival.

The incorporation of folk religious practices in Uyghur life transition ceremonies is seen clearly during birth and death rituals. Most Uyghur women give birth to their first child in their parents' home, to which they return a month or so before delivery. Others stay at their new homes and use the services offered by female doctors or midwives there. When a child is born, a small swath of red cloth is placed on the doorpost to announce the happy occasion and to warn people away. The new mothers are not allowed visitors for forty days.[10]

The parents bury the newborn's afterbirth in the mud wall of the house but never tell the child where. Uyghurs in Turpan believe that if the afterbirth is simply disposed of or buried in the ground, the child's eyes will always be cast down. Likewise, if the afterbirth is buried too high in the wall, the child will constantly look upward. So it is buried at adult eye-level and, because of Turpan's arid environment, the afterbirths dry and do not rot. In other areas of Xinjiang the placement of afterbirths varies. Most Uyghur intellectuals in Urumchi were shocked to learn of the existence of these practices, which they had never heard of or observed. Hans were also surprised and considered such a practice a waste since they know the afterbirth to have health benefits and so make it into medicine or simply eat it.

In asking about this Uyghur practice I found regional variation. In the southern Xinjiang city of Kucha, Uyghurs bury afterbirths in the ground inside the front gates of their homes, to ensure that children will stay close to their families.[11] Writing about the Karakhanid times, named for the first Islamic empire that asserted its influence on Xinjiang, Mahmud Kashgari in *Divan Lugat at-Turk* (1075 C.E.) states "The afterbirth is said to be the companion of the child in the womb. Women draw a good omen from it and they also pray to it for fertility. Woman pray the words, 'umayqa tapinas ogul bulur'—One who worships the afterbirth will give birth to a son" (Dankoff 1975:73). The afterbirth is called *hämra*, meaning "companion," and is seen as the constant companion of an individual through life. *Hämra* is also the name for satellites that accompany planets and a popular name given to females.

Infant mortality in Xinjiang is fairly high. A child who dies is buried according to Islamic tradition, as are aborted fetuses of more than five months. A Uyghur child is named three days after birth, and only when the parents believe the child will survive. Uyghur women speak frequently about children dying of disease in the first year, many of dehydration resulting from diarrhea. One of the water distributors (*mirap*) of Üzümchilik was the father of eight children, four of whom died in their first year. However, infant mortality statistics were not recorded by the hospital staff in Subeshi's clinic.

Medicine is available in even the most remote villages. Each village has its own hospital staffed by health-care workers who have received six months' training in Western medicine. Uyghurs prefer using Western medicine for common illnesses because it is faster acting. Uyghur medicine, which is a combination of Greco-Indian (*Unani Tibb*), Chinese, and Western traditions, is used at home for longer-term illnesses.

When medicines do not work or an individual dies, the community is informed by neighbors in a quiet, somber manner. When a Uyghur male dies, the *molla* is alerted. An attendant from the mosque washes the body and wraps it in a white sheet. The corpse is placed in a covered stretcher resembling a casket and taken to the mosque, where it is kept until the burial the following day. The procedure is similar for a woman, except that the attendant is a funeral specialist called a *büwä*, not an attendant from the mosque.

Burial is performed the day following the death. Men carry the corpse on its covered stretcher from the mosque to the graveyard in a large procession. They dress in black with white sashes around their waists and wrap their *doppa* caps with white turbans. Women wear white veils. Older men and women ride to the cemetery in the backs of trucks. When the procession arrives at the gravesite, the attendant places the corpse in the grave and the prayers commence. Graveside prayer is done in a segregated fashion, the men praying first and the women after. The men circle the plot and a *molla* leads them in prayers; the women are then led in prayers by a woman of the community who has gained respect through wisdom in dealing with community affairs and negotiating conflict. Tomb size indicates both family status and wealth. Sometimes, after a person has been buried for some time, family members may decide to build a larger tomb; in this case, they transfer the deceased's bones in bags and rebury them.

After returning from the grave, the deceased's family holds a funeral ceremony (*nazir*) in their home. Mourners comfort the family members, and friends and neighbors provide *suyuk ash*, a filling soup made of noodles and mutton. As in most Uyghur ceremonies, men and women gather in different rooms. Close family members remain in mourning for one year. Women wear a white veil that partially covers their faces and men wear white turbans. The color white, or the absence of color, symbolizes loss for Uyghurs as it does for Hans and Tungans. Mourners hold another commemoration, *nazir*, on the fortieth day after the person's death and on each subsequent anniversary of the death. During the *nazir*, mourners tell stories about the deceased and, by recalling the intravillage relationships that connect themselves through her or him, reaffirm the strength of their community.

[margin annotation: White for Mourning]

In Turpan, jars of paper and medicine are burned on top of or near tombs in Uyghur cemeteries to appease the *jin* of the dead.[12] At the beginning of the century, Mannerheim also noted the use of fire in a cemetery, though in this case it was not a means of protection from the dead but to protect the sick:

> In passing a Mohammedan cemetery I witnessed an old Sart's efforts to exorcise the illness of a young one, who seemed to be paralyzed in both legs. A small fire was lighted in front of the patient and the old man was trying, by waving some bits of wood round the head and body of the sick man, to drive out the evil spirit, after which he started reading from the Koran in a loud voice.   (1969 [1942]:79)

The numerous burned-out jars in Uyghur cemeteries show that such practices are still widespread. These jars of medicines, ineffective in treating patients before they died, are placed on the graves to indicate familial intentions to do their utmost to bring health to the deceased when he or she was still alive and, now that he or she is dead, to restore health to the deceased's spirit in the afterlife.

MARRIAGE RITUALS

The rituals surrounding courtship and marriage powerfully contribute to strong Uyghur local identities, oasis loyalties, and intervillage oasis solidarity. It is essential to examine marriage rituals in depth, for the wedding festivities, while similar throughout Xinjiang, vary not only at the oasis level but also at the village level. These marriage practices play an important role in reinforcing Uyghur Islamic ideology, but most interesting are the deviations from Islamic orthodoxy displayed in marriage rituals, for they highlight Turpan's unique syncretism between Islamic traditions and folk religious practices.

While marriages between Uyghurs and Tungans are rare, marriages between Hans and Uyghurs are almost unheard of. In Turpan, Uyghurs hold weddings on Sundays and Tungans hold weddings on Saturdays, enabling each to attend the other's weddings. Hans only attend Uyghur and Tungan weddings in the capacity of work supervisors. Their visits are generally short, obligatory appearances.[13] The rare instances of marriage between Hans and Uyghurs have mostly involved Uyghur students who have gone to China proper for their education. These Uyghurs are invariably disowned or told not to return to Xinjiang. Children of mixed Han and Uyghur parentage, known in Mandarin as *erzhuanzi*, are stigmatized; they are not allowed to attend Uyghur funerals, have difficulty finding marriage partners, and are mistrusted throughout their lives.

Although the legal age of marriage is eighteen, in the countryside men and women often marry as young as fifteen. This is easily accomplished by families who forge birth certificates or simply lie about the age of their children. I met a seventeen-year-old religious-school student from Aydingköl, a village in southern Turpan, when he was on his way to obtain government permission to marry a fifteen-year-old girl from Üzümchilik. Several days later I received an invitation to his wedding. Obviously, both had lied about their ages.

Men and women of marriageable age often meet at cinemas or at weddings. A favorite spot for young men and women to meet in downtown Turpan is the outdoor roller-skating rink, where they shyly eye one another from opposite sides. In the countryside, meetings are held between the parents of prospective marriage partners even before their children meet; the parents arrange to have the son pay a visit to the daughter's home. Later, both sets of parents will exchange opinions on the match. If the prospective partners do not like each other, the matchmaking is called off; if they do, they are permitted to see each other again.

The practice of oasis endogamy places prime importance on the building of intervillage social networks that can be called on for assistance in times of need—for extra labor in the fields or for financial assistance with burials, circumcisions, weddings, and pilgrimages to Mecca. Thus, the calculations by each family as to a couple's suitability can be somewhat complicated. It is essential to have parental permission for marriage. According to Chinese law, one can marry legally without it; however, Uyghur parents often disown children who do so. A twenty-four-year-old Uyghur woman fell in love with a man of mixed parentage (Uyghur and Han), whose mother was Han but had converted to Islam. The woman's parents refused to allow the marriage, the couple married anyway, and consequently the bride was disowned by her parents.

If a match is viewed as suitable by all parties, the parents arrange the marriage. Regardless of how this is done, Uyghurs have three distinct stages of courtship. The first meeting between the parents is known as *körüshüsh*. During the second meeting, the *tazim* (formal bowing), the parents agree on the match. At this meeting, the man's parents bring food and clothing to the woman's family. The third stage of engagement, the *chay* (literally "tea"), occurs two to three weeks before the wedding. The groom's family brings the food required by the bride's family for the wedding feast, including two sheep, one to be eaten at the *chay* and the other to be saved for the wedding feast. The groom's side must also give the bride's relatives clothing and betrothal gifts. All of this is very expensive; the total cost for the *chay* and the wedding can typically reach 5,000 to 10,000 *yuan* (US $1200–2500). At the wedding the bride's family gives the couple household items such as carpets, blankets, and housewares. However, in Turpan these items are often purchased by the groom's family, even though they are presented as if coming from the bride's family. Among Urumchi intellectuals, the families of the groom and bride divide the cost of the wedding equally, but in Turpan the majority of the cost is shouldered by the groom's family, according to tradition.

Young Uyghur intellectuals, both male and female, who go to the capital of Urumchi to study or work often marry someone from their home oasis who also lives in the capital. This makes visiting both sets of parents easy, perpetuates oasis endogamy, and further strengthens ties to the home oasis. It simultaneously forges strong local alliances within the capital city, where local oasis relationships are maintained by an active social life with fellow natives.

In the rare instances when Uyghurs marry someone from outside their oasis, the wedding is held in the bride's oasis. Family and friends of the groom take a bus to the bride's oasis for the wedding ceremony and later return to the groom's home for a celebration there as well.

3.3   A wedding of intellectuals in Urumchi (1985).

According to Uyghur informants who work at the Family Planning Office, the divorce rate among Uyghurs in Turpan is low, though it is extremely high in the south of Xinjiang. Turpan Uyghurs explain that this is because fewer betrothal gifts, viewed as "cement" for the marriage, are given in the south; there, marriage is not an expensive endeavor and divorce does not result in a loss of invested capital.

Turpanliks claim that in southern cities such as Kashgar, men seek out beautiful women for marriage to gain prestige. They claim the most beautiful women have been married nine or ten times, initiating divorces to get better husbands if unhappy in their present marriages. Less beautiful women are not as likely to initiate divorce because they have fewer opportunities to remarry. Skrine referred to this practice in the early 1900s: "A Kashgar beauty dates her past life by her successive husbands, just as a racing enthusiast in this country dates his by Derby winners" (1926:202). On the other hand, Albert von Le Coq (1985 [1928]:37) regarded the rumors of such permissiveness among the inhabitants of the southern Tarim oases as invented stories. Regardless of the veracity of these accounts, they point to the long-standing rivalry between the east and the west Xinjiang oases.

According to Chinese law, women, including Muslims, may initiate divorce. Although according to the Koran, Muslim men are allowed to have four wives, marriage is always monogamous in Communist China, though I discovered that some Muslims were able to continue polygynous marriages in Turpan. One man, a well-known elderly doctor, maintained adjoining compounds for his two wives, whom he married prior to Communist control, visiting them on alternate days. In Turpan, unlike in Kashgar, divorced Uyghur woman are stigmatized and find it difficult to marry unless with widowers or men with undesirable traits such as birth defects, slight mental retardation, alcoholism, or ugliness. Divorced men are also considered less desirable, but are not as heavily stigmatized.

The wedding ceremony, a joyful celebration involving the entire community, brings together and highlights fundamental aspects of Uyghur life. Kinship ties are extended and reinforced. Family values are displayed in shows of hospitality and choice of spouse. Courting strategies are developed by unmarried men and women who meet at the celebrations. Islamic marriage rituals and folk Islamic practices are employed during the wedding. The complexity of interethnic relations among Uyghurs, Tungans, Hans, and other minorities is evident in the duration that each group stays and the formalities that are exchanged. Finally, the rules of presentation are clear and express the different respect accorded to each family member and fellow villager. Marriage ceremonies also provide opportunities for social mixing among peasants, merchants, and intellectuals and reveal Uyghur variations in cultural practices within formal and religious settings. During my fieldwork, I was invited to seventeen weddings—thirteen Uyghur, two Han, and two Tungan—and served as photographer and videographer for each. I used the video footage later to solicit participants' views about wedding and marriage symbolism.

A week or two prior to the wedding ceremony, invitations on red paper (red is the symbol of happiness) are sent to the guests.[14] On the evening before the wedding, the bride's and groom's families serve their guests a feast. Men and women are segregated and entertained in different rooms of the house; thereby, according to Uyghur thought, both men and women, though perhaps especially men, have greater freedom. Uyghur women do not smoke tobacco or drink alcohol, and it is considered impolite for men to smoke and drink in front of them. It is also disrespectful for men to smoke in front of their parents.

Once the men are gathered, they are served a strong alcoholic beverage, made of sorghum, called *haraq* (a type of *Maotai*) in Uyghur. The most famous brand is known by its Mandarin name, *Ilidaqu*, and is produced in the Ili oasis. While the meal is served by the women, who bring it to the door of the men's room, the men toast each other in ritual fashion.

One man toasting another forces the other to join him in downing his shot of the alcohol, which tastes similar to gasoline. Then both men grimace, their eyes bulging, showing that the drinks did not go down smoothly. This demonstrates that they drink to honor the other person, not because they like to drink. They then chase the alcohol with a small bowl of tea. This formal toasting continues around the table several times. The toasts are generally related to the virtues of the groom and his father.

After the men finish eating, the groom and his young male friends gather in a room that, because it is the only place these youths can smoke out of their parents' view, quickly fills with cigarette smoke. There they continue to make speeches but use different protocol. They toast each other with small sherry glasses, but the person making the toast holds one hand over his heart while speaking—generally about his happiness at seeing so many good friends sharing in the occasion or about the virtues and goodness of the groom and his family.

While the groom and his male friends are toasting, the hired musicians are fed and the female family members and guests help with food preparations for the following day. By midnight, the musicians begin to beat their drums outside the house, and both male and female guests go outside to dance. At traditional weddings, Uyghurs dance only with members of their own sex. Single men, in particular, use the opportunity to express their interest in the women among the crowd that encircles them as they dance. It is often here that single men first make their intentions known to potential brides. A man who finds a particular woman attractive will direct his dance toward her and bow while holding his hand over his heart. The men dance sensuously, beating their chests and raising and lowering their eyebrows. The women look on nervously and giggle. This is a contrast to other kinds of dances—at home gatherings and in dance halls—in which mixed Uyghur couples dance the fox-trot and waltz. Mixed-couple dancing, however, is a deviation from Uyghur Islamic religiosity.

The musicians number from three to five men who play traditional Central Asian instruments; one plays the *sunay*, a reed oboelike instrument with a whining sound, and the others form a troop of drummers. The *naghra* drums, covered in cowhide, resemble bongos in both sound and appearance. They are beaten with foot-long poplar sticks. The drum tempo varies throughout the wedding to dramatize the emotional tenor and character of events, heightening the excitement of the ceremony and marking its transitions.

The next day the religious wedding ceremony (*nika*) is performed at the bride's home, where only male family representatives, generally the grandfather, father, or brother from both households, meet with a *molla*, who presides.[15] No guests are invited. During this short ceremony, Islamic scriptures are read and the groom's father promises before God that he will ensure the bride is well cared for. The *nika*, symbolizing the union between the families and an acknowledgment of their mutual responsibilities and obligations, must take place before the wedding can commence. Only in southern Xinjiang are both the bride and the groom present at this ceremony.

On the same morning, trucks take the groom's guests to the bride's village. Two green wooden wedding chests (*sanduq*), one containing betrothal gifts and the other a conjugal fund, are placed on the truck. Both chests are provided by the groom's family, but the conjugal fund is later presented as if given by the bride's family. In regions of wealth, such as Turpan, the groom's family provides both chests; in poor regions and in Urumchi, each side provides its respective chest. Once the trucks are prepared for departure, guests pile in, women and children in separate trucks from the men. The musicians are usually in the lead truck, which carries the unmarried or recently married men of the groom's age group. As they make their way through the groom's village, the musicians beat their drums fast, creating a mood of expectation and excitement.

As the caravan proceeds through the village, the young male guests make sexual-sounding catcalls at the young women—from ten-year-olds on up—who are on the street. The drums incite the men into an almost frenzied state while the women, in the rear trucks, sit passively, watching the men and laughing. As momentum builds among the men, the catcalls become more animal—expressing both threatening urgency and raging sexual desire. Women on the streets run to get out of sight, giggling as they hide. Some flee with genuinely fearful expressions on their faces. Smaller children, upon hearing the approaching trucks and music, come out of their homes and begin to dance in the traditional Uyghur fashion, alternately extending their arms outward from the chest and snapping their fingers. The musicians continue to beat their drums until reaching the farthest extent of the village, resuming only as they near the bride's village. The men's catcalls also resume.

Near the bride's home, villagers erect barricades, often consisting of bolts of cloth or rope stretched across the street, to obstruct the passage of the trucks. When they encounter the barricades, the trucks stop and the groom's best man jumps out to dance in front of the bride's family and coax people to take down the barricades.[16] He hands money to people, as if making a bribe, and shakes their hands in a jovial manner. Friends and

3.4   Musicians on a wedding caravan truck in Keriya, east of Khotan (1985).

relatives of the bride then bring him tea and eventually the barricade is taken down. Other men from the groom's village may also join the best man and dance for the bride's villagers. There can be as many as five barricades near the bride's home, and each is treated in the same way.

When the trucks finally arrive at the bride's home, the men and women are again segregated. The guests file into the rooms one at a time, and are given pieces of flat bread (*nan*), which they dip in sugared tea and eat. This symbolizes the hope that life's sustenance and relations between the families and villages will be sweet. Before the meal of *polo* (pilaf) and mutton is served, the father of the bride brings a basin and a water jug and washes the hands of each male guest; each nods and smiles, in turn, to show his appreciation. The mother of the bride does the same for the female guests. During the feast, men from the bride's village eat with those of the groom's village, building camaraderie among themselves through conversation, drinking, toasting, and telling jokes. The young men joke with the groom, usually about sex, trying to put him at ease. When the men finish eating, they say a prayer (*duwa*) with their palms held upward, as if holding a book. At the end of the prayer, they bring their hands to their own faces, moving them in a circular motion as if stroking their beards. If alcohol is being served, some Uyghurs will not say a prayer. In more formal feasts, when a *molla* is likely to be present, all alcohol is hidden.

While the men eat and pray, the bride remains secluded with her closest female friends. The mother of the groom or the matriarchs of the groom's family bring the chests containing the betrothal gifts and the conjugal fund to the matriarchs of the bride's family, who thereupon throw candy and sunflower seeds into the air. This is a symbolic gesture meant to bring happiness and fertility to the newlyweds. A female representative of the groom's family, or the groom's mother, presents the betrothal gifts (from the groom's family) of clothing and jewelry to the bride's mother. Then the second chest, the conjugal fund (symbolically from the bride's family), containing household items such as thermoses, blankets, teapots, and serving platters, is opened. The jewelry and clothes are taken to the bride so that she may dress in her new clothes for her journey to the groom's family. After the meal and the presentations, the musicians begin beating their drums and the men dance in the street, where crowds gather to watch.

The bride emerges from the cloistered room after the men have finished dancing, wearing her new clothes and a thick veil, through which she can barely see. Throughout the festivities, she remains veiled. Upon entering the matriarchs' room, the bride lets out high-pitched wails to express the grief she feels about leaving her parents. While wailing, she bids her family members farewell. Three *nan* are brought to the *molla*, who circles them over her head to bless her with wholeness and sustenance throughout her life.[17] He randomly opens pages of the Koran in front of her face, blesses her, and prays that she always follow the Islamic teachings. He then places the *nan* below the bride's eyes so that her tears may fall on them to demonstrate that her pain is real. These *nan* are kept by her parents.

After saying farewell to her family again, the bride continues to wail and her body becomes limp—another expression of pain at leaving her family. An uncle or brother carries her to a van or car as the groom's co-villagers and friends pile into the trucks to return to the groom's village. In southern oases, the bride's male family members carry the veiled bride, seated on a carpet, outside the gate of her home. There they gently bounce her several times on the ground to symbolize that she is no longer part of her parents' household. The bride and groom sit in the lead car—the groom in the front passenger side and the bride in the back with her best friend, mother or, though less common, her father. Her sobbing and wailing continue.

On the return trip the musicians change their beat to a slower tempo, mixed with lots of quick beats, as if declaring their victory in obtaining the bride. Often the wedding caravan detours through the center of downtown Turpan just so that as the trucks make their way down the main boulevard the young men can again shout out catcalls at the women on the streets.

As the bride's car nears the groom's home, a fire is lit in the road and the car runs over it. A fire is also lit at the groom's doorway, or coals are placed in a ladle at the doorstep, which the bride walks over.[18] The burning of plants and seeds to ward off evil is common throughout Central Asia. As mentioned earlier, Uyghurs also use fire to ward off evil spirits, *jin*, in cemetery rituals and during the swaddling ceremony when a child is placed in a crib for the first time.

Upon the bride's arrival at her new home, a female friend of the groom's family or the groom himself escorts her into a private room, where the groom's mother consoles her, saying such things as "You are welcome here, please don't cry." Meanwhile, the groom and the remainder of the men rest to prepare for the arrival of the bride's family, upon which the wedding festivities will continue. Later, the veiled bride is brought into a room where the matriarchs of the groom's family are seated with other women and children. A female friend of the groom's family formally introduces the bride to the matriarchs. She sits facing them on a blanket on which a large rock is placed to symbolize the groom's family's hope that her stay will be long-lasting. When the bride stands, the matriarchs throw candy and sunflower seeds into the air once again to bring happiness, fertility, and sweetness. The bride then changes her position to sit beside the matriarchs. This shows that her acceptance of the groom's

3.5   A veiled bride carried out of her home gate on a carpet. Notice the teacup-shaped hat pinned to a woman's head covering in center of photo.

family and their acceptance of her has been confirmed. About an hour later, the bride's family and co-villagers, who remained in the bride's home to clean up, arrive at the groom's home. The musicians play as a gesture of welcome. The guests are fed a reciprocal feast. In the courtyard, an architectural feature of all traditional Uyghur homes, the cooks carry on at a tremendous pace, passing plates to the guests seated inside. After the meal, dancing resumes outside the main entrance, and finally the bride's co-villagers, and the bride, pile back into the trucks and return to their village. Later in the evening the newlyweds will be reunited when the father of the bride brings her back to her husband's home.

FOUNDATIONS OF OASIS UNIQUENESS

Uyghurs maintain status relations across horizontal age grades, and relations between sibling sets are emphasized. Weddings serve an important function by creating opportunities to build strong relations across age grades and strengthen age sets at the same time. Men and women of similar ages eat together. Unmarried men have opportunities to acquaint themselves with eligible women, specifically, each other's sisters. Overall, the wedding festivities reinforce Uyghur Islamic ideology while simultaneously deviating from Islamic orthodoxy: gender roles are both practiced and reinforced and segregation between the sexes is strictly maintained, but the drinking, dancing, and sexual overtones of the festivities are clearly Uyghur innovations. Similarly, the syncretism between Islamic traditions and folk religious practices creates particular variations of Uyghur culture unique to individual oases.

Distinct social practices have created varied cultures that foster strong oasis identities and perceptions of difference among Uyghurs throughout the region. In addition, Uyghur oases were, and are again becoming, in closer contact with the regions bordering them on the outside than with each other. The development of distinct and separate identities is greatly reinforced by the isolation of the Xinjiang oases and their unique manner of proceeding through the life cycle. When the focus of the oases turned inward after 1935, the separate oasis identities were temporarily masked; the opening of Xinjiang to the outside world in 1985 has caused the geographical forces that traditionally divided the oasis dwellers to reemerge. These distinct oasis identities challenge Uyghur intellectuals' attempts to create a nationalist awakening and a Uyghur nationalist ideology. But they are finding it even more difficult to craft nationalist ideologies that are accepted at the local level by the three social groups— peasants, merchants, and intellectuals—who maintain vastly different notions of Uyghur identity.

Social Group Identity in Turpan 4

> I worry for your lives,
> So I am calling you to awaken.
> —"Uyghur," "Awaken! (*Oyghan*)"

ENTERING THE TURPAN OASIS

Passengers' ears pop during the descent into the Turpan depression, but entering Turpan is a relief after the daunting and repetitive barrenness of the *gobi* sands. The oasis of Turpan lies 180 kilometers from Urumchi and the journey takes four hours by public bus. From China proper, Turpan is the first major railway stop in Xinjiang. Since the oasis lies deep in the Turpan Basin (the second lowest place on earth), the train skirts it north on higher ground. After disembarking, passengers on their way to Turpan continue on a fifty-kilometer bus ride. The road they follow traverses the barren *gobi*; the bus jolts along the rocks and sand as the road intermittently disappears. Lines of concentric mounds of sand and rock, eerie and bunkerlike, descend toward the town. These are the shaft wells of the *karez* irrigation system, a network of underground irrigation canals that form Turpan's lifeline.

A particularly noticeable feature of Turpan is its climate. In summer the heat is oppressive, with temperatures reaching 48°C (125°F). To withstand this heat at night, people sleep on wooden beds in their courtyards or on the roofs of their homes; during the day they seek shelter in rooms with floors several feet below the ground. In winter the temperature drops below -7°C (20°F). In spring, powerful 100-mile-an-hour winds blow the desert sand around like baby powder. These winds, known as *qara buran* (black wind), turn the sky black, destroy crops, overturn vehicles, and damage homes. Grit and sand cover everything.

When travelers reach the oasis, the colors of Turpan soothe the eyes—the reddish mud homes, green grapevines, and dusty tree-lined streets are welcoming variations in an otherwise bleak landscape. Bus passengers are unloaded in the center of town, across from the central bazaar, which explodes with color and activity (see figure 4.1). Uyghur women stroll along the streets in multicolored silk skirts and nylon stockings, their gold earrings dangling, and call out to one another in high-pitched tones. Uyghur men, in square brimless skullcaps, shout at friends with a whining "whoa" sound. Some sell colorfully inlaid knives from the western town of Yengisar. Others prepare shish kebabs, contributing to the heavy smell of spices and smoke in the marketplace. Young Uyghur men are on the lookout for tourists, whom they approach with the greeting "chanjee marney" (change money), their arms outstretched so that the newcomers can read the black market exchange rate written on their palms.[1] Hans haggle over prices with gold-toothed Uyghur women who answer them in monotone Mandarin. Young Uyghur girls, their heads covered in sheer silk, walk arm in arm in red-heeled shoes. Old bearded Uyghur men, in turbans and knee-high black leather boots, answer the call to prayer that periodically rings out from the many mosques decorated with Arabic calligraphy. Tungan men answer similar calls from mosques bearing Chinese characters.

In the bazaar, a converted storeroom serves as a movie theater where Uyghur, Han, and Tungan men watch films, chewing sunflower seeds and smoking cigarettes made from tobacco stems rolled in newspaper. The only women in the audience are Hans who are passing through Turpan—they watch the films while waiting for their buses to leave. Just a block or two from the bazaar, along the back alleys of the villages, donkey carts bounce through dust-filled lanes, their drivers cracking whips and yelling "*posh posh*" to clear people out of the way.

At night, the bazaar is filled with disco sounds booming out of the top of a five-story modern department store where young Uyghur men dance in pairs, cigarettes dangling from their mouths. Once evening falls, fast-food stands open up in the outdoor markets. Male customers fill the Uyghur, Tungan, and Han restaurants, which take on the aura of social clubs: as they eat, the men smoke and spit on the floor, many of them becoming drunk and boisterous. Pool is a popular game through-

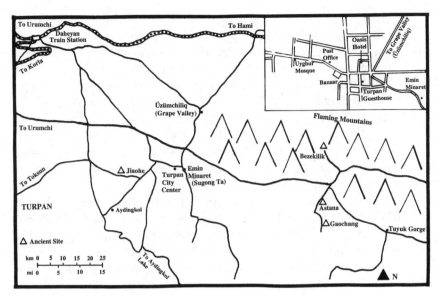

FIGURE 4.1   Turpan in 1989–1990. Adapted from Bonavia (1988:135).

out the oasis, and men crowd around a pool table that a savvy bookseller has placed inside his shop. Some read books, others watch the game. At night, street life is dominated by men. Other than the few who work with their husbands selling food at the bazaar, most women are at home with their children.

The town of Turpan is divided into "old" (*qona*) and "new" (*yengi*) sections. The "new" part of town is said to have been built during the rule of Yaqub Beg (1864–1877), the military leader from Andijan who invaded the region and drove the Qing forces out of Xinjiang. On a map made by C. G. Mannerheim in 1923, the two towns are called the "Chinese Town" (*qona*) and the "Sart Town" (*yengi*) (see figure 4.2). However, the "new" (*yengi*) or "Sart Town," located eight kilometers to the west of the "old" (*qona*) section, is today older than this "Chinese Town," which was for the most part demolished to make way for the modern government buildings, gaudily decorated with Chinese versions of Islamic motifs, that form Turpan's municipal center.

The Islamic building façades are inspired by the Communist government's decision to make Xinjiang look more Uyghur, in keeping with its designation as the Uyghur Autonomous Region. Since 1985, the government has incorporated stylized Islamic motifs in architecture and building projects throughout the region. Most of the rest of Turpan's downtown structures were erected in the 1950s and are Russian in style and design. These were built with the help of Soviet architects and building contractors prior to the Sino-Soviet split in 1962.

In 1949, the Han population amounted to only 1 percent (640) of the total population (67,319) in the city of Turpan, which includes seven outlying villages. Their numbers have since increased steadily, reaching 20,586 in 1966 and jumping to 37,152, or 24 percent of the population, by 1974. Uyghurs, however, still make up the majority of the population today (see table 4.1) and are concentrated in the oasis's seven villages outside of the city center.

The ethnic composition in Turpan City (including its seven outlying villages) is 70 percent Uyghurs, 20 percent Hans, and 10 percent Tungans, and each group is distributed in a clear pattern throughout the city. Most Han government workers live inside the "old," or "Chinese," town; the rest of the Hans live in neighborhoods that are separated from the

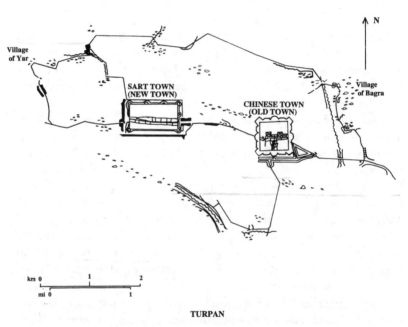

FIGURE 4.2   Map of Turpan, c. 1907, Showing the Sart (New) and Chinese (Old) Towns. Adapted from Mannerheim (1969 [1942]:351).

TABLE 4.1

Population Growth in Turpan City, 1912–1985

Year	Total	Uyghurs	Hans	Tungans	Others
1912	46,014				
1949	67,319	60,189	640	6,466	24
1956	75,982	67,033	2,137	6,795	17
1958	83,525	71,905	5,030	6,534	36
1959	97,000	72,355	18,054	6,559	32
1966	111,952	82,144	20,586	9,151	86
1970	130,865	94,254	26,143	9,323	145
1973	141,931	103,206	27,877	10,776	88
1974	154,788	106,191	37,152	11,331	112
1985	196,847	140,244	41,869	14,410	324

SOURCE: Tulufan Shizhi Bianjishi (Turpan City Historical Collections Department). Internal documents.

Uyghurs. Grape Valley Village (Üzümchilik), in northeast Turpan, is predominantly Uyghur. In the settlements south of the Turpan central bazaar, Uyghurs and Tungans live together as they have done for at least five generations. Tungans and Hans also live in some of the same areas. Thus, while the Han and Uyghur populations are segregated, Tungans live among both.

EFFECTS OF RADICAL MINORITY POLICIES

After Xinjiang was officially incorporated as an autonomous region of China in 1955, the Communists believed they had consolidated themselves sufficiently to attempt harsher policies in the oases aimed at fusing Uyghur culture with Chinese communism. These radical minority policies began with language—a building block to both ethnicity and self-awareness and the basic means of cultural production—by introducing script changes in Uyghur. This, they believed, would create a break with the past and move the Uyghurs toward "modernity." Kemal Atatürk implemented Latin script changes in Turkey in the 1920s to achieve a similar break with the past.

By 1956 the Communists had replaced the Arabic script with a modified Cyrillic alphabet for Uyghurs, Kazaks, and Kyrgyz. This was primarily done to undermine Islamic influence, given that Islamic teachings are written in Arabic, and purportedly to eliminate the high illiter-

acy rate in Xinjiang. It also followed the alphabet policy of the Soviet
Union toward Central Asia. With the deterioration of Sino-Soviet relations in 1960, the Communists decided to change the Cyrillic alphabet to
a Latin script, reflecting the Chinese desire to eliminate Soviet influence
in Xinjiang and, more important, sever ties between the indigenous
peoples of Xinjiang and their kinsmen across the Sino-Soviet border
(McMillen 1979:120).[2] A modified Arabic script was reinstated in 1978 as
part of a series of cultural and religious reforms. Today, while many
Uyghurs are able to read the Arabic script, many are unable to either
read or write it, especially Uyghur adults who were educated between
1960 and 1978. About one half of the publicly posted political commen-
taries, written frequently by Uyghurs working in government offices or
businesses about the political speeches of Communist Party leaders in
Beijing, are still written in the Latin script.

The decision to launch the Great Leap Forward (1958–1961) in Xinjiang was partially based upon Chinese determination to exploit the natural resources of the border region. Their major interest was to exclude
Soviet interests and to eliminate pro-Soviet influence among the region's
minorities. This turbulent time was characterized by an "anti-local
nationalist" campaign that purged many Uyghur cadres and non-Party
intellectuals, both in the capital and in the oases, charged with retaining
pro-Soviet or anti-Chinese Communist Party sympathies.

In the oases, the closure of rural bazaars, attacks on Islam, and
emphasis on assimilationist policies during this period caused considerable destabilization and increased discontent among the Uyghurs.
Uyghurs were forced to collectivize in communes, material incentives
were abolished, and private land holdings were eliminated. A critical
threshold was reached in 1962, when relations between China and the
Soviet Union deteriorated precipitously. After 60,000 to 120,000 minority nationals fled from the Ili region to what is today Kazakstan in 1962,
the borders were sealed. At the same time, construction was completed
on a rail line linking Urumchi to China proper. With these events, the
communist Chinese gained unquestionable control of the Ili–Three
Regions area, which had for so long been a pro-Soviet stronghold on
Chinese soil (McMillen 1979:123). China had attained its goals: to control Xinjiang's natural resources and to eliminate Soviet influence.

In reaction to the Ili turmoil of 1962, Wang Enmao, Xinjiang's top Party
and People's Liberation Army leader, adjusted regional policies along
more moderate lines aimed at achieving order and gradual economic and
social development. At the same time he sought to insulate the region
from outside influence and military threat by settling Hans to work in the

abandoned Ili regions and expanding units of the Production and Construction Corps in the Three Regions area. Fear of possible Soviet intervention in Xinjiang was fed by Moscow's intervention in Budapest in 1956 and in Czechoslovakia in August 1968. Most threatening were the series of Sino-Soviet border clashes in Xinjiang from March through August 1969.

In mid-1969, Wang was removed from power as a result of the Cultural Revolutionary political struggles in the Central Communist Party in Beijing. For the next decade, the Xinjiang region experienced a succession of leaders and policies that fluctuated according to these high-level party struggles. The Cultural Revolution was carried on with particular fervor in Xinjiang. Uyghurs who supported Wang Enmao and those who did not fought bitterly. One Uyghur informant, strongly opposed to Wang Enmao, spoke to me about an occasion on which pro-Wang Uyghurs attempted to seize him. Fearing the typical torture—being hung upside-down by the ankles inside a *karez* well—the informant fended off the attack with several well-thrown hand grenades.

In 1978, following Mao's death, the fall of the Gang of Four, and the rise of Deng Xiaoping, the Chinese government promulgated cultural and religious reforms to bring order and stability to minority areas and reestablish trust. Policies of reform and liberalization, such as the responsibility system allowing farmers to keep a percentage of their crops to sell on the open market, were introduced to reverse slumping productivity. These policies, however, were not instituted in Xinjiang; the government awaited the results of the responsibility system in other areas.

By 1980, there were reports of serious economic dislocation and impoverishment in southern Xinjiang. In Kashgar, in April of 1980, frustrations led to a clash between soldiers and civilians, comprised of both Uyghurs and Hans, and several hundred people were reportedly killed or wounded (McMillen 1984:575). By mid-1981 it had become obvious that the overall situation in Xinjiang demanded a Party leader who could steer the region out of its continuing turmoil. In late October Wang Enmao was sent back to Urumchi to resume the post of first secretary of the regional Party committee. Sensitive to the region's special conditions, Wang Enmao also demonstrated his dedication to the goal of consolidating Xinjiang into the modern Chinese state (McMillen 1984:581).[3]

Uyghur Memory

Uyghurs claim that the disruption brought about by the Cultural Revolution was most intense in small villages and among Uyghurs with the least education. Indeed, the remaining traces of the Cultural Revolution are most apparent in small villages throughout Xinjiang. Vestiges can still be seen on the road from Urumchi to Turpan—one crumbling building retains on its walls faded red script reading "Raise high the red banner of Chairman Mao." Faded slogans, as well as paintings of Mao, Marx, Engels, Lenin, and Stalin, are prevalent on public buildings throughout Turpan's villages. In a village in the distant mountains of Turpan, one building has Mao's portrait painted on each of its six outside doors. Some Uyghur homes still contain mirrors inscribed with the Cultural Revolutionary phrase *"Jingzhu Maozhuxi Wansui Wujiang"* (Respectfully wish Chairman Mao boundless long life). Some of these mirrors show paintings of the Cultural Revolutionary play "The White Haired Girl." Most of these mirrors were received as wedding presents, and strangely enough, Uyghurs are not ashamed to display them. This contrasts sharply with practices in China proper, where Hans have long since thrown away or hidden images reminiscent of this brutal and bitter era. Most Uyghurs, however, shrug this period off as a time of Han foolishness, placing full blame on the Hans for the suffering inflicted on the Uyghur people and China as a whole.

During the Cultural Revolution, Uyghurs obediently carried Chairman Mao's *Little Red Book* and, upon greeting friends, would raise it in the air saying "Long live Chairman Mao." The Red Guards, including Hans, Tungan, and Uyghurs, beat those who did not reply in kind. The Red Guards also enforced a dress code—Uyghurs were not allowed to wear either their traditional *doppa* or white funeral turbans. Uyghur Islamic leaders, *mollas*, were severely attacked and forced to shave their beards; Korans were burned, mosques were destroyed, and prayer had to be done in private. *Mollas* were often paraded through the streets with dunce caps on their heads and were chided with the curses *jin, alwasti,* and *shaytan* (evil spirit, ogre, Satan) by passersby.

Intellectuals in China were faced with more persecution than others during the Cultural Revolution and, in fact, throughout most of the Communist period. They were victims of the 1957 Anti-Rightist Movement (against right-wing liberal thinkers) and, after the failures of the Great Leap Forward in the early 1960s, were subjected to tests of loyalty. During the Cultural Revolution they were considered class enemies and designated as the lowest category, the "stinking old ninth."[4] During this period all schools were closed. Universities were not fully reopened until 1978. Intellectuals were restricted to educating the masses in socialism, and the government used campaigns and framing strategies to imprison any intellectuals considered dangerous. Dissident voices were rarely heard.

Uyghur intellectuals have not forgotten the devastation inflicted by the Chinese Communists during the Cultural Revolution and often speak of the suffering they experienced. For example, a Uyghur teacher, while drinking with his schoolmate, a Uyghur village official, explained that he looked twenty years older than the official because he had been tortured during the Cultural Revolution. As a young man, the teacher had the Latin letters H.U.H.K. tattooed on the four fingers of his right hand. H.U.H.K. stands for *"Khälq Üchün Khizmät Qilayli,"* the Uyghur equivalent of the Communist motto "Serve the People" (*wei renmin fuwu*). Although he had attended college and was a Party member, he was refused employment because his family's landlord background placed him in an undesirable category. He worked as a peasant and was brutalized—his face was beaten and burned and part of his ear was crushed.

Another Turpan Uyghur intellectual now living in Urumchi became a teacher at age seventeen and wrote children's stories about friendship and good work habits. During the Cultural Revolution, at the age of twenty, he was sentenced to eight years of hard labor. His crime (*guna*) consisted of telling a friend that he liked a particular type of Russian candy. His friend interpreted this as his having Soviet leanings and reported him to the authorities. One week later the friend was arrested for a similar crime, and they were ordered to build roads and irrigation ditches and to collect human waste. In the evenings the teacher often was made to stand before groups of people who shouted abusive words at him. For eight years he was confined to a small village. In 1967, only one month after he had been sentenced, his wife divorced him because he had brought her so much shame; almost thirty years later, their only daughter still refuses to have contact with him.

UYGHUR KINSHIP

On the northeast outskirts of Turpan, near village stores and restaurants, a large sign depicts two couples, one with only one daughter, the other with two children, a girl and a baby boy. Above the picture are the words: "All nationalities have the responsibility to practice family planning." Both men are dressed in Western-style suits and are shown walking through a modern city with high-rise buildings. Both women wear summer dresses and neither wears head-covering. The only way to iden-

4.1　Birth control sign with Uyghur (left) and Han (right) families. The sign reads, "All nationalities are responsible for carrying out their duty to practice birth control" (1990).

tify one couple as Uyghur is by the square brimless hat (*doppa*) the father wears and by their two children.

The government's effort to limit Uyghurs' birthrate threatens both their kinship and economic systems, making opposition at the local level as well as an increasing return to the insulation of Islamic practice a future possibility. Rumors of government interference in family planning began in 1985, when I first visited Xinjiang. There was some evidence that the rumors were well-founded. Government officials placed inconspicuous signs in hotels frequented by Hans, who were already limited to one child per family, that read, "All nationalities have the obligation to limit family size." By May 1989, government policy mandated that rural minorities limit their families to three children and urban minorities to two children; propaganda signs were commonplace.[5]

Although the government has made efforts to educate Uyghurs about the new laws, considerable confusion remains among the villagers.[6] One thirty-one-year-old male peasant from Üzümchilik with a daughter and two sons, wanting another daughter, insisted that the birth-control law did not apply to a couple with only one daughter. I was also told that a family with three daughters was allowed to have another child in an attempt to have a son. However, the law specifically levies a one- to two-thousand-*yuan* fine for exceeding the three-child limit. A fifth child would bring a fine of 6,000 *yuan* (US $1,500). Nevertheless, during 1989 and 1990 I did not learn of any couples who were fined as a result of the law's enforcement.

The majority of Uyghur peasants determine their social networks and relationships through kinship ties, which are influenced by relations of production. Based on African material, Claude Meillassoux argues that lateral filiation is encouraged by relations of production, as opposed to relations of reproduction: "Lateral succession implies continuity between people of neighboring age, the producers' strength being an important factor in the constitution of small communities in which agricultural labour is predominant" (1981:48). For example, grape cultivation in Turpan depends on labor assistance from affinal kin. Because planting and harvesting occur at different times depending on the location and altitude of the land within the basin, farmers in the lower regions, where crops ripen earlier, will be the first to call on their kin. They will reciprocate a week or so later when the crops in the higher regions ripen.

4.2   Uyghur kin working together after the harvest to bury and protect grapevines from Turpan's winter (1990).

The Uyghurs are the only Central Asian people who practice oasis and village endogamy. As Lawrence Krader observes,

> The Uyghurs favor marriage within the village. These people stand in great contrast to their neighboring Kirgiz, Kazakhs and Uzbeks by favoring village endogamy. Or put in other terms, the greater the proximity or vicinity of the two families, the more to be preferred is the marriage. This we call vicinal marriage.   (1971:143)

Oasis endogamy is principally a result of the strong oasis identities created by the distances that have historically separated Xinjiang's oases. Uyghur kinship is unilineal, through the father, and stresses lateral filiation, or horizontal relations among both male and female siblings. Uyghurs also maintain status relations across horizontal age grades and use specific terms to designate whether a particular affine is older or younger. Relations among sibling sets and age grades are emphasized.

Uyghurs prefer families that include as many sons as possible and at least two daughters. One unusual feature of the Uyghur kinship system is that females attempt to remain in their natal village or oasis, often marrying men from the same village, and marriage between two sisters from one family and two brothers of another is not uncommon. Sister marriages serve to consolidate the kin upon which a daughter's family may call for assistance. Fathers maintain that they prefer at least two daughters because this provides each with a confidante. They fear that a single daughter would grow up to be too masculine and end up interfering in family affairs. Furthermore, should a daughter with no sister divorce (an infrequent occurrence in Turpan), she would have no one to live with. The most important consideration, however, is that with two daughters, *baja*, a special relationship between husbands of sisters, with at least two brothers-in-law will be established. *Baja* enables the two families to unite in economic cooperation.

The prohibition against patrilateral parallel cousin marriage, between the children of two brothers, further aids the formation of exogamous family networks. A marriage between such cousins, although permitted by Islamic law, is considered by Turpan Uyghurs to be a form of incest because the cousins belong to the same patrilineage and hence the same bloodline. However, patrilateral parallel cousin marriage is said to be practiced in southern oases like Khotan and Kashgar when a grandfather desires to keep his wealth within his lineage. Marriages of children of two sisters or of a brother and sister are practiced, but are ideal rather than the norm.

CHINESE REFORMS AND UYGHUR SOCIAL CHANGE

Kinship practices of the Turpan Uyghurs, which emphasize cooperative sharing of work, have placed them in a strong position to take advantage of the dramatic economic changes in their oasis. Since 1985, a large number of fields in Turpan have been converted from subsistence and cotton crops to grape cultivation. In the same year, the Chinese government floated the price of Turpan's most valuable commodity, the golden seedless raisin produced only in Turpan, and the oasis experienced an economic surge. Since then, raisin production has become even more lucrative. In 1990 Uyghurs sold their raisins for six *yuan* per kilo (about US $1.50), up from the 1984 price of 1.7 *yuan* per kilo (about 55 cents). One *mu* (one sixth of an acre) of grapes earns from 600 to 1,000 *yuan*, nearly twice as much as cotton, at 400 to 500 *yuan* per *mu*. As a result, since 1985 most Uyghurs have converted their fields to vineyards and have become more wealthy. They invest most of their wealth in the construction of brick houses to replace their traditional mud homes, which are easily damaged by the strong winds that blow in the spring. Brick construction is dramatically changing the face of Turpan: wealth is now measured by the amount of bricks used in a home. Those with less means build their front gates with brick gateposts and wait hopefully for more income with which to complete the rest of their houses later.[7] Such wealth has led the majority of peasants to be satisfied with Chinese government reforms.

These reforms have caused major changes within Turpan society, including the creation of wealthy merchant and peasant groups and a new form of social stratification. This is an enormous difference, since in 1958 Uyghur villages were collectivized into people's communes as part of the Communist government's reorganization. Although most of China's communes were decollectivized in the late 1970s, they were not officially dissolved in Turpan until 1985 when village (*xiang* or *yeza*) governments with political and administrative functions took their place. This change constituted a return to a small-scale peasant economy that depends on individual family initiative, the same kind of economy that existed, at least in principle, before collectivization.

Turpan villages with 25,000 people were divided into brigades (of up to 2,000 villagers) and teams (of up to 500 villagers) for administrative purposes such as taxation, medical care, water distribution, and judicial mediation. Fixed purchase quotas formerly determined peasant crop yields; now village work brigades and peasants generally make contracts with one another. Among the poorer brigades, no contracts are made at all. As Hoppe found in 1985, peasants devote themselves to subsistence production and are free to sell surplus products on the market (1987:232).

Chinese development projects also have changed the physical structure of Turpan. In the 1960s, forest shelter belts were planted to protect Turpan from the brutal winds and fine dust that used to submerge the streets. Describing changes in Turpan since his arrival from Shanghai in 1961, a Han water management official said moving through the streets used to require walking in brown silt up to one's shins.[8] Another dramatic change came when the road connecting the main bazaar with the outlying villages was built. Uyghurs living in more distant villages no longer use the donkey cart for transportation but rather the satellite taxi, a covered flatbed mini-truck with seats in the rear. The trip from the community of Subeshi, located in the hills northeast of Turpan at the top of Grape Valley, to the central bazaar used to take two and a half hours by donkey cart on a road only ten feet wide. The road has now been doubled in width and blacktopped (*qara may yol*), and the trip takes only twenty-five minutes.

The new reforms have brought a dramatic increase in wealth to Uyghur peasants in Turpan, especially to farmers in the north whose land is more fertile. This is exemplified by one wealthy peasant who works as a cook (*ashpäz*) at Uyghur ritual celebrations even though he is the richest man in a village located to the west of the Turpan city center. He owns 100 *mu* of land, about 17 acres, planted with wheat, sorghum, and grapes that he began to cultivate in 1981 when the government decided Uyghurs could begin to own private plots. In 1985, he had proved himself so successful that his brigade asked him to farm more land. After getting the brigade to provide pump irrigation for the fields, from 1985 to 1988 he invested 13,000 *yuan* in farming. In 1989, he made 8,000 *yuan* in profit and signed a 15-year contract for the land with the government to secure the continuity of the arrangement. In three years he planted 20,000 poplar trees and 1,000 grapevines worth one million *yuan*. During this period he employed twelve Uyghur permanent laborers, for whom he built homes, and hired over 300 Han Chinese day laborers to assist him. To take advantage of the brick building boom in the villages, he also built, owns, and operates a large brick factory.

Economic Specialization and Social Group Identity

In Turpan, economic specialization in grape production has promoted localized identities and has undercut a strong commitment to a pan-Uyghur identity. Grape cultivation is both vital and integral to Turpan life; it is the center of Turpan's economy and recent wealth and makes Turpan unique among the oases of Xinjiang. It accentuates peasants' reliance on cooperative labor, both kin and nonkin, and has led Turpan's merchant Uyghurs to focus on trade with China proper, where they sell most of Turpan's raisin crop. Turpan's Uyghurs are also oriented toward China because of their relative satisfaction with Chinese reforms. Consequently, they are greatly influenced by Chinese culture even though other opportunities for trade are available to the west. This separates them from Uyghurs in oases to the west, which have not experienced the same economic prosperity, express more dissatisfaction with the Chinese administration of the region, and are more open to cultural innovations and economic development from neighbors across their borders.

While economic advances have created a new social order that distinguishes merchants from peasants, they have also raised expectations for a better standard of living. For now, the merchant and peasant groups have not become entrenched opponents, and social mobility is possible from one rank to the next. This is especially true within the grape economy that has led to prosperity in the Turpan oasis and has also played an important part in shaping Turpan Uyghur consciousness.

Merchants

Most Turpan merchants have developed extensive trading contacts with Hans and Tungans (Huis) in China proper and are involved in the long-distance raisin trade with China. To establish contacts with Han merchants before the crop arrives, merchants frequently send their kin, both consanguineal and affinal, to the eastern Chinese cities. There they build trade networks with Hans and develop impressions, generally favorable, of their Han counterparts. Because of this profitable relationship, Turpan Uyghur merchants express positive attitudes about being citizens of the Chinese state.

One of the wealthiest merchants I met lived in Subeshi, a small neighborhood of 1,000 Uyghurs located in the mountains at the northern extent of Üzümchilik. Subeshi is unusual for several reasons, but particularly because the village head is a woman and there is a strong social welfare program fostered by merchant wealth. Subeshi produces almost 3 percent (45 tons) of Üzümchilik's 1,700 tons of raisins, and as a result of the raisin price increase in 1985, villagers have become wealthy (see tables 4.2 and 4.3).[9]

The house of Mämät Imin, the main raisin merchant of Subeshi, is constructed of brick and has the aura of a castle. In 1989, Mämät Imin made over 80,000 *yuan*. He and his four associates buy raisins, for which they pay 5.5–6 *yuan* per kilo, from families throughout Turpan. After collecting twenty tons of raisins they travel to Beijing, where they sell them at seven to twelve *yuan* per kilo and gross about 190,000 *yuan*.

Peasant life in Subeshi follows a yearly boom-and-bust cycle. There is a money crunch for most of the villagers from April to November, during the grape growing season. Consequently, most weddings and circumcisions, which are expensive, take place between November and March when farmers have received money for their crops. Mämät Imin, in cooperation with the female head of the village, Jamilikhan, provides villagers with financial assistance. When Subeshi grape growers cannot fund funerals, weddings, or other social events, Mämät Imin provides interest-free loans, which are later repaid with raisin crops. If a family is very poor, Mämät Imin will give them more than the six *yuan* per kilo of raisins or will forgive their debts altogether. Mämät Imin's generosity has led the community to hold him in high regard. While not a Party member, he is an active member of the village entrepreneurial organization, which includes all merchants in Üzümchilik village. Because of his generosity and coordinated efforts with Jamilikhan, Turpan Uyghurs consider Subeshi the best neighborhood organization in all of Turpan.

TABLE 4.2
Population and Income Statistics from Subeshi (December 1988)

Households	172
Population	1,025
Workers	520
Total income	88,375 *yuan*
1988 average income (per capita)	812 *yuan*
1985 average income (per capita)	483 *yuan*

SOURCE: Interview with Niyaz Kuaiji, February 21, 1990.

TABLE 4.3
Census of Subeshi Total Village Value (November 7, 1989)

	1st Team	2nd Team	3rd Team	Total
Population	309	380	378	1,067
Households	59	64	64	187
Tractors	10	20	6	36
Motorcycles	9	9	7	25
Bicycles	15	14	43	75
Refrigerators	6	1	2	9
Color televisions	0	2	4	6
B/W televisions	32	20	35	87
Tape recorders	36	37	38	111
Electric fans	29	23	37	89
Sewing machines	27	19	35	81
Washing machines	0	2	1	3
Cows	7	9	6	22
Donkeys	15	6	18	39
Donkey carts	14	7	17	39
Sheep	116	207	173	496
Ewes	68	109	98	275
Rams	50	98	75	223
Goats	7	4	19	30
Goats (female)	6	1	13	20
Billy goats	1	3	6	9
New homes	13	6	0	19
New homes (square meters)	150	144	0	294
Total value (yuan)	149,050	172,700	132,600	454,350

SOURCE: Niyaz Kuaiji, February 21, 1990.

Few regions in Xinjiang are able to produce grapes, and the Chinese government's regulation of agricultural production assures the continued health of Turpan's grape economy. The village of Üzümchilik (Grape Valley), to the northeast of Turpan, has experienced the greatest increase in wealth of the Turpan villages because of its specialization in grapes.[10] Its wealth is reflected in the goods available in the village store, which is well stocked with bicycles, heaters, and fabrics. Another noticeable feature in the village is the large number of homes made of bricks, usually built by Han laborers from China proper, who come to Xinjiang as migrant laborers.[11] In one Üzümchilik graveyard, Uyghurs have begun to construct tombs out of bricks to display their status and wealth. Uyghurs in Üzümchilik are also buying tractors with attached flatbeds for 6,000 to 7,000 yuan ($1,500–1,700). The tractors are used to haul agricultural equipment and products, and also to transport friends to the bazaar. People frequently ride up and down the mountain in this way. Other wealth indicators include the number of privately owned satellite taxis that shuttle people up and down the mountain.

One taxi driver comes from a family who owns eighty grapevines. From these his family earns 80,000 *yuan* ($20,000), a sharp contrast to the average family income of 4,500 *yuan* ($1,125) earned from four to five vines. His family also owns livestock: ten sheep and one donkey. To further promote his prestigious status, he pulled the Chinese brand name off his Jilin pickup and wrote *Toyota* on it, a common practice similar to the American practice of placing stickers on car bumpers with slogans like "My other car is a Mercedes." Although in eastern China, in cities like Beijing and Shanghai, Japanese products are widely regarded as top quality, Han Chinese also have held protest marches against the influx of Japanese products, viewing them as another Japanese conquest of China. Uyghurs, on the other hand, without any reservations, view Japanese products as status symbols that represent power and wealth, both of which they aspire to. Perhaps the most telling sign of Üzümchilik's wealth is the fact that the village opened up its own trade office in the Shenzhen Special Economic Zone near the Hong Kong border. Clearly, trade in grapes with China proper is a major factor in shaping Turpan Uyghur views of the world and in focusing their attention eastward.

Intellectuals

Intellectuals' personal decisions and experiences have a profound effect on the inhabitants of their home oasis villages. Most intellectuals in Urumchi frequently return to their natal oasis homes and are intimately involved with local cultural developments, sponsoring conferences on historical figures or regularly writing for the many local oasis journals. Oasis inhabitants eagerly extend invitations to these intellectuals to attend weddings and circumcisions, as well as more informal social gatherings in homes. As the most educated and well-known representative of the village oasis, the intellectual confers a certain degree of prestige to the ceremony. At these gatherings, intellectuals are frequently the center of attention and lead discussions about Uyghur history and the future of the Uyghur people. It is primarily through such occasions that ideas developed in intellectual circles in the capital are quickly spread at the local level. But it is also here, at the oasis level, where the intellectuals face their greatest challenge. Peasants have the power to accept or reject intellectual notions of Uyghur identity and history and thus can make or break the projects of the intellectuals.

Today, most Uyghur intellectuals live in the capital, Urumchi, a modern city of one and a half million inhabitants that is 85 percent Han Chinese. Urumchi was founded as a garrison town and though a small number of Uyghurs lived there, they were never in the majority and were never in control of Urumchi's day-to-day affairs.[12] Today the city's non-Uyghur environment has a profound effect on intellectual views of Uyghur identity. Urumchi's buildings consist largely of drab apartment blocks. Winters are long and harsh, and the ice-covered streets and sky are blackened by coal dust. The city stretches along a north-to-south axis extending between two branches of the Tianshan Mountain range. The majority of Uyghurs live in the south near the government center; many of the post-1949 buildings inhabited by Hans lie to the north. Although the PRC government attempted to change the look of the city in 1985 with the construction of ten major architectural projects featuring Islamic design motifs, Uyghur inhabitants cannot avoid being extremely self-conscious of their Uyghurness in this Han environment: pork slabs are pulled on wheelbarrows through the streets, buses are packed with Mandarin-speaking Hans, and fashionable Western dress is the standard.

Most Uyghur intellectuals are employed at Chinese government institutions staffed by Hans. While they have been lured to work within the Communist state apparatus, where they acquire education and prestige, this integration has not ameliorated the pervasive Han prejudice against them. In this environment intellectuals begin to accept the Hans' pejorative views of the Uyghur people, particularly of those living in the oases of Xinjiang.

Only since the cultural and religious reforms of 1978, and the opening of Xinjiang to foreign trade and tourism in 1985, have Uyghur intellectuals begun to create their own versions of Uyghur national culture and put forward various nationalist ideologies. Much of their work has been shaped by the ethnic environment of Urumchi and the difficult decisions they must make about the degree of cultural assimilation their own families should undertake. They are constantly confronted with their Uyghurness in the face of Han Chinese culture in Urumchi. The choices they make—such as whether to send their children to Han-language or Uyghur-language schools—are fraught with the potential danger of cultural assimilation on one hand, and possible opportunities for individual career advancement and the attainment of skills needed to promote Uyghur causes on the other. As more and more

Hans enter Xinjiang, the pressure to come up with a Uyghur strategy to make Uyghur culture resilient to Han Chinese cultural hegemony has caused a fierce competition among intellectuals over Uyghur nationalist ideologies.

This competition to place salient historical events or personages into prominence has great and ominous ramifications for the Uyghur people. It is a clear indication of a future breakdown of Uyghur identity. Intellectuals make historical events and individuals powerful and politically significant. This serves to challenge the Chinese government's official versions of Uyghur history and to mobilize sentiment, and consequently political activism, among the Uyghur people. Uyghur historiographers and authors seek to create nationalist ideologies that will inspire their people toward unity and national consciousness without posing an overt threat to the Chinese government. But by proposing diverse conceptions of Uyghur identity which, though nationalistic, have strong oasis biases that correspond to the propagator's birthplace, intellectuals are actually fueling a renewal of the historic rivalry among the oases. The competition undermines the possibility of a cohesive intellectual leadership and inhibits adoption of a pan-oasis ethnic unity.

[handwritten margin note: oasis bias undermines intellectuals' efforts]

UYGHUR SOCIETY AND SOCIAL GROUPS

Although radical Chinese efforts at social engineering attempted to create a classless society, recent Chinese reforms have allowed the three main traditional social groups—peasants, merchants, and intellectuals—in Uyghur society to once again differentiate themselves. Peasants are those who are involved in agricultural production, mainly grape cultivation in the case of Turpan. Merchants engage in local or long-distance trade. Intellectuals work as educators or administrators (Party officials, writers, historians, and professors). This tripartite division within Uyghur society was described similarly by C. G. Mannerheim, the founder of modern Finland, who explored the region in the early 1900s. Mannerheim's colleague, Kustaa Vilkuna, writes,

Socially the population is divided into three classes: (1) manual labourers and tillers of the soil, (2) merchants, (3) representatives of the sarjat (ecclesiastical courts) and of Mahammedan science (kazi, agljami, mufti, imam, ishan or dervishi, muddarrisi and mullah). The representatives of the sarjat and science usually gain a livelihood by their profession, but in addition many of them engage in farming.   (1969:122)

All three groups are mixed within the villages of the Xinjiang oases. At the local level these three groups maintain diverse conceptions of identity that eclipse Uyghur intellectuals' attempts to instill an overarching Uyghur national identity. This has not led to the abandonment of "Uyghur" as a classificatory term, but instead to an attempt by local groups to make themselves the defining core of the ethnic label.

Had I only examined how oasis identity in Turpan is defined at the local level, the relationship of identity to social group and the widely differing conceptions of Uyghur identity within the oasis would not have entered into this analysis. However, by tracing extremely divergent conceptions of identity within various webs of social and economic relationships, I found that identity is formed according to social class and occupation rather than family type, descent, or pan-oases solidarity.

In Turpan, for example, middle-income and poor peasants, who for the most part do not travel outside the region, identify strongly with Islam and maintain strong Turpan (*Turpanlik*) oasis identities. Merchants who trade in China proper, in cities to the east such as Beijing and Shanghai, and wealthy peasants benefiting from China's development policies identify themselves as citizens of the Chinese state.

Uyghur intellectuals who reside mostly in Urumchi describe themselves as being in opposition to the Hans, who comprise 85 percent of Urumchi's population. For the most part, they are pan-Turkic nationalists and identify with the larger Turkic world of western Central Asia and Turkey that lies to the west of Xinjiang. Though they consider themselves Muslims, they are secularists and express virulent anti-Islamic sentiments. Their citizenship in a multiethnic Chinese state does not play a large role in their identity. Though they reside in Urumchi, most intellectuals maintain residences in their home oases and return there for social gatherings, cultural events, and conferences. Those originally from Turpan return to spend the spring there because the weather is warmer.

In contrast, peasants in Turpan do not recognize the word *Turk*. When I pointed this out to Uyghur intellectuals in Turpan, who identified themselves principally as "Turks" or "Eastern Turkestanis," they refused to believe me until they confirmed my observations through their own questioning.[13] They then declared that the peasants' ignorance of their identity was a result of the culturally subversive PRC policies.

In informal interviews with 87 Uyghurs of the three social groups, in which 81 gave complete answers, Uyghurs ranked five words, in descending order, that best described them: *Junggoluq* (pan-PRC Chinese, a member of the Chinese [Zhongguo] state as opposed to Han), Uyghur, Turk, Muslim, and Turpanlik. I also elicited comparisons of these terms. For example, I asked whether individuals felt more Muslim than Uyghur, more Turk than Chinese, or more Muslim than Turk. The percentages in table 4.4 reflect the number of Uyghurs who selected the term chosen by the majority of individuals from a particular social group as their first, second, third, fourth, or fifth choice.

Uyghur peasants blurred the distinction between Uyghur and Muslim, and a majority insisted that Uyghurs and Muslims were the same. In addition, almost all of the peasants interviewed said that Uyghurs were not Turks. The few who recognized the term *Turk* said that Turks were people from Turkey. To older peasant Uyghurs, the term also meant "ignorant." This understanding recalls the meaning of the word during Ottoman times, when *turk* meant an ignorant, uncultured person. The majority of peasants placed Muslim and Uyghur as their first choices and Turpanlik as their second. Peasants retain a strong Muslim identity that links them with the international Muslim community (*ummah*).[14]

Similarly, most merchants interviewed maintained that Uyghurs were not Turks. When I asked directly if they were Turk, they answered "*Yaq, Musulman*" (No, Muslim). Merchants and wealthy peasants in Turpan, especially merchants involved in long-distance trade with China proper, express a very positive attitude about being part of China. Rarely did these merchants express ideas of pan-Turkism. I found a strikingly unique attitude in merchants who placed *Junggoluq* (pan-PRC Chinese) as their first choice and Turpanlik as their second; they ranked Uyghur as their third choice and Muslim as the fourth. They rarely mentioned the choice *Turk*.

TABLE 4.4
Self-Definition by Social Group

Social Group	1 (most frequent)	2	3	4	5 (least frequent)
Peasants (n=47)	Muslim 74%	Uyghur 51%	Turpanlik 64%	Junggoluq 77%	Turk 89%
Merchants (n=15)	Junggoluq 80%	Turpanlik 73%	Uyghur 73%	Muslim 67%	Turk 87%
Intellectuals (n=19)	Turk 74%	Uyghur 63%	Turpanlik 79%	Muslim 63%	Junggoluq 63%

TABLE 4.5
Peasant Self-Definition

	1 Muslim	2 Uyghur	3 Turpanlik	4 Junggoluq	5 Turk
Peasants	74%	51%	64%	77%	89%
(n=47)	(most frequent)				(least frequent)
19	Muslim	Uyghur	Turpanlik	Junggoluq	Turk
11	Muslim	Turpanlik	Uyghur	Junggoluq	Turk
6	Uyghur	Muslim	Turpanlik	Junggoluq	Turk
5	Muslim	Uyghur	Turpanlik	Turk	Junggoluq
5	Uyghur	Turpanlik	Muslim	Junggoluq	Turk
1	Junggoluq	Turpanlik	Muslim	Uyghur	Turk

In startling contrast, intellectuals ranked themselves as Turks first, Uyghurs second, Turpanliks third, Muslims fourth, and finally *Junggoluq* (pan-PRC Chinese). The intellectual community is more influenced by international events than the other groups, and members see themselves as part of the larger Turkic world. As stated previously, the majority of Uyghur intellectuals are highly nationalistic and strongly reject Islamic conservatism.

One Uyghur author refused to have his son circumcised by a *molla* but had it done in the Uyghur hospital. He later doubted his decision when the wound became infected. Intellectuals often express dissatisfaction with Communist development of Xinjiang, especially in terms of the education of the Uyghurs. Some intellectuals rhetorically ask how Xinjiang could be developed, when the Hans in charge are so technologically primitive in comparison to the Japanese. They consider the economy impressive in contrast to forty years ago, but they claim that this development has enriched only the Chinese government and not the Uyghur people themselves.

TABLE 4.6
Merchant Self-Definition

	1 Junggoluq	2 Turpanlik	3 Uyghur	4 Muslim	5 Turk
Merchants	80%	73%	73%	67%	87%
(n=15)	(most frequent)				(least frequent)
10	Junggoluq	Turpanlik	Uyghur	Muslim	Turk
2	Turpanlik	Junggoluq	Muslim	Uyghur	Turk
2	Junggoluq	Uyghur	Turpanlik	Turk	Muslim
1	Muslim	Turpanlik	Uyghur	Junggoluq	Turk

TABLE 4.7
Intellectual Self-Definition

Intellectuals (n=19)	1 Turk 74% (most frequent)	2 Uyghur 63%	3 Turpanlik 79%	4 Muslim 63%	5 Junggoluq 63% (least frequent)
7	Turk	Uyghur	Turpanlik	Muslim	Junggoluq
5	Turk	Uyghur	Turpanlik	Junggoluq	Muslim
3	Uyghur	Turk	Turpanlik	Muslim	Junggoluq
2	Turk	Turpanlik	Uyghur	Muslim	Junggoluq
2	Junggoluq	Turpanlik	Turk	Uyghur	Muslim

Uyghur Intellectuals:
The Path of the Strong

Those who are weak are those with the most enemies.
Illiteracy is the path of the weak.
—"Uyghur," "Unsettled (*Ich Pushush*)"

INTELLECTUALS AND THE PEASANTRY

Although government reforms have allowed Uyghur intellectuals to participate in the process of defining Uyghur nationalist ideologies, intellectuals view these reforms as a threat to their people. The government's cultural policies have met with considerable favor among the Uyghur peasantry—especially the policy of religious tolerance, which has brought about a resurgence of Islam. Intellectuals fear these reforms will cause the majority of the Uyghurs to withdraw into cultural isolation and Islamic religious fervor—the insulation of what peasants view as Uyghur tradition. They fear the peasants will not face the challenges to modernize brought by the government's social and cultural changes.

As we have seen, the majority of Uyghur intellectuals are isolated in Urumchi and have grown out of touch with the Uyghur peasantry in the oases. They are, for the most part, against the resurgence of Islam, believing that it contributes to Uyghur passivity by stifling secular educational development and modernization. While they identify themselves as Turk and consider themselves Muslim, they are against Islamic traditionalism.

Uyghur intellectuals hold that hope lies in secular education. But this places them in a dilemma. If Uyghur children are to compete with Hans, they must know the Mandarin Chinese language. Thus, intellectuals struggle to preserve their Uyghur culture and language while maintaining and developing the ability to compete on a national level. The question of whether to send their children to Han-language or Uyghur-language schools is one facet of this dilemma.

Intellectuals perceive a weakening of Uyghur identity. They are strongly anti-Chinese and resent the large influx of Chinese to Xinjiang, fearing that soon the Uyghurs will become a minority in their own autonomous region. The region's population of Hans has increased from 200,000 in the 1940s to almost six million in 1994. The Han migration, which originally was a strong force in coalescing modern Uyghur nationalism, has become a divisive issue as peasant oasis dwellers realize that the Uyghurs, even if united, will never gain control of the region. Therefore, Uyghur intellectuals have begun to develop optimizing strategies that take advantage of the open borders—yet by doing so, they inadvertently strengthen local oasis cultural identities. Many Uyghur intellectuals perceive that this strengthening is a result of the outward focus of the oases.

Uyghur Ideologies and the Chinese State

The majority of Uyghur intellectuals consider China's liberalization of religious policy, which has fostered positive feelings among the Uyghur peasantry toward the Chinese government, detrimental to the future of the Uyghur people. These intellectuals hope to harness disaffection for the Hans and mobilize the peasantry toward a cultural and nationalist awakening that will strengthen the Uyghurs in relation to the Hans, instead of causing them to retreat into Islamic and cultural traditionalism. Policy reversals by the Chinese government, especially the halting of mosque construction and limitations on family size, could result in the kind of disaffection intellectuals can manipulate for their purposes. Still, oasis identities at the local level, such as those of residents of Turpan (Turpanlik) and Kashgar (Kashgarlik), are extremely strong and pose a great challenge to the acceptance of nationalist ideologies developed by Uyghur intellectuals.

The paucity of well-known Uyghur intellectual figures today has heightened the influence of the few that have recently become prominent. We must remember that from 1911 to the early 1980s, the Chinese government stifled and curtailed Uyghur intellectual expression. It was only after the cultural and religious reforms of 1978 and the opening of Xinjiang to foreign trade and tourism in 1985 that Uyghur intellectuals were able to develop historiographies and take on a political role in Xinjiang.

The competition over nationalist ideology among intellectual elites, like that occurring in Xinjiang, is a common feature in minority resistance movements against the central governing power of a state. Intellectuals redefine their people's history by manipulating the interpretation of historic individuals and events, infusing them with new symbolic meaning for political and social ends. The nationalist ideologies Uyghur intellectuals develop can become politically significant, mobilizing the indigenous population at the local oasis level.

The role of intellectuals in the state-building process is presently at center stage in the scholarly analysis of political interest group formation. Critical to that debate is a definition of what constitutes an intellectual. In Xinjiang, intellectuals are those involved in education or administration, including Party officials, politicians, writers, historians, professors, economists, journalists, doctors, artists, and lawyers. In Islamic terms, they are all "men of the pen." They are differentiated from two other important social groups found in Uyghur society: merchants, who buy and sell goods; and peasants, who are involved primarily in agricultural production.

Uyghur intellectuals fall under the definition set forth by Katherine Verdery, who views all intellectuals as playing a privileged role in creating and disseminating ideologies that shape cultural values and influence identity formation (1991:17). However, with regard to Xinjiang, I include politicians and those who occupy formal political positions within this social category, because they too are intimately connected with legitimating nationalist ideologies, since this is a socialist society. By virtue of their privileged positions, they hold the power to manipulate cultural knowledge and historic symbols.

This definition of *intellectual* is similar to the People's Republic of China's definition, though in the latter there are strong Marxist political implications. Goldman and Cheek's subdivision of intellectuals in China into high-level intellectuals (*gaoji zhishi fenzi*) and high-level officials (*gaoji ganbu*) (1987:2) is also relevant to Uyghur contexts. In China, most of the high-level intellectuals—including writers, artists, doctors, scientists, journalists, economists, social scientists, and lawyers—are part of the official establishment. All the institutions (*danwei* or work enterprises) in which they work are controlled by the government (1987:2). Thus Chinese intellectuals hold an ambiguous position, for they are both potential opponents of the state and at the same time its beneficiaries, employed to legitimate the state's scientific socialism.

URUMCHI HANS AND UYGHUR CONSCIOUSNESS

Hans in Urumchi know little about Uyghur culture and history and denigrate the Uyghur language, dress, food, and social customs. Such views tend to be strongest in the capital, where Han culture dominates and Hans are in positions of power, able to air their bigoted views without recrimination. They view their own culture—the Han—to be one of progress, opportunity, science, and reason, and Uyghur culture to be backward, poor, weak, superstitious, and, worst of all, "feudal." While many Uyghur intellectuals in Urumchi still express pride in being Uyghur, in enumerating the differences between Uyghurs and Hans they too criticize their people as being lazy, too traditional, and socially and politically naive. Adoption of the Hans' negative stereotypes of Uyghurs is typical.

Among Hans, particularly those in Urumchi, "feudal" is the Chinese equivalent of a curse and a pervasive conceptual category; it is comparable to such negatively charged Western terms as *primitive, fanatical,* and *backward.* Hans use the word *feudal* to dismiss something without critical evaluation. To them, traditional Uyghur culture is an aberration, an archaic remnant; Islam and other religions are "feudal" superstitions. To support their views, Hans in Urumchi frequently refer to the Uyghurs' conviction that it is not appropriate for their Muslim children to marry Hans. Han men, in particular, speak of this practice with anger, because in Chinese lore Uyghur women are considered to be the most beautiful. Han men also contend that Uyghur women actually prefer them to Uyghur men because "Hans are more intelligent, do not drink heavily, and do not beat their wives." But negative views are not reserved for Uyghur men. Hans view Uyghur women as being promiscuous.

Hans often categorize their own names' origins, when they are not such Communist-inspired ones as "army," "red," or "party," as being outdated. For example, *ping* is a common woman's name meaning "seaweed"; a daughter will marry out of the family, and is therefore like seaweed that grows in the ocean without roots, flowing with the current. Hans say this name reflects a feudal mentality, expressing a negative image of daughters and their importance to the family. This view is even more common today because Hans are limited to one child and the government encourages them to give daughters as much importance as sons.

Han intellectuals in academic institutions frequently remark that ethnic consciousness itself is feudal. Referring to the ethnic resurgence currently underway in Xinjiang, one Han woman, a highly educated Japanese-language interpreter, said the minority nationalities' assertion of their cultural background was a regression into a feudal mentality. She pointed out that in Xinjiang all non-Muslim ethnic groups used to say they were Hans, to distinguish themselves from the Uyghurs and other Muslim indigenous nationalities. Now, these people often describe themselves as belonging to non-Turkic minority nationalities such as Bai or Zhuang. This self-identification frequently occurs in university settings, because minority students are given extra points on college entrance test scores according to China's affirmative action-type policies. Others claim minority status to take advantage of the government policy allowing minority nationalities more children per family.

The question of nationality often becomes a matter of who eats pork and who abstains—in other words, who is not Muslim and who is. One Han intellectual claimed that Uyghurs eat pork when alone and, furthermore, that they secretly aspired to be like Hans. "The main problem with the Uyghurs," he maintained, "is that they don't know anything about their own history and this is their own fault. Uyghurs are lazy, they think only of enjoying themselves."

The prevalence of these pejorative attitudes in Urumchi and throughout China undermines individual Uyghurs' sense of self-worth and results in internalization of self-doubt and swallowed anger that occasionally becomes explosive. Uyghur intellectuals are convinced that the increase in alcohol consumption among male Uyghur students and intellectuals is directly related to their marginalized sense of self-worth, which produces an anger spiral they direct toward one another. Uyghur men drink great amounts of alcohol in the evening while socializing with friends, and these occasions often turn into brawls or angry fistfights. Many intellectuals claim that the Uyghur men who drink most heavily are not peasants, who rarely drink to excess, but those employed in government organs, where they interact with Hans. Many of these drunken Uyghurs curse the "mother-screwing Hans" (*Anangga ski Hanzular*). At a circumcision party, a drunken bank official blurted out, "They say that we are lazy and stupid. But we are great, we are Turks." "They," of course, are the Hans.

Uyghur intellectuals are frustrated with the Han attitudes they encounter daily in the workplace. They see little hope for change—either altering Han attitudes or developing the Uyghurs into a strong, modern

5.1   Drunken Uyghur supported by friends in Khotan (1985).

nationality capable of contributing significantly to the world. When Uyghur intellectuals accept negative stereotypes of their own people, they provide further justification for China's control of Xinjiang. In the search for mutual support and relief from their frustrations, Uyghurs turn to their families and to their extended kin and oasis networks.

In the capital city, Uyghur couples no longer live in their native villages and are often separated from their immediate kin. As a result, strong relationships often develop between sisters who live in the capital, where transportation is convenient and allows them to keep in close contact. In Uyghur oases, when women marry into other villages their contact with their sisters and other family members diminishes markedly. As mentioned previously, in Uyghur society a special relationship develops between husbands of sisters, who are known as *baja*. When sisters live in Urumchi, frequently *baja* relationships become stronger than elsewhere, for here *baja* are more dependent on their wives' kin—particularly if they are based in Urumchi and the husband's kin are in the native oasis. Often *baja* relationships gain greater importance than relations with other family members, since *baja* are usually around the same age. In one family, all four of the married sisters maintain daily contact with one another. Their husbands, drawn into their wives' family orbit because their own families remained in the home oases, are also close.

Another strategy that preserves strong oasis ties involves child care. In Urumchi, Uyghur families are conjugal; city life is not conducive to the maintenance of extended families because living quarters are too cramped. However, precisely because of these conditions, many intellectuals prefer to send their children, newborn to five years old, to their parents in the local oasis. For example, a professor at the Medical College in Urumchi whose husband is a professor at the Economics Institute there decided to leave her child with her parents in Turpan until she reaches the age of five.[1] Since Urumchi is only a four-hour bus ride from Turpan, the parents return to Turpan every other weekend to see their child. This is a common practice among Turpan intellectuals in Urumchi.

Min Kao Han

Uyghur intellectuals believe education is central to Uyghur identity, and this issue is at the core of a major Uyghur dilemma. Uyghur children have the option of studying in either Han- or Uyghur-language schools. Intellectuals are divided on whether it is best to enroll their children in Han-language schools, which would facilitate their participation within Chinese society, or to keep them in Uyghur schools, where they maintain more of their culture but lose opportunities for professional advancement.

Uyghur children who study in Han-language schools are known as *Min Kao Han* ("Minorities tested in the Han language") because they will take their college entrance exams in Mandarin Chinese. There is a strong desire among intellectuals that their children learn to compete successfully with Han children; those who favor *Min Kao Han* education contend that Uyghurs in these schools are often at the top of their classes. The most recent Uyghur hero, Urkesh (Wuerkaixi), a student leader in the Tiananmen protest, was educated in Han-language schools in Beijing and is pointed to as a successful product of *Min Kao Han* education.

The debate about education among Uyghur intellectuals breaks down along oasis lines. Uyghur intellectuals in Urumchi who come from the Khotan and Kashgar regions favor Uyghur schools because they prevent assimilation. Urumchi's Uyghur intellectuals from Ili, Turpan, and Hami favor Han-language schools, believing these will enable their children to compete on a national level and improve their lives in general.[2]

Many *Min Kao Han* students do not speak Uyghur well and use Mandarin at home. Uyghurs fluent in their own language refer to Mandarin-speaking Uyghurs as the "fourteenth nationality" (*ön-tötinchi millät*), referring to the fact that there were thirteen officially recognized nationalities in Xinjiang before 1949 and thus implying that another nationality has come into existence: Uyghurs who mainly speak Mandarin.[3] These hybrid minorities consider themselves both Chinese (*Junggoluq*) and Uyghur, but feel alienated from both nationalities.[4]

The Uyghurs opposed to assimilation of any kind frequently tell the same joke about the fourteenth nationality: older Uyghurs on a bus are seated behind two young, well-dressed Uyghur women who are speaking to each other in Mandarin. When the bus stops short, someone steps on the foot of one of the Uyghur woman and she cries out, in Mandarin, "*Ah, teng de yao ming!*" (Ouch, that really hurts!). One of the older Uyghurs then says: "See how revolting these fourteenth nationalities are? Even when they are in pain, it is Han pain."

The same disdain is held by the *Min Kao Han* for the *Min Kao Min* (Uyghurs educated in Uyghur schools). For example, I arranged to meet some Uyghur friends, and the one who was a *Min Kao Min* misheard the time and arrived several hours late. My *Min Kao Han* friends told me this was typical *Min Kao Min* stupidity. On another occasion, in a conversation with two brothers-in-law, one of whom was a *Min Kao Han* and the other a *Min Kao Min*, the *Min Kao Han* argued fervently that Uyghurs and all minorities should be educated in Mandarin. He argued that if the Uyghurs did not learn Mandarin well and compete with the Hans on their terms they would become like the American Indians, separated from society's mainstream and placed on reservations. His *Min Kao Min* brother-in-law argued that Uyghurs who study in Han-language schools do not learn to appreciate their own culture. The *Min Kao Han* countered by challenging his brother-in-law to list the classic Uyghur literature he had read, as a proof of his grounding in Uyghur tradition. While the *Min Kao Han* listed numerous books, his brother-in-law, who had studied in Uyghur-language schools, could name only a few.

Uyghur intellectuals in favor of *Min Kao Han* education argue that the best curricular materials are written in Mandarin, and therefore the same quality of education cannot be attained in Uyghur schools. Also, in university settings, only those already proficient in Mandarin can study both English and Russian; those who are not must study Mandarin as their only foreign language. One Uyghur, opposed to *Min Kao Han* education, found it intolerable that some Uyghurs call themselves "*Urgoy*," a variant pronunciation of Uyghur: "Those who mispronounce the name of their own nationality are like all *Min Kao Han* who know nothing of their own culture. The most important thing to know in life is where one comes from and the ability to answer the question 'Who am I?'" Most *Min Kao Han* students know neither the Han nor the Uyghur language well. The majority of Uyghurs look down on them; Hans, who do not consider them "real" Uyghurs, nonetheless hold them in contempt.

Uyghur Intellectuals and the Chinese Government

Uyghur intellectuals have adopted strategies similar to those used by the Jadids of western Central Asia almost a century earlier. They stress the importance of education as a means of transcending the opposition posed by Islamic and conservative anti-intellectual trends. It is crucial in Uyghur intellectuals' attempts to create a historical awareness they hope will revitalize the Uyghur people and strengthen their collective national identity.

At the same time that the Chinese government seeks to win over Uyghur intellectual support by approving of Uyghur cultural projects, it undermines the intellectuals by encouraging Islam. Religious freedoms have brought about the reopening of mosques and a flurry of mosque construction throughout Xinjiang. In Turpan alone, over 350 mosques were constructed between 1979 and 1989. Today, *mollas* again officiate at Islamic weddings, and the Holy Koran and other Islamic texts are once again sold openly. The Islamic threat to intellectuals is strengthened by Chinese government encouragement of Uyghur Party officials' participation in religious events; this is justified as part of Uyghur "tradition" and separate from religious beliefs, which contradict Communist doctrine. As part of this policy, the government even provides financial support to members of the Uyghur Party elite so that they can make the *hajj* to Mecca. The *hajj* is considered by Uyghur government officials to be linked more to Uyghur cultural tradition than to religion, and therefore increases their political prestige and influence at the local level.

These new cultural policies are a dramatic reversal of earlier attempts at cultural subversion: the government has concluded that a controlled "revival" of cultural and religious affairs will encourage stability and economic development in the region and at the same time undermine nationalist movements and antigovernment protests. This liberal and pragmatic approach, however, is filled with dangers—a strategy of selective toleration and cautious liberalization could give rise to increasing demands for further freedoms and greater autonomy (McMillen 1984:579).

5.2   Repairing a mosque in Urumchi (1985).

[handwritten note: 1985 Student demonstration]

Such dangers became real in Urumchi on December 10, 1985, when about 1,000 Uyghur students demonstrated in front of the Regional People's Committee Building. The regional government described this as "the most serious political event since the 1949 liberation of Xinjiang, even considering the Great Cultural Revolution" (Yuan 1990:71). The demands of the students were wide-ranging: they called for a ban on the use of Lop

Nor as a nuclear test site and opposed the volatile population policies. The students protested the regional government's family planning policies, which were applied to indigenous ethnic groups of Xinjiang (excluding the immigrant Hans), and argued that ethnic minorities had a right to choose their family size. The students also protested the regional government's deportation of Han prisoners to Xinjiang and demanded restriction on the entry of self-drifter immigrants from eastern China (Yuan 1990:71). The demonstration reflected Uyghurs' fears that the Chinese would render them a minority in their own autonomous region by allowing the influx of Han Chinese from China proper while limiting the Uyghur birthrate. Government policies were indeed moving in this direction: in 1987, families of Uyghur party officials were limited to only two children. Two years later, the government decreed that Uyghur families living in the villages would be limited to three children.

At this point the government began to worry about the pace of the Uyghur religious revival. Its worries increased dramatically on May 19, 1989, when a protest broke out in Urumchi against the recent publication of a book, *Sexual Customs* (*Xing Fengsu*), written by a Han author.[5] Among other offensive descriptions in the book, a history of sexual customs around the world, the author compares the architecture of mosques to various parts of women's anatomy. The protest, involving about 4,000 people, lasted three hours; during it a rock was thrown through a window of the central government building. In the protest's aftermath, the government halted mosque construction and closed many of the village Islamic schools, which were meant to train students eighteen years and older but which had, in fact, begun enrolling children as young as twelve years of age.

The emergence of Urkesh at the forefront of the Beijing Tiananmen student protests in 1989 was also an extremely significant event. The first time most Uyghurs heard of Urkesh was when he appeared on national television on May 18, 1989. He was filmed scolding Li Peng, the Chinese premier, for being late to a meeting with student leaders; Urkesh then collapsed to the floor as a result of his hunger strike. Uyghur intellectuals feel considerable pride that of all the hundreds of thousands of people involved in the demonstrations, it was a Uyghur who led the movement. Most Uyghurs believe that by attaining world recognition, Urkesh has put Uyghurs on the map. In the aftermath of Tiananmen, many Uyghur boys were named Urkesh. I was constantly asked about Urkesh when I first arrived in Xinjiang;[6] even when I was accompanied by Professor Xia Xuncheng, the Han director of the Xinjiang Desert Research Institute,

Uyghurs did not seem nervous asking "Where is he? We hear he is in America." By December 1989, with the collapse of Eastern European communism and increasing sensitivity and repression on the part of the Chinese government, these questions were asked in whispers or ceased altogether.

Still, Uyghurs followed Urkesh's story closely and were relieved when he escaped from China. When peasants spoke of their heroes, some named Ähmätjan Qasimi, the leader of the East Turkestan Republic centered in Ili (1944–1949), and Mähmud Qäshqäri (Mahmut Kashgari), the eleventh-century scholar from Kashgar. Some even mentioned Marx and Lenin. Invariably, however, all would speak of Urkesh. One intellectual simply stated: "Urkesh is our only hero."

During 1989 and 1990, with the breakdown of the Soviet Union and the fall of Eastern European communism, the atmosphere in Turpan grew more tense and the government became increasingly sensitive to ethnic rumblings. In February of 1990 newscasters announced over Uyghur television that "hoodlum elements" were causing disturbances in the Kashgar region. In April of the same year, fighting broke out in Akto, near Kashgar, because of the enforcement of birthrate limitation and the halting of mosque construction.[7] Newsweek reported that as many as sixty people were killed; the government claimed only twenty-two.

The cultural reform policy presented dangers not only to the Chinese but also, ironically, to Uyghur intellectuals who were alarmed by the liberalization. As mentioned previously, Uyghur intellectuals fear that Chinese government liberalization policies are causing the Uyghur peasantry to retreat into cultural isolation. They believe the peasants will be lulled into passivity by the cultural and economic reforms, and they do not favor the strengthening of local oasis identities through the reestablishment of cross-border trade. The intellectuals view this as weakening their attempts to promulgate an overarching Uyghur identity, in which they have a stake: this mission provides them with influence and legitimizes their roles as Uyghur culture brokers within Chinese government institutions.

Intellectuals also oppose the ever-increasing number of Han immigrants to the region. The Han influx, once a strong coalescing force for Uyghur nationalism, is now a major source of division: Uyghurs realize they will soon be outnumbered by the Han, and this has decreased the viability of a pan-oases Uyghur identity as a strategy for gaining power and wealth in Xinjiang. Instead of focusing inward, establishing economic and political relations with one another to gain collective strength, the oasis dwellers have begun to take advantage of the border openings for trade. Kashgar and Ili in particular have new opportunities unavailable to Turpan or Hami, because they are located on the borders with Kyrgyzstan and Kazakstan. These developments have made Uyghur intellectuals' endeavors to create nationalist ideologies all the more intense. But because the majority of Uyghur intellectuals are isolated in Urumchi, they are out of touch with the Uyghur peasantry. This makes the acceptance of their nationalist ideologies difficult at the local level. Because of his opposition to Han immigration—his contention that Hans should immigrate to Xinjiang only after all unemployed Uyghurs have jobs—the popular Uyghur leader and chairman of Xinjiang, Ismail Ämät, was removed from his post and sent to Beijing in 1985 to head the Minority Affairs Commission. Removal to Beijing is a common government practice; prominent and controversial minority politicians are sent there to fill posts that have little effect on their homeland.

Uyghur intellectuals also oppose the growing influence of the Kazaks in the region, especially since Kazakstan recently became an independent country. The traditionally nomadic Kazaks have been settling in cities in ever-increasing numbers, and their power continues to grow. The Hans are manipulating the traditional opposition between the sedentary Uyghurs and the nomadic Kazaks, placing a greater number of Kazaks in visible positions of power in provincial and county government offices. Some Uyghur intellectuals refer to the decade of the nineties as "the Kazak era" and predict that the Kazaks will gain control of Xinjiang's regional government. But, in fact, a majority of Uyghurs respected the Xinjiang Kazak leader Janabil more than they did the Uyghur leader and former chairman of Xinjiang, Tömür Dawamät, whom they considered a well-meaning incompetent.

Uyghur Intellectuals During the Communist Period

The modern history of intellectuals in Xinjiang follows the same general pattern as in China proper. It can be argued that Han intellectuals continue the Confucian scholar-official (literati) tradition of ancient China. In a similar way, Uyghur intellectuals continue the tradition of Sufi religious mystics who were extremely influential in the Islamic development of Central Asia, including Xinjiang. In Xinjiang secular Muslim intellectuals gained influence in the 1930s, the period in which the modern Uyghur identity was being redefined. Since then, Uyghur intellectuals have been subject to several convulsive events leading to their death, imprisonment, or flight to the Soviet Union. For example, hundreds of Uyghurs were educated in Soviet universities during the late 1930s and early 1940s.[8] When they returned to Xinjiang, many were killed by Sheng Shicai, the Han warlord governor of the province.

During the Communist period (since 1949), Uyghur intellectuals have been strictly controlled and subject to volatile Chinese government policies. Today, while the Uyghurs make up less than one percent of China's total population, their importance continues to be disproportionate to their numbers—for their location raises issues of security that concern the Communist Chinese. Upon Communist takeover, the most politically sensitive region in Xinjiang was the northwest Three Regions area (Ili, Tacheng, and Altay), where the East Turkestan Republic had existed during the previous five years. Thus, the Chinese took a very careful political approach: they consolidated their control of Xinjiang from 1949 to 1956 while leaving the system of local rule by native leaders from the East Turkestan Republic regime unaltered (McMillen 1979:42). Intellectuals of the Three Regions area were allowed to remain in power even though they were pro-Soviet.

Under the leadership of Mao Zedong, intellectuals were subject to political campaigns designed to punish and denigrate them. This strategy was used to foster ideological loyalty while simultaneously severely limiting intellectual autonomy. Many Uyghur intellectuals have been imprisoned, beginning with the Anti-Rightist Movement of the late 1950s; still more were imprisoned, killed, or forced to do brutal manual labor during the decade of the Cultural Revolution (1966–1976). During the various social and cultural Communist campaigns, notably the Great Leap Forward and the Cultural Revolution, the Communists paid close attention to Xinjiang. For example, the Red Guards overturned and destroyed traditional Chinese culture and society throughout China, but their attacks on "feudal" cultural practices were considered too dangerous to the security of Xinjiang and were suspended in 1967.

The Communists secured their control of the area through the use of the Production and Construction Corps and the People's Liberation Army.[9] Party power was patiently and firmly consolidated as minorities were coopted into the government under the leadership of Wang Enmao.[10] From 1949 on, when first Party secretary Wang Enmao entered Xinjiang as field commander of the Communist First Field Army that took control of Xinjiang, he was the major political force in Xinjiang.

In the post-Mao period in China, intellectuals have again become prominent as the political leadership has recognized their importance to the nation's modernization. The training of cadres and activists from among the minority nationalities was a crucial task in the province. First priority was given to retraining political and administrative cadres in Party and government-run schools.[11] Special training sessions were organized for minority cadres according to the government's functional needs in commerce, agriculture, animal husbandry, justice, and translation. Many Uyghurs were sent to Tashkent, in the Soviet Union, for training (McMillen 1979:86).

The system developed during this period to train Uyghur and other minority intellectuals remains unchanged today. Many Uyghur intellectuals are trained at the Central University (formerly Institute) for Nationalities in Beijing. The Communists educate Uyghurs in large numbers and then select those whose views dovetail their own for placement in government positions; the rest, though excluded, believe they are entitled to influence society because of their newly gained knowledge. While in a position to challenge the government, they are often blocked from doing so by rival Uyghur intellectuals who have acquiesced to the government's goals.

The Chinese in power have alternated between extreme caution in dealing with the Uyghurs and a firm tightening of control in the region. These fluctuations are due to the experimental nature of Communist integration and assimilation of the Uyghurs and other non-Han groups. For example, from 1949 to 1956, the government's policies were tempered and the Party refrained from pursuing strong policies, especially with regard to Islam, fearing that doing so would increase tension between Hans and Uyghurs and further aggravate the widespread anti-Han sentiments.[12]

Ultimately the influential position of the Muslim clergy was slowly undermined: a number of religious institutions were closed, the land and property of the mosques (*vaqf*) were confiscated, and People's Courts took over the judicial functions of the Islamic courts, *qadi*, in both civil and criminal matters (McMillen 1979:114). From 1957 to 1961, the Chinese Communist policies became more Maoist in approach, and concerns unique to Xinjiang—such as religion, ethnic culture, and the desert ecosystem—were not taken into serious consideration. Initially after their takeover of the region, the Communists simultaneously attacked both local nationalism and "Great Han Chauvinism," seen as counterrevolutionary tendencies. However, to the Communists' credit, it was "Great Han Chauvinism," or Han bigotry toward minority nationalities, that they most violently opposed. Han cadres were instructed to cooperate with their minority counterparts, respect minority customs and beliefs, and implement party policies according to local cultural and environmental conditions (McMillen 1979:89).

During this time the Chinese produced official histories of the region that described Xinjiang as an inalienable part of China since well before the arrival of the Uyghurs in the region in the ninth century. The displays at the Provincial Museum in Urumchi stressed this very point.

> In the two main halls, introduced by the usual Chairman Mao quotes, "Make the past serve the present," there is not a single item related to the history of the 12 different minority peoples living in Xinjiang. The collection is made of exhibits recording the over 2,000-year-old presence of the Hans in the region.   (Terzani 1985:63).

In 1985, the government decided the displays were too overbearing and changed them so they would better represent the multiethnic cultures of Xinjiang.

The Communists wrongly assumed that Uyghur culture and Islam in Xinjiang would be undermined by the economic, social, and educational advancements launched by the government. Uyghur Muslim customs can be practiced under current conditions without difficulty. Circumcision, marriage, burial rituals, the Ramadan fast, *Qurban Heyt*, and dietary restrictions—all powerful components of Uyghur identity—have continued, even within modern cities like Urumchi. Islam has proven to be more than a superstitious "feudal" faith and, indeed, is the one common characteristic shared by all Uyghurs. As such, it forms the basis of national and religious Uyghur consciousness.[13]

Despite its persistence, Islam has remained a relatively inchoate force and has not brought unity to the Uyghurs.[14] While a minority of intellectuals believe that Uyghurs can gain strength and unity through their common religion, most intellectuals who see themselves on the front lines in the development of Uyghur identity view Islam as a negative force. They believe Islam has stifled modernization and made the Uyghurs passive; they maintain a Marxist view of Islam as an opiate of the masses. Indeed, the Uyghur peasantry has reacted to the Chinese government's relaxation of religious restrictions by returning to an overt attachment to traditionalism and Islam. Now Uyghurs tithe the mosques instead of giving their financial support to secular schools. In response, one famous Uyghur author even went so far as to advocate blowing up all Xinjiang mosques to break Islam's popularity.

The majority of intellectuals identify themselves as Turks; they accept the cultural practices and heritage of Islam, such as circumcision and wedding and burial rites, but are indifferent to the religious faith and are opposed to conservative Islam. Their attitudes are shaped by their networks of relations within Urumchi, where most live. Within the city environment, intellectuals use three different methods of constructing Uyghur identity. They romanticize and mythologize the Uyghur past; they attempt to emulate Han cultural practices and assimilate into the modern "advanced culture" of the region; or they promote a strong image of the Uyghur people that is defined in opposition to the Han Chinese. Most intellectuals choose the last strategy—basing a Uyghur identity on anti-Chinese views.

The Chinese claim a four-, even five-thousand-year history that includes their control of Xinjiang since early Han dynasty times, two thousand years ago. The Uyghurs' notions of identity, though effective as ethnic markers, lack the historical depth claimed by the Hans. To compensate, some Uyghur intellectuals argue that Uyghurs were in Xinjiang before the birth of Mohammed in the sixth century C.E. Using archaeological finds to buttress their claims, they argue that the extant culture in Xinjiang dating back 6,000 years is Uyghur. They further assert that the Uyghurs who lived in Xinjiang 6,000 years ago moved northeast into Mongolia, only to return when their empire was destroyed in 840 C.E. These claims compete with those of the Hans but also reduce Islam to a secondary component of Uyghur identity. Therefore, peasant Uyghurs, who are devout Muslims and for whom history begins with Islam, reject these views.

Chinese Versions of Uyghur History

Until 1979 the Communists prevented the study of local history, condemning it as a feudal practice. History was meant to serve the state and legitimize its authority. The Chinese, like the Soviets in Central Asia, developed denigrating histories of the Central Asian peoples before conquest, saying it was the Chinese presence that had a civilizing influence on this population.

Despite the fact that Deng Xiaoping permitted the writing of minority histories in 1978, elementary and high school textbooks in Xinjiang today refer to the Uyghurs only in the context of Chinese history, stressing the point that Xinjiang has been an inalienable part of China since well before the arrival of the Uyghurs in the region in the ninth century.[15] A placard in the Turpan Museum, before it moved to a new location in 1990, described the abundant Confucian texts found in Turpan from the pre-Tang dynasty period and illustrated the Han-centric bias of most history available to the public:

> In the Turpan region a great number of writings and tomb elegies of the Han Chinese, in the languages of our nationality brothers, have been unearthed. Many of these can be dated precisely. Royal edicts and family records recovered reflect the political and social control exercised during the Jin and Tang Dynasties. Many commercial records of sales, ancestral property holdings, and goods borrowed, reflect the deep and bitter conflict between feudalism and the social classes of that time. Among the historical materials have been found copies of Confucius' *Analects*, the *Classic of Filial Piety*, etc. which reflect that period's propagation in great force of the method of Confucius-Mencius thought for social control. This was a means of poisoning the people's thought and for maintaining feudal control. These materials completely illustrate that during ancient times, the government, economy, culture, and education were the same as those in the interior of China.   (my translation)

One of the new museum's curators, Ablim, is also the secretary general of the nascent Turpan Studies Society, founded in November of 1988 and consisting of only two members, Ablim and Li Nong, a Han. Ablim, about thirty years old, stated that he had a somewhat superficial knowledge of Uyghur history and that the Society had few historical materials. He planned a trip to museums and research institutes in Beijing to collect some.

Since 1985, the government has been using historical materials in radically different ways. One is by promoting Uyghur culture, sometimes in superficial and inadvertently comic ways. Just as the Chinese use the Great Wall and the panda as trademarks in advertising, Chinese enterprises now use Uyghur historical figures and relics in Xinjiang. A soap called "Fragrant Concubine" is named after the famous Uyghur concubine, Ipar Khan or *Mämrusin* (known as *Xiang Fei* in Chinese) who has become a symbol of the Uyghur past.[16] She died after one year of service as Qing Dynasty emperor Qian Long's concubine. Her maternal grandfather, Apaq Khoja, was an ancestor of the leaders of the rival Black Mountain and White Mountain Sufi sects, which brought strife to Xinjiang from the seventeenth to the nineteenth centuries. The picture on the soap depicts the Apaq Khoja Mausoleum in Kashgar, a burial ground for prominent Uyghurs and Muslim clerics. Other consumer goods use famous historical localities. There is a Lou Lan wine named after the ancient settlement near Lop Nor, and a wine cooler from blazing hot Turpan appropriately called "Turpan Cooler."

One way the Chinese disassociate Uyghur history from Islam is by claiming Buddhist origins for Uyghur Turkic texts.[17] Uyghurs claim that Yusuf Khass Hajib Balasagun's book, *Kutadgu Bilig*, is one of the first Uyghur masterpieces on the aesthetics of the Turkic language. Balasagun was born near Kashgar, and Kashgar Uyghurs are proud of his role in the development of Turkic literature. His mausoleum in Kashgar has become an historical site and attracts many local tourists. However, in a Chinese article, this eleventh-century work is given a Buddhist origin on the basis of its frequent references to the pain experienced in the world—a concept foreign to Islam but in keeping with Buddhism.[18] Of course, it would make sense that Turks from the Kashgar area would be influenced by Buddhism, since the large Buddhist center at Khotan was only five day's ride east.

The Chinese also support Uyghur cultural heroes, artists, and historical personages whose lives and works are viewed as politically neutral. They have popularized Uyghur folk hero Nasruddin Khoja, known as A-fan-ti in China, and stories about him are known throughout all of China.[19] Similarly, the Chinese have established national dress styles for minorities to wear at national and government celebrations, and in recent years have promoted ethnic sporting events such as wrestling and tight-rope walking. Sometimes these innocuous events are given a nationalistic twist by the minorities involved. Uyghurs, for example, claim that European football (soccer) was invented in Kashgar. The ethnic games held in Urumchi in the mid-1980s had a strong symbolic function: contributing "to the maintenance of minority identities still rather recently acquired, and in convincing most minority group members of relatively benign intentions of the Han-dominated center" (Hann 1987:24–25).[20] Since 1979, most Chinese attempts to foster minority cultures appear to have had these purposes in mind.

However, the Chinese have also used scientific technology to contradict minority histories. For example, they have attempted to give a chronological date to the *karez* wells, the ancient underground canal sys-

FIGURE 5.1   Poster of Yusup Khass Hajib Balasagun, author of *Kutadgu Bilig*

tem in Turpan, to prove that the technology was introduced by Chinese and not by Iranians or other peoples to the west of Xinjiang. The Uyghurs believe that the *karez*, which are unique in China to Turpan and similar to the *qanat* system found in Iran, are a symbolic link to the Islamic world to the west. They also hold that the *karez* have been in Turpan for at least

1,000 years. The Chinese, on the other hand, claim that Han Chinese introduced *karez* technology to Turpan in the seventeenth century.

In reports from travelers who passed through the Turpan region over the eight centuries up to the seventeenth century, no mention is made of the *karez*, a very impressive and obvious feature. This lends credence to the Chinese claim. At a Chinese-organized *karez* conference held in Urumchi and Turpan in 1990, Chinese scientists and Japanese scholars announced their discovery that the sedimentation that accumulates at the mouth of a *karez* can be distinguished for each year; this, like the formation of tree rings, makes it possible to establish the age of an underground canal by counting the layers. The oldest *karez* prove to be from the seventeenth century; this supports Chinese claims but does not end the debate as to who introduced the *karez* canals.

Some Uyghur *karez* diggers claim that the underground canals were developed by Hans who came to the region 400 years ago as wage laborers for the Uyghurs. Another interesting addition to the *karez* controversy was offered to me by a noted Xinjiang historian, Ji Dachun, a Manchu who was an assistant to Burhan Shahidi, the first Xinjiang governor in the Communist period. He maintains that a Qing emperor sent prisoners to the King of Lukchun (in the Turpan region) to be used as slaves for *karez* construction. He said the slaves intermarried with the Uyghurs and that is why the Turpan Uyghurs look like a "mixed breed."

Regardless of the veracity of the Chinese government's claims, Uyghur historians are mistrustful of any history that relies on Chinese texts. The sources for most of the recorded history of the Uyghurs are Chinese, so Uyghur intellectuals maintain that this history is, by its very nature, biased against the Uyghurs. The controversies surrounding the history of the region are not simply intellectualizations. They directly reflect and feed into the troubled ethnic relations between Hans and Uyghurs that have existed during the more than forty years of Chinese Communist rule.

Since 1985, the government has taken a utilitarian stance toward Uyghur intellectuals in Xinjiang in hope of developing the region's human resources and stemming minority uprisings. The Chinese Communist government needs the collaboration of Uyghur intellectuals to control Xinjiang and maintain power. Today Uyghur intellectuals, no longer completely loyal to the Party, have been given limited freedom to create and disseminate nationalist ideologies to the Uyghur populace. As part of this effort the government has allowed the publication of a large number of diverse Uyghur books.

Still, despite government leniency, the paucity of well-known Uyghur intellectual figures has heightened the influence and notoriety of a few, placing them under strong surveillance by the Chinese government. They are viewed as dangerous because their ideas about what should be done to help the Uyghur people differ from those of the government. To counter this danger, the Chinese government attempts to control the cultural productions of Uyghur intellectuals, believing that "no socialist regime can countenance the production of ideological effects contrary to its purposes, effects that would reveal its nakedness" (Verdery 1991:90–91). Nonetheless, the symbolic aspects of Uyghur writings have often been overlooked by government censors and, once published, have had a profound influence on the hearts and minds of the general populace. This is especially true for those writings that stimulate a sense of Uyghur nationalism and a rejection of Han domination. Because it is only since 1985 that Uyghur intellectuals have had the opportunity to create nationalist ideologies that inspire the Uyghur people toward unity and national consciousness, they know they must do so in a way that does not pose an overt threat to the Chinese government.

6

The Future of the Uyghur Past

Open your eyes wide and look about you.
You must contemplate the future.
—"Uyghur," "Awaken! (*Oyghan*)"

The struggle currently taking place to manipulate history and heroes in
the definition of Uyghur nationalist ideologies is as much between
Uyghur intellectuals and the Chinese state as among Uyghur intellectuals. Each Uyghur involved in this definition process attempts to create a
nationalist ideology that places his own oasis at the forefront of Uyghur
history, in order to facilitate the acceptance of a national identity in his
own oasis.

Intellectuals have a vested interest in promoting the concept of
Uyghurs as a national group. But they do not push this national agenda
when it conflicts with the concerns of their own local oases. Though they
constantly strive toward an ideology distinct from Hans and other major
groups, such as the Tungans and Kazaks, the nationalist picture they
paint of Uyghur identity is actually parochial and riddled with oasis
chauvinism. As Bernard Lewis writes, "When there are conflicting loyalties or clashing interests, each will have its own version of the past, its
own presentation of the salient events" (1975:55–56).

Challenges are therefore made to intellectuals from other oases, not
necessarily to deny their histories a place but to make them less salient.
Intellectuals believe that their particular version of history will lead the
Uyghur people to a rejuvenation of Uyghur nationalist culture and con-

sciousness, especially within their respective oases. Through the images and rhetoric they use, their selection of heroes and histories, these intellectuals are, in effect, struggling over the future of the Uyghur past.

In the Turpan oasis we have seen that there are strong differences among intellectual, peasant, and merchant conceptions of Uyghur identity. Uyghur intellectuals believe that peasants have withdrawn into Islamic traditionalism, while peasants see Islam as intrinsic to Uyghur ethnic identity and view secular intellectuals who oppose it as out of touch with their own people. Merchants have accepted a *Junggoluq* (pan-PRC Chinese) identity. In contrast, the majority of intellectuals are anti-Islamic and believe that science and Western education are the means by which to bring progress to the Uyghurs. Several Uyghurs believe that the resurgence of Islam among the Uyghur peasants would place them in a position analogous to that of the American Indian. "What are we to do?" one Uyghur political official asked, "retreat into our culture so that Hans can come watch us like animals in a zoo? No! We must compete with the Chinese on their terms."

Most intellectuals believe that the Uyghurs must forge an identity in a creative and powerful way to give them strength to live within the Chinese state. In 1989, prior to the breakup of the Soviet Union and with the number of Hans in Xinjiang growing to parity with the number of Uyghurs, many Uyghurs believed that Xinjiang would never be independent. A Turpan economist pointed out that many nations were given independence in the aftermath of World War II, and somberly remarked that the only hope for Uyghur independence from China would come after World War III. Since 1985, many intellectuals have been cut off from their home villages and they live within the predominantly Han world of Urumchi. In effect, these intellectuals are alienated from their own oasis identities. But it is this alienation that, at least theoretically, puts intellectuals in the best position to create a pan-oasis identity, a unifying identity not prejudiced in favor of any local oasis.

It appears, however, that the opening of Xinjiang's borders to neighboring countries is leading to radical changes in Uyghur oasis dwellers' world views and notions of what constitutes Uyghur ethnic identity. Long-held rivalries among the oases are beginning to resurface, and seem to be leading to further fragmentation of Uyghur identity along traditional lines. In Turpan, oasis rivalries and particular world views were strengthened by the opening of borders and the development of tourism and trade. Intellectuals seize on these world views to create nationalist ideologies that influence local notions of Uyghur identity.

Therefore, it was through the study of Uyghur intellectuals and the promulgation of their ideologies at the oasis level that Uyghur nationalism and its local oasis biases came to be understood.

Uyghur scholars write histories and historical novels to influence their fellow oasis dwellers' views about themselves and, consequently, about all Uyghur people and their relationship to the Chinese state.[1] Intellectuals are the Uyghurs most capable of articulating and shaping notions of ethnic identity, national consciousness, and cultural values. However, their success depends on acceptance by the peasantry at the local level.

The intellectual strategies discussed below document the work of both admired and not-so-respected writers who have introduced competing ideologies that may shape interethnic conflict or cooperation with the Chinese state. At the regional level, these intellectuals' definitions of Uyghur nationalist ideology vary according to which historical figures and events they believe are more likely to find acceptance with the peasantry, merchants, and other intellectuals in both their home oases and throughout Xinjiang. These strategies indicate these particular historical figures and events to be not only the most ideologically significant, but also the most important for awakening Uyghur consciousness.

PORTRAIT DUELS

In May 1987 members of the Turpan Uyghur intellectual elite organized a conference in the Turpan oasis on the contributions made by a local poet, Abdukhaliq (1901–1933), to modern Uyghur literature. A young nationalistic poet whose pen name was "Uyghur"—in fact, one of the first to use that word in its modern context—Abdukhaliq was killed by Chinese government representatives in retribution for the ethnic uprising known as the Hami Rebellion (1931–1934). The goal of the conference was to place Abdukhaliq "Uyghur" in a prominent position within Uyghur history and among Uyghur historical figures. The Turpan intellectuals also hoped that the poetry and person of "Uyghur" would compete favorably as motivators of peasant nationalism with historical personages proposed by intellectuals in other major oases of Xinjiang.

This was not the first such effort. In 1989 a popular poster depicting the eleventh-century scholar Mähmud Qäshqäri was widely distributed throughout Xinjiang. In Ili, which lies in the northwest of the region, pictures of the 1940s revolutionary leader Ähmätjan Qasimi were numerous. But an unusual difficulty faced the Turpan intellectuals in their effort to promote Abdukhaliq "Uyghur." Unlike for Ähmätjan Qasimi and Mähmud Qäshqäri, no visual representations of Abdukhaliq "Uyghur" existed. While Abdukhaliq's poetry seemed certain to stir Uyghur national feelings, intellectuals felt that a portrait was needed to give a focus to those emotions.

To rectify this situation, a local Turpan artist, Imin Hasil, sought to create an image of the poet from descriptions by the poet's brother, his sister, and other Turpan peasants who had known him. After five failed renderings Imin began to panic. In an act of desperation, a few days before the Turpan conference, Imin went to Abdukhaliq's grave and exhumed his remains. After taking cranial measurements, he was finally able to render an image of the poet. In viewing the final painting, Abdukhaliq's sister was moved to tears. Turpan's intellectuals had their symbol (see figure 6.1).

POETRY OF RESISTANCE

The Turpan conference, attended by scholars from oases throughout Xinjiang, produced an edited volume of papers with titles such as "The Importance of Abdukhaliq's Poetry to Uyghur Literature," and "Abdukhaliq Our National Hero." The meeting was successful in spreading Abdukhaliq's name throughout the Uyghur intellectual community. His words were frequently quoted in the Uyghur press and are now disseminated in Uyghur literature textbooks used in middle schools. Imin's renderings of Abdukhaliq hang in Turpan schools, and many college students tack sketches of the poet on their dormitory walls.

It is interesting that intellectuals consider Turpan, the historical heartland of original Uyghur culture, as culturally backward as Khotan, which lies in a remote part of southern Xinjiang. In fact, Uyghurs frequently use the expression "Turpan level," to describe other Uyghurs they consider provincial. Turpan lies at the second-lowest elevation in the world, next to the Dead Sea, and Turpanliks are said to assume the low quality of the depression itself. Despite these attitudes, Turpan intellectuals successfully advanced their local hero, Abdukhaliq "Uyghur," who has now become a major source of government concern.

Abduhaliq's most famous poem is a call to action. Written two years before his death, it describes the pitiful condition of the Uyghur people

FIGURE 6.1   Imin Hasil's Portrait of Abdukhaliq "Uyghur".
SOURCE: Abdurusul Ömär (1986).

and calls on them to awaken from inactivity and take control of their future through rebellion. At the time, Abdukhaliq "Uyghur" realized that the Turks of Xinjiang were not conscious of their situation and were living as if in a dream. Like a biblical prophet, he believed it was his mission to open their eyes and warn them of their fate.

Awaken! (*Oyghan*)
Hey! Uyghur, it is time to awaken,
  You haven't any possessions,
  You have nothing to fear.
If you don't rescue yourselves
  From this death,
Your situation will become very grave.
Stand up! I say,
  Raise your head and wipe your eyes!
Cut the heads off of your enemies,
  Let the blood flow!
If you don't open your eyes and look around you,
  You'll die pitifully, helplessly.
Your body appears lifeless,
  And yet you don't worry about dying.
I call out to you but you do not react,
  It seems as though you want to die unconsciously.
Open your eyes wide and look about you.
  You must contemplate the future,
  Think about it a long time.
If this opportunity should fall from your grasp,
  The future will bode much hardship, much hardship.
My heart breaks for you my Uyghur people,
  My brothers in arms, relatives, my family.
I worry for your lives,
  So I am calling you to awaken.
Have you not heard me yet?
  What has happened to you?
There will be a day when you will regret,
  And on that day you will understand,
  Just what I have been telling you.
"Damn!" you will say when you realize
  That you missed your only chance,
And on that day you will know that
  I, Uyghur, was right.

Abdurusul Ömär, ed. (1986:13–14)(my translation)

As a youth, Abdukhaliq read the historical classics of China and learned about the Uyghurs and their civilization. He studied Arabic and Persian in religious school, and also knew Russian, Mandarin, and, of course, the eastern Turkic dialect, now called Uyghur, which is very close to Uzbek. He discovered that Uyghurs were not called *chantou* (turban heads) throughout their history, as they were by Hans during his own lifetime. In 1916, Abdukhaliq went to Russian Central Asia with his grandfather (*chong dadisi*), returning a second time in 1923 and staying for three years (Abdurusul Ömär 1986:1). There he made the acquaintance of many Soviet Turkologists, studied Uyghur history, and adopted "Uyghur" as his pen name.[2] After returning to Xinjiang in 1926 he continued to write poetry and to travel throughout Xinjiang reciting it.

In an earlier paper, I suggested that it was the Soviet diplomat Garegin Apresoff, invited to Xinjiang in 1933, who might have encouraged the use of the term *Uyghur* to refer to Xinjiang Turkic oasis dwellers.[3] However, it is now clear that Abdukhaliq also profoundly influenced the Chinese government's selection of the ethnic name *Uyghur* in the mid-1930s. The close friendship between Abdukhaliq's family and the family of Burhan Shähidi, the first governor of Xinjiang during the Communist period, gives credence to this view. Burhan played a central role in the first Xinjiang Nationalities Congress held in 1934, one year after Abdukhaliq's death, and it was there that the term *Uyghur* was first proposed for use in China. Burhan later became the provincial governor under both the Nationalist and Communist regimes (1949–1955).[4]

When the Hami revolts broke out in 1931–1932 after Governor Jin Shuren sought to depose the hereditary ruling family, Xinjiang military commander Sheng Shicai, later to become governor of the province, labeled Abdukhaliq a traitor and a pan-Turkist because of the content of his poems. A Tungan rebel named Ma Shiming and his family hid out in the old city of Turpan. In an attempt to get Turpan Uyghurs to betray Ma and to punish them, Sheng Shicai arrested and executed famous Uyghur intellectuals. Twenty-seven Turpan intellectuals were killed, including Abdukhaliq "Uyghur" (see figure 6.2).

During the Three Regions Revolt (1944–1949) and during the brief time that the Ili revolutionary Ähmätjan Qasimi was part of the central government, some of "Uyghur's" poetry was published in the *Xinjiang Gazeti* (*Xinjiang News*), the newspaper edited by Abdurehim Ötkür.[5] But "Uyghur's" poetry was later nearly forgotten. In 1978, the government, in the spirit of reform, dropped the ban on its publication. Since then, many Uyghur intellectuals have been stirred by Abdukhaliq's poetry and have begun to study his work and discuss its importance to Uyghur literature.

When Muhammät Shah Niyaz began the journal *Turpan*, in 1981, the first issue was devoted to Abdukhaliq "Uyghur." In a conference on

FIGURE 6.2   Depiction of Abdukhaliq "Uyghur"'s Execution.
SOURCE: Khewir Tömür (1987).

Uyghur literature held in Kashgar that same year, local Uyghurs placed a large poster on which they handwrote the entirety of "Uyghur's" poem "Awaken! (*Oyghan*)" on a prominent wall in the city, clearly making a statement against the Chinese government. The Kashgar police, in reaction to the inflammatory message, cordoned off the city and conducted handwriting tests in an effort to find the culprit. They did not realize that the poetry had been written in the 1930s and published in 1979 with government approval. When finally informed of this, the police gave up their search.

In the mid-1980s, in an atmosphere of interoasis struggle over cultural heroes, "Uyghur's" fame spread. A series of papers was presented at the May 1987 five-day conference on Abduhaliq "Uyghur" held in Turpan. The proceedings were published in Uyghur in a book entitled *Abdukhaliq Uyghur wa Uning Ädibiyatimizdiki Orni* (*Abdukhaliq Uyghur and His Position in Our Literature*) (Iminjan Ähmidi and Isma'il Tömür 1988). A Uyghur middle-school student referred to "Uyghur's" poetry as "the voice of the Uyghur conscience awakening the Uyghur people from their sleep." Yet this voice had no visual representation, for there were no photographs of Abdukhaliq "Uyghur." As mentioned earlier, to meet this need the Turpan artist Imin Hasil, trained in reconstructing portraits from skulls in art school, exhumed Abdukhaliq "Uyghur's" remains and rendered a portrait of the poet. Many Uyghurs refuse to believe that Imin actually exhumed the remains, but he insists that he did, to the extent of giving me precise measurements of Abdukhaliq "Uyghur's" cranial circumference, the length of his jaw bone, and the dimensions of his eye sockets. Imin described how he washed and ritually purified himself before opening the grave. He found three bodies inside and identified Abdukhaliq by a severed left arm that had been sliced by a sword immediately before he was killed. Only later did Imin admit to Abdukhaliq's family that he had dug up "Uyghur's" bones in order to reconstruct his image.

Abdukhaliq "Uyghur's" brother, Sattar Haji, who still lives in Üzüm-chilik, said that Abdukhaliq started to write poetry in 1918, at a time when no one in Turpan called themselves Uyghur. When Abdukhaliq began to use the name "Uyghur," the Hans considered it to be national-istic and wanted him to desist. Abdukhaliq refused. Some of Sattar Haji's favorite poems reflect his brother's Uyghur pride and conviction that the Uyghur people should stand up to Han exploitation. The poem below stresses the shortness of time and the brief opportunity open to the Uyghurs for action:

It Is Close at Hand (*Yäqin Boldi*)
Arise. Time is at hand.
It is very close.
Stand up brothers. Do you want to die lying there?
We now face our deepest winter.

Arise.
Time is very short but we still have time.
If we miss this chance,
The winter will freeze our lives.

Abdurusul Ömär, ed. (1986:47)(my translation)

The following poem, written by Abdukhaliq "Uyghur" in prison before his death in 1933, calls attention to the Uyghur people's great historical legacy and demands that they take action for themselves through force of arms and literacy:

Unsettled (*Ich Pushush*)
We have a world renowned name, Uyghur.
We are not less than these fools,
We are not crippled.
They have made such slanderous attacks on us.
They call us "turban heads" (*chantou*).
They put us in the same room with animals.
We have no more patience left.
Is this the life for us?
We must take up arms and begin our struggle.
We will cross all the dark mountains.
I heard of the fighting in Qomul (Hami),
It filled me with excitement.
I jumped up from my bed.
This war will shake the power of our oppressors.
Our enemies have attacked,
And we have retreated.
The situation is grave,
We must liberate ourselves from exploitation.
Those who are weak,
Are those with the most enemies.
Illiteracy is the path of the weak.

Abdurusul Ömär, ed. (1986:98–100)(my translation)

The anger expressed in "Uyghur's" poetry speaks to the Uyghur present: his rage was directed toward the Chinese warlord regimes that had ruled Xinjiang throughout his life, but the message can be just as easily applied to the Chinese Communists. While Abdukhaliq "Uyghur's" historical understanding of Xinjiang and the Uyghur people led him to develop a highly political message, his gift for poetry is what gives the message such power.

Most young people had not heard of "Uyghur" until 1985, but today there is a strong popular awareness of the poet in Turpan. Many children are named after Abdukhaliq. High school students regularly read his work, and his poetry is extremely popular among university students. In the teacher's room at the Number One Middle School in Turpan City there is a large picture of Abdukhaliq "Uyghur"; its caption reads "National Patriot Poet." During Beijing Spring (1989), Uyghur students in Urumchi protesting against the government chanted lines from "Uyghur's" poem "Awaken! (*Oyghan*)": "Stand up! I say, / Raise your head and wipe your eyes!;" and "I worry for your lives, / So I am calling you to awaken." At present, government officials, including many Uyghurs, feel that "Uyghur's" work is too inflammatory and should not be published. Communist government officials and Uyghur intellectuals debate whether Abdukhaliq "Uyghur" was a patriotic hero (*wätänpärwär*) or a dangerous Uyghur nationalist. Consequently, the government has prohibited the printing of Muhammät Shah Niyaz's book on Abdukhaliq "Uyghur's" life until a clear official policy is established and ethnic problems in Xinjiang calm down.

THE LEGACY OF ISLAM

An Islamic challenge to China has recently mounted in Kashgar, causing authorities to fear the spread of Islamic fundamentalism. Only in Kashgar do women wear thick brown cloth veils that cover their heads completely. Hundreds of thousands of Muslims travel there during *Qurban Heyt*, the day on which pilgrims make their *hajj* to Mecca. And Koranic schools are more numerous in Kashgar than in any other region of Xinjiang.[6] Therefore, in contrast to intellectuals in Turpan, Kashgar intellectuals have emphasized heroes associated with Islam.

Kashgar is held to be the traditional cultural center of the Uyghur people, for it is there that Islam, now perceived as intrinsic to Uyghur culture, first took root. The Karakhanid ruler Sutuq Bughra Khan's conversion to Islam in the mid-tenth century is an extremely significant event, marking the beginning of Islam in Xinjiang. The eleventh-century scholar Mähmud Qäshqäri is also part of Kashgar's Islamic cultural legacy to the Uyghur.

Kashgar remains the most volatile of the Uyghur oases in terms of pan-Turkic and anti-Chinese sentiments. To keep control of the region, the Chinese government has officially sanctioned Mähmud Qäshqäri, author of *Divan Lughat at-Turk*, an encyclopedic dictionary of eastern Turkic culture, as a cultural hero. However, although posters and articles promoting Mähmud Qäshqäri are widely circulated throughout Xinjiang, Uyghur intellectuals from Kashgar are distancing themselves from this personage (see figure 6.3). A central reason for their disavowal is Qäshqäri's written claims that only the Buddhists from the Turpan region are Uyghurs, not the people of Kashgar. There is also speculation that the author was not a Turk, but an Arab.[7]

It must be stressed that only since the 1980s has information about Uyghur cultural heroes such as Mähmud Qäshqäri and classical works

FIGURE 6.3   Eleventh-century famous Uyghur linguist Mähmud Qäshqäri.
SOURCE: Ghazi Ämät, Kashgar Uyghur-Language Press, 1983.

such as the *Divan Lughat at-Turk* and the *Kutadgu Bilig* been made public. Prior to the cultural liberalization of 1978, the desire to learn about pre-Communist history was considered feudal and antisocialist; history belonged to the feudal past.

The former Uyghur leader of Xinjiang, Säypidin Äzizi (b. 1914), the son of a merchant family from Artush, near Kashgar, launched another approach (see figure 6.4). As chairman of the Xinjiang government from 1955 to 1978, he supported, or most likely had no choice but to support, the policy of sending Hans from China proper to populate Xinjiang. He is discredited for this and because his children married Hans, and he is not held in high regard by Uyghurs; in fact, many intellectuals consider him a traitor and hate him vehemently. In 1985, a well-known Uyghur author told me that if Säypidin attended the National Day Celebration, a commemoration of the thirtieth anniversary of the Xinjiang Uyghur Autonomous Region, he would try his best to kill him.

In 1987, Säypidin attempted to restore his image by publishing a one-thousand-page historical novel, *Sutuq Bughra Khan*, about the life of the first Karakhanid ruler, who adopted Islam in the middle of the tenth century. The effort to place Sutuq Bughra Khan in the pantheon of major Uyghur heroes was meant to emphasize Kashgar's position as the Islamic heartland of Xinjiang and of the Uyghur people. Although Sutuq Bughra Khan's conversion to Islam is significant for Uyghurs because it emphasizes their Muslim identity, this historical figure does not have the same impact as the great eleventh-century scholar Mähmud Qäshqäri. Mähmud Qäshqäri's scholarly achievements are a symbol of Uyghur intelligence and wisdom; he embodies the very characteristics that have been denigrated by the Hans. Säypidin's widely acclaimed book raised many Uyghurs' estimation of Säypidin, but not their historical or ethnic consciousness.

ANTEDATING MUMMIES

Some Uyghurs have redefined their history by adopting myths that tell of Uyghur superiority over Hans. Symbolic formulations and mythologies of origin and descent are socially constructed ideologies by which the Uyghurs confront the Chinese state. Some of these myths, as described earlier, involve the Uyghurs' affirmation of their relation to Hitler and Nazi Germany's Aryan ideology, claiming that Hitler consid-

FIGURE 6.4   Säypidin Äzizi. SOURCE: Säypidin Äzizi (1987).

ered both Uyghurs and Germans as Hun descendants. Other myths, involving the early origin of the Uyghurs, maintain that they settled in the Tarim Basin before it became a desert over 8,000 years ago. In these stories, ancestors of the Uyghurs moved to the northwest Mongolian steppe when the Tarim Basin became desiccated and then returned to the oases after the fall of the Uyghur Empire in 840 C.E.

A Uyghur translator at the Academy of Sciences denigrated the significance of Han Chinese culture for the Uyghurs by pointing to the example of the Great Wall: "The Chinese take immense pride in the Great Wall. But think of it. It was built to keep us Uyghurs out." A middle school teacher told a group of guests at a circumcision party that the Uyghurs originally came from the Anatolian Peninsula. When someone asked him about the Karakhanids, he said they too were Uyghurs. He then added, "Of course we all know that Uyghuristan and East Turkestan are the same thing. The Karakhanid [932–1165 c.e.] was a period of great unity for all of the Turks. It was during that time that the Uyghurs in Turpan converted to Islam. Before they were either Christians or Buddhists." While certain aspects of many of these histories can be verified, much of the information is jumbled and questionable; it is this kind of history that will be taught to children with the liberalization of school curricula.

When Kashgar intellectuals began to see that neither Mähmud Qäshqäri nor Sutuq Bughra Khan could become a symbol strong enough to embody the nationalist spirit of Kashgar, they developed a new approach, best represented by Kashgarlik Turghun Almas's 1990 book *Uyghurlar* (*The Uyghurs*), a highly nationalistic version of Uyghur history. The book reached stores in February 1990 but was banned and removed from the shelves one week later. Part of the controversy was due to the stylized wolf motif on the cover, a blatant pan-Turkic symbol (see figure 6.5)[8] (according to legend, the Turkic peoples are descended from a wolf). The main point of contention, however, was the author's claim that the Uyghurs have a 6,000-year history. When I met Turghun in 1985, he told me that a corpse of a female, carbon dated at over 6,000 years old, was found wrapped in cloth woven with Uyghur symbols and motifs.[9] Turghun included such discoveries in his book.

While it is almost certain that there were people in the Xinjiang region over 6,000 years ago, it is quite unlikely, perhaps impossible, that they are linked to the Turkic people known as the Uyghurs, who first appeared in history about 1,500 years ago and did not arrive in Xinjiang until 840 c.e. Uyghur histories that promulgate claims impossible to prove are similar to other historical accounts, examples of the "triumph of ideology over reality, of will over fact" (Lewis 1975:101). One is reminded of Mark Twain's advice to the young Rudyard Kipling: "Young man, first get your facts, then distort them as you please" (in Spalek 1972:86).[10] Turghun's claims resemble those of Afrocentric intellectuals in the United States who believe that black Africans built the Egyptian pyramids. The question remains whether the symbol of blacks as ancient pyramid builders can help African Americans heighten their twentieth-century cultural pride and social position. Will Turghun's claim of a 6,000-year history raise the modern Uyghurs' national pride and social position?

Turghun's strategy to educate Uyghurs in their own history and to negate the official Chinese view appeared to have failed in its nascent stage when the government banned his book. However, the Uyghurs, like other minority or oppressed peoples under totalitarian regimes, see book-banning as an indication of the government's fear—fear that both validates the truth of the writings and leads to a perception that these banned books might strengthen the minority peoples beyond government control. In Turpan, in the final month of my fieldwork, three people pulled me aside and offered me Turghun's book. Each had a similar message: "Take this out of the country and publish it. This is the true his-

FIGURE 6.5   Turghun Almas. SOURCE: Turghun Almas (1990).

tory of our people. The government has banned it and because of that we know it must be true."

The future implications of Turghun's views cannot be known in their entirety, though it is certain that they will become the basis of underground propaganda for Uyghur nationalism. This has already begun. In February 1991, one year after the publication of Turghun Almas's book, the government organized a conference in Urumchi devoted specifically to criticizing the book, and invited Uyghur and Han historians of Xinjiang to participate. The conference was also attended by several dozen scholars from Beijing. Later, Uyghur exiles in America told me that Uyghurs in Chinese government work units were writing a pamphlet, entitled "One Hundred Mistakes of Turghun Almas's *Uyghurlar*" and describing the historical flaws in the work, which government workers later were forced to study. The fact that the government has taken such strong measures to attack Turghun Almas's work is evidence that it is widely known among the Uyghurs and is considered dangerous by the government. By distributing the pamphlet throughout the region, the government's efforts achieved the opposite of their intended purpose: many more Uyghurs were exposed to Turghun Almas's ideas in the pamphlet than could have obtained copies of the original banned book, and many found Turghun's historical account very compelling. In the summer of 1995, Turghun remained under virtual house arrest in a weary and broken condition.

SEPARATIST LEADERS

The historical period significant to Uyghur intellectuals from Ili took place after Xinjiang's last warlord, Sheng Shicai, was replaced by representatives of the Nationalist government under control of Chiang Kaishek. Muslim opposition arose once again and ignited a nationalist movement, beginning with the Three Regions Revolt (also known as the Ili Rebellion) and culminating in the formation of the independent East Turkestan Republic (ETR) (1944–1949). The ETR led the most powerful Uyghur nationalist movement in Xinjiang's history. The main political organization within the ETR was the *Yashlar Täshkilati*, the East Turkestan Youth Party, which at its height claimed some 300,000 members (Benson 1990a:161).

In 1946 and 1947, Uyghurs and other non-Han nationalities of Ili won remarkable concessions from the Chinese government when a brief peace accord was made. Its major points, which indicate that the ETR hoped to take control of the region, included protection for freedom of thought and written expression; unrestricted publishing, association, residence, and movement; the guarantee of women's equality; the means by which to solve conflict between civil law and religious law; the granting of local elections based on universal suffrage and secret balloting; and permission to use both the Chinese and Muslim languages (*Huiwen*) in government and legal matters (Benson 1990a:188). During this period, ETR leaders traveled throughout Xinjiang spreading their nationalistic message.[11] However, because of violations of the accord, the coalition government comprised of Chinese government and ETR officials fell in 1947. The ETR survived, independent, until 1949, the eve of Communist establishment of the People's Republic of China (PRC). Uyghurs in the ETR were poised for autonomy within China and the leaders of the Republic, centered around the charismatic figure of Ähmätjan Qasimi, built themselves into a viable political force.[12] This strength would, however, be undermined by Communist maneuvers.

Prior to the establishment of the ETR and at the end of Sheng Shicai's rule in 1944, nationalistic Turkic pamphlets were widely distributed throughout Xinjiang. Their message of outrage against Chinese rule stressed the fundamentals of nationalism and made passionate appeals that East Turkestan be considered the Uyghur homeland. The Uyghur writers lament the loss of the Uyghur leadership due to Sheng Shicai's brutal governance of the region and call on the native populace of East Turkestan to take revenge on the Chinese.

Hail, people! Let all men know well:
That these helpless, unfortunate people in the prisons of Sheng [Shicai] Tupan [warlord governor], drawing their last breaths of life before dying, turn upon us the eyes of their souls and in their moaning say to us: "For the suffering which we have endured at the hands of the savage Chinese, you must avenge us. We are pouring forth our blood and yielding up our souls for our people: for this also you must avenge us."

At the present time, in our territory of East Turkestan, all of the ruling power is in the hands of the Chinese alone. We are a people who have lost all human rights. It should be known by every man of knowledge that when the rule is in the hands of the Chinese, there is no equality and no justice. Only when the throats of the Chinese fascist oppressors have been cut and they have bled to death will we come again into the life of light.   (Benson 1990a:201–2)

With the development of the East Turkestan Republic these powerful sentiments became the basis for a sophisticated rhetoric created by foreign minister Ähmätjan Qasimi. ETR nationalistic views found expression in the Ili paper *Minzhu Bao* (*Democratic Daily*), published in five languages, including Mandarin, and in the *Xinjiang Gazeti* (*Xinjiang Newspaper*), published in the Uyghur Turkic language. Uyghur writings during this period, like those written against Russian rule during the Jadid period in Russian and Soviet Central Asia, were more concerned with vilifying Chinese government policy than with recording Uyghur history. However, the advent of Communist control of Xinjiang in 1949 put an end to the growth of Uyghur nationalism.

To maintain and foster allegiance in the minority areas, the Communist government absorbed minority leaders into the pantheon of officially promoted pan-PRC Chinese (*Zhonghua*) heroes. Sometimes their policy took on ridiculous proportions, as when they celebrated the birth of Genghis Khan, claiming that since the Mongols are minorities of China, Genghis Khan was "Chinese."[13] Ähmätjan Qasimi, the Uyghur hero promoted by Ili intellectuals, was one of the central national leaders co-opted (see figure 6.6).[14] Educated in the Soviet Union and fluent in Uyghur, Mandarin, and Russian, he was an important leader of the East Turkestan Republic and played a major political role during the Ili Rebellion from 1944 to 1949. His leadership was cut short when he and his co-revolutionaries were killed suddenly a month before the People's Republic was established in 1949, in a mysterious plane crash en route to talks with Mao Zedong about autonomy for the region.

Although the political line of the East Turkestan Republic was characterized by anti-Han rhetoric, the Communist government during the People's Republic period has adeptly reinterpreted this rhetoric as being anti-Kuomintang (KMT Nationalist) and therefore patriotic (McMillen 1979:42). However, while Ili intellectuals today support the promotion of Ähmätjan as a Uyghur hero, they do not accept Chinese versions of his political message. They still consider his speeches against Han Chinese oppression in Xinjiang relevant to Communist policies today.

Ähmätjan was a sophisticated, young, charismatic leader, and he symbolizes the unique qualities of today's Ililiks, including greater sophistication and political awareness as compared to Uyghurs in the rest of Xinjiang. It is a matter of pride for Ililiks that photographs of Ähmätjan show him wearing Western suits. In general, Ililiks wear up-to-date Western fashions, stay current on global events, and are the most secular Uyghurs in their views and lifestyles. In Ili, women do not veil and there are no Islamic schools. Most Uyghurs in the Ili area still call themselves *Taranchi* (tillers of the soil), the same ethnonym used until 1949 by the Chinese and Soviets to name Ili Uyghurs as a distinct ethnic group. The cultural superiority that the Ililiks feel over other Uyghurs is reinforced by the Chinese government: the Ili dialect has become the standard Uyghur language used in schools and on television and radio broadcasts.

FIGURE 6.6   Ähmätjan Qasimi. SOURCE: Abdurakhman Äbay (1984).

The Historical Novel

One of the most respected of recent Uyghur nationalist intellectuals is Abdurehim Ötkür, who published three historical novels: *Iz* (*Traces*) in 1985, *Oyghanghan Zemin I* (*The Awakening Land, Part I*) in 1987, and *Oyghanghan Zemin II* (*The Awakening Land, Part II*) in 1994 (see figure 6.7). In his novels, Abdurehim Ötkür, who died of cancer in 1995, describes his native oasis, Hami, and the events during the 1930s that show its privileged place in Uyghur nationalistic resistance as well as its revolutionary spirit. Uyghur university students are Abdurehim's greatest admirers and view his novels as well-disguised nationalistic literature.[15] Because Abdurehim wrote of the time before the Communists came to power in 1949, he described events essentially similar to today's while not directly criticizing either the Communists or the Hans.

FIGURE 6.7   Abdurehim Ötkür. SOURCE: Abdurehim Ötkür (1986).

Abdurehim has added Hami, an oasis whose contribution to Uyghur history has been long neglected, to the Uyghur historical tradition.[16] Abdurehim was born in Hami and as a youth moved to Urumchi for schooling. In the 1930s, during the boom in Uyghur native intellectual literature, Abdurehim wrote plays that reached a large audience and taught literature at a school for young women (Allworth and Pahta 1988:19). During the Ili Rebellion of the 1940s, he became the chief editor of the Uyghur-language political newspaper, *Xinjiang Gazeti*. In 1949 he tried to flee Xinjiang but was captured by the Communists and imprisoned until the late 1970s. Abdurehim Ötkür spent almost half his life behind bars. After his release and what the Chinese called his "rehabilitation," which was to them the clearing of his record and name, he began to write once again and, in the liberal atmosphere following Mao's death and the opening of Xinjiang in 1985, to publish his novels.

His books deal with the Hami Rebellion, which led to the formation of the Turkish Islamic Republic of East Turkestan (TIRET) in the early thirties; with Khoja Niyaz Khan, one of the leaders of the rebellion who was hostile to the Tungans; and with the cruel Han leader Sheng Shicai.[17] It was only after he reached his sixties that Abdurehim became the most respected and popular Uyghur intellectual. His popularity stemmed from Uyghurs' perceptions of his fearlessness; he appeared unafraid to write about Uyghur history and heroes, even though in doing so he risked his life.

Abdurehim viewed the historical novel as the most powerful tool for educating Uyghurs and one that the Chinese government is less likely to censor because its polemics are disguised in a fictional context. There is considerable freedom within the medium to express themes and beliefs pertinent to the present, though they must be cloaked in analogous historical situations. By writing about a situation prior to the arrival of the Communists, Abdurehim was able to refute suggestions that he was making a political statement.

The Chinese government clamped down on Abdurehim Ötkür's work in 1992 because he became too popular and because it viewed the political statements made in his books as too obvious. However, permission was granted for the publication of the second part of his book, *Oyghanghan Zemin II* (*The Awakening Land, Part II*), in 1994. Abdurehim became one of the most stirring voices in the Uyghur "poetic awakening," and one that the government found difficult to still even momentarily. Unfortunately, in 1995 death from cancer cut Abdurehim's writing career tragically short. His novels are certain to live on.

Abdurehim's novels owe their profound impact to the relation between the depicted historical reality of the past and the nationalistic concerns of the present. His characters wrestle with problems that are as acute now as they were in the past. Georg Lukacs states that the historical novel is important not only for providing information, but for "the poetic awakening of the people who figured in those events" (1983 [1962]:42). Abdurehim Ötkür presents the lessons of the past as a means of awakening today's Uyghurs to three important aspects—and potential advantages—of their identity as a people: Uyghur cultural heroes, their great historical heritage, and their pressing current situation. Uyghur intellectuals concur that it is by understanding their history that the Uyghur people will ultimately be able to understand themselves and their present, and take charge of both. In doing so, they will truly awaken.

7

"Hey! Uyghur, it is time to awaken."

—"Uyghur," "Awaken! (*Oyghan*)"

Expressions of Uyghur nationalism vary greatly by social group and by location in Xinjiang. For the most part, modern scholars have viewed Xinjiang as a single entity; lacking a clear understanding of the region's geography, their studies have fundamentally misread Uyghur identity and the Uyghur nationalist struggle. In contrast, I argue that Xinjiang is composed of four distinct geographic regions, each influenced by a different bordering culture, and that this geographic legacy influences the nature of Uyghur nationalism.

As we have seen, the opening of Xinjiang's borders to outside countries has radically changed Uyghur world views and notions of what constitutes Uyghur ethnic identity. Traditional trade and cultural ties with outside cultures have been reestablished, causing rivalries between the oases to resurface and leading to further fragmentation of Uyghur identity. Uyghur intellectuals throughout Xinjiang are competing to place historical events and personages related to their home oases into prominence; this competition actually undermines the possibility of a cohesive intellectual leadership and inhibits pan-oasis ethnic unity. The Uyghurs' nationalist ideologies are crucial to the development of national pride and self-respect, both aspects of psychological and cultural cohesion that form the basis of group action. However, it is clear that if intellectuals' versions of Uyghur historiography and identity are to succeed, they must resonate with the Uyghur peasantry.

At the oasis level, Uyghur identity is not unified but fragmented along the same lines that separate social groups. In Xinjiang, social groups are defined by occupation, not family type, descent, or pan-oasis solidarity. Thus, the three social groups in the Turpan oasis, intellectuals, merchants, and peasants, hold diverse conceptions of identity. Uyghur intellectuals define themselves in opposition to the Hans and identify strongly with the larger Turkic world of western Central Asia and Turkey that lies to the west of Xinjiang. They are secular, virulently anti-Islamic, pan-Turkic nationalists. In contrast, middle-income and poor peasants, who for the most part do not travel outside their region, are devout Muslims and maintain strong oasis identities. Uyghur merchants who trade in China proper, in cities like Beijing and Shanghai, and wealthy peasants who benefit from China's development policies identify themselves as citizens of the Chinese state. These divergent Uyghur self-identifications at the local level pose the greatest challenge to intellectuals' efforts to shape an overarching Uyghur nationalist ideology.

It is best to view these contending versions of Uyghur nationalist ideology as negotiable experiments with history, subject to trial and error. The development of Uyghur nationalist ideology in this way follows Mahatma Gandhi's theory of cultural history, which is produced through struggle and experiment. Regarding Gandhi's theory, Richard Fox writes, "Opposition and struggle cultivate indeterminate outcomes precisely because the outcomes result from the experiments" (Fox 1989:29). This book has examined some of the outcomes of Uyghur intellectuals' struggles to develop and disseminate nationalist ideologies among an ethnic population that, more often than not, favors a localized and particularistic understanding of ethnic identity and shows little or no interest in pan-Uyghur notions. For example, intellectuals have added certain heroes to the present Uyghur genealogy, holding them up for emulation even though, historically, it is difficult to claim that these people would have considered themselves Uyghur. If a selected personage does not have the desired effect on the Uyghur populace after several years, another is adopted and the previous figure abandoned.

This is typical of the nationalist ideology definition process in the greater Turkic area and nationalist revitalization movements throughout the world. Historical events and personages are infused with meaning and can be mobilized for modern political purposes. The creation of nationalist ideology is not a dialectic process, in which one ideology wins out over the others; instead, it is dialogic: several approaches coexist, holding more salience in some regions than in others. Changes can be made within these ideologies if a strategy does not have the desired effect.

Uyghur intellectuals' writing of history aims to remove what is distasteful from the past and embellish that which is considered glorious and complimentary to Uyghur culture. In this way, intellectuals create a view of the past that is more conducive to the development of Uyghur pride and self-respect. Like a mental patient who cannot become healthy without first understanding his personal past, so too an ethnic nationality cannot become strong without discovering its collective past—whether mythic or real.

As Bernard Lewis in *History—Remembered, Recovered, Reinvented* points out, however, such work is sometimes subversive and potentially dangerous to the governing power:

> Sometimes the purpose . . . is not to legitimize authority but to undermine it—to assert new claims and new arguments, sometimes even a new identity, in conflict with the old order. An obvious example of this is nationalist history—usually of little value to the historian, except for the historian of nationalism, but invaluable to him.   (1975:64)

The struggle over history now being waged in Xinjiang between the Uyghur intellectuals and the Chinese state is filled with both opportunities and dangers. Uyghurs may encounter great danger should they function purely within the confines of an abstract intellectualism, failing to address the urgent problems of social justice in Xinjiang in favor of an esoteric preoccupation with the past. Uyghurs critical of projects such as those that claim non-Uyghurs as heroes believe these projects renounce the present and the future in the name of a mythical past, ultimately leading nowhere. Bernard Lewis explains,

> Historical choices have their dangers. . . . Care is needed not to carry history beyond the stage of recovery to that of illusion. Dedication and courage are both noble and necessary—but they must not lead again to destruction in a dead end of history.   (1975:102)

History is always illusory in some sense, but, like the historiographers Lewis cautions, Uyghurs fighting for social change and government amelioration of their people's condition should avoid indulging in a mythic past that prevents them from focusing on present, more pressing needs.

Although Islam causes a religious and ideological separation between the Uyghurs and the Hans, the Chinese liberalization of policies related to religion has been an important factor in fostering positive sentiment among Turpan Uyghur peasants and merchants toward the Chinese government. The growth of Islamic tradition at the local level is extremely significant because it can encourage resistance to Chinese acculturation, or at least simple indifference to and withdrawal from the overarching PRC-Chinese society. Thus, the Chinese government is caught in a familiar and recurrent dilemma: if it suppresses the local religion (in this case, Islam), Uyghurs will feel oppressed and oppose the government; if it encourages Islam, the Uyghurs, though more content with the government, may feel more separate from Chinese society. It is the same dilemma that confronts China in Tibet and with Chinese Muslims throughout China.[1]

China and the Islamic world meet in Central Asia; Xinjiang has now become the "pivot of Asia," as Owen Lattimore called it. Ethnic barriers and profound interethnic disputes pervade Central Asian countries. Tajikistan is afraid it will be eclipsed by Uzbekistan, Uzbekistan and Kazakstan are competing with each other for dominance of Central Asia, and there are too many Russians in Kazakstan for Kazak nationalism to be viable. The region may seem a natural unit, but as in the case of Xinjiang, a common language and religion cannot transcend its subcultures.

Economic development is as key to stability in China and Xinjiang as in Central Asia. By promoting economic development in Central Asia, China could maintain stability on both sides of the border and assert its influence. However, Beijing continues its attempts to bolster Xinjiang's industry by relocating more Hans there, seemingly without considering whether these development schemes are sustainable or whether they will cause environmental destruction and/or undermine local cultures. This kind of development has proven politically dangerous in the recent past; such projects and social programs have led to rioting.

In April 1990, Uyghurs and Kyrgyz clashed near Kashgar over the suspension of mosque construction and over birth-control policies. An estimated fifty people were killed and the province was closed for several months. In September of 1991, there were reports of guns being smuggled into Xinjiang from Afghanistan and Pakistan. In February 1992, at least six people died in a bus bombing in Urumchi. There were also rumors of a "Front for the Liberation of Uyghuristan" planning its operations from Kazakstan (Harris 1993:118). In the summer of 1993, a bomb blast ripped through a building across from the Seman Hotel in Kashgar, killing three people. In 1995, Uyghurs rioted in Khotan after government officials failed to clear the streets of mosque worshippers who were so numerous their overflow blocked traffic, and arrested the head *molla* of the mosque, who refused to help.

An even greater escalation of violence, creating tremendous Uyghur disaffection, took place in 1996 as the government launched its "Strike Hard" anticrime campaign, broadening it to crack down on Uyghur national splittist (separatist) groups. In one of the most serious incidents, nine Uyghurs armed with guns and homemade bombs were killed by police in Kucha. Xinjiang Public Security announced that more than 2,700 terrorists, murderers, and other criminals, presumably of various ethnic groups, as well as 4,000 sticks of dynamite, 6,000 pounds of explosives, 30,000 rounds of ammunition, and 600 firearms were captured in two months (Macartney 1996).

In response to the "Strike Hard" campaign, Uyghur antigovernment protests, violence, and terrorist activities have reached levels unprecedented since Communist control of Xinjiang. A grave series of protests began in Ili on February 5 and 6, 1997, as over 100 Uyghur students brandishing blue East Turkestan Republic flags and seeking an end to China's rule in Xinjiang were fired upon by police. As many as 31 were killed and nearly 200 were wounded. Following these riots, more than ten anti-Chinese demonstrations took place in Ili, one involving more than 5,000 Uyghurs. In response to the Ili deaths, Uyghur separatists first derailed a train filled primarily with ethnic Hans traveling from Lanzhou to Urumchi on February 12, and then on February 25, in a shocking act of contempt and disrespect, bombed three Urumchi buses to coincide with the state funeral for Chinese leader Deng Xiaoping. As many as 23 were killed and 74 injured. Ten days later, Uyghur separatists, in the first attack on China's capital, exploded a pipe bomb on a bus in Beijing's busiest shopping district, Xidan (Jiang An 1997). The following week, Uyghur separatists targeted the Chinese military, bombing an installation in southern Xinjiang. Two exiled Uyghur groups in Kazakstan, the United National Revolutionary Front and the Organization for East Turkestan Freedom, have claimed responsibility for most of the bombings and warn that more bombings will come until independence is won for Xinjiang.

CAUSE FOR HOPE

There are Uyghurs who dream of independence and claim that their absorption into the Chinese state is as much a form of colonization as

Britain's control of Hong Kong. Many call for an independent East Turkestan nation within territorially defined borders; they claim that without a state they are both deprived and exploited. The danger of such a belief is that it can lead Uyghurs into self-destructive actions and behavior resulting in the degradation of their people. Many Uyghurs, especially those who influence Uyghur popular opinion, believe that this danger must be taken seriously.

There are also Uyghurs who believe it possible to push for a revitalization of their people within the political and social framework of the Chinese government—without threatening the Chinese state. For example, some intellectuals have proposed to unite with religious leaders to carry out a health education campaign combined with a religious campaign against alcohol. Focusing on health can downplay the religious implications of the movement and diminish government resistance to such a program.

Some Uyghurs draw hope from current policies that indicate it is in China's interest to foster the development of historical trade networks. They believe it is also beneficial for China to increase the number of Uyghurs who leave the country to visit relatives, and thereby increase and strengthen trade networks. In this way, as some Uyghur economists believe, the historical role of Uyghurs as middlemen will be revitalized and will help to connect China with the world to the west. Xinjiang Uyghurs are in a position to play a major role in forging these relations.

Growing awareness among Uyghur intellectuals of the importance of historical knowledge, combined with the relaxation of restrictions in educational curricula, is leading to greater use of texts about Xinjiang history in schools. These intellectuals hold that Uyghur pride, enhanced by knowledge newly gained about the history of their people, especially their long relationship with China, is crucial to the future of the region. Unlike the Central Asians in the Soviet Union, who were taught by Soviet ideology that they were a backward people awaiting the civilizing influence of the Russians, Uyghurs are learning that they are the inheritors of a great civilization with its own glorious achievements, upon which they can build their national pride and self-respect. Hope for the Uyghurs lies in understanding their history as disseminated by teachers and writers and their subsequent action upon that understanding. Uyghur historians and writers, like Hami's Abdurehim Ötkür and Turpan's Muhammät Shah Niyaz, have argued that Uyghurs must not treat their situation as an evil imposed by an enemy, to be rebelled against through destructive means. Instead, Uyghurs must view it as a challenge that will allow them to display their best and create a Uyghur nation worthy of their history.

Understanding Uyghur history, it is possible to envision a future breakdown of the modern Uyghur people along historical and geographical lines—somewhat like that of the former Yugoslavia, though probably much less bloody. But perhaps in their growing recognition of these historical divisions, the Uyghurs will be able to work with, rather than against, the Chinese government. Otherwise, as one Turpan intellectual conjectured, if the struggle over Uyghur nationalist ideology becomes an "us vs. them," Turpan poet Abduhaliq's prediction will come true: "The future will hold much hardship, much hardship."

The Uyghur people are faced with a conscious historical choice. They can either build their future, or renounce the present and that future in their preoccupation with the past. The latter choice could lead to destruction, to open and violent confrontation with the Chinese state resulting in tragic massacres such as the one at Tiananmen Square in 1989. With the example of authors such as Abdurehim Ötkür guiding the Uyghurs, however, the recovery of their history may and can lead to a better future.

In Abdurehim Ötkür's book Iz (Traces), a camel caravan through the Täklimakan Desert is the symbol of the history of the Uyghur people. The desert is a metaphor of the eternal flux of history and the caravan is the finite events that lead to a destination in an unforeseen way. According to Abdurehim, no experience in the past is in vain, for traces of the paths taken by one's ancestors provide lessons for the future (Allworth and Pahta 1988:19). These traces will never be swept away—they are waiting to be discovered by the generations to follow. The opening stanzas of Abdurehim Ötkür's novel come from his famous poem, also entitled Iz (Traces)(see figure 6.8):

If the sand blows hard,
  Even if the dunes shift,
They will scarcely bury our trace.
From the route of the ceaseless caravan,
  Although the horses grow terribly thin,
Our grandchildren, our great grandchildren
  Will most assuredly find
This trace one day,
  Without question.
Abdurehim Ötkür (1985:1), translation adapted from Allworth and Pahta (1988:20)

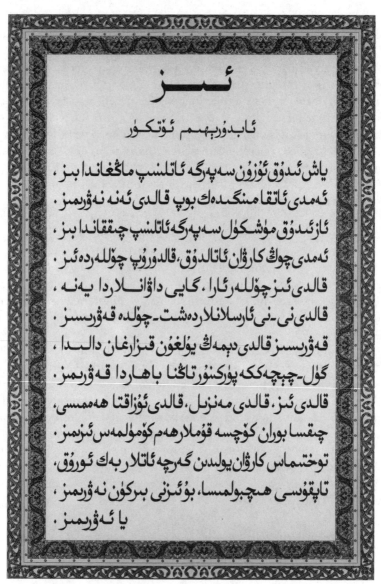

FIGURE 6.8   Poem *Iz (Traces)* by Abdurehim Ötkür.
SOURCE: Xinjiang Youth Press, Urumchi, 1994.

The search for history, the wrestling with and recovery of local heroes and oasis identities, may propel the Uyghurs to a better future, with prospects for greater autonomy, heightened respect from the Han Chinese, a better standard of living, freedom of travel and trade with the independent Central Asian republics, and perhaps—though unlikely— independence from China.

History leaves the traces in the desert of which Abdurehim speaks. Most Uyghur intellectuals feel that it is their task to recover these traces and make them live again, as if breathing life into their ancestors' desiccated bones. In the end, it is up to all Uyghurs to use these traces, these bones, for their collective awakening—as the words of the Turpan poet Abdukhaliq "Uyghur" say:

Hey! Uyghur, it is time to awaken.

Notes

You have nothing to fear.
—"Uyghur," "Awaken! (*Oyghan*)"

Introduction

1. On the Uyghur Empire, see Mackerras (1972 and 1990). For trade between China and the Uyghur Empire, see Mackerras (1969). On the symbiotic relationship between China and the Uyghur Empire, see Barfield (1989).

2. The notations C.E. (Common Era) and B.C.E. (Before the Common Era) denote years corresponding to A.D. and B.C., respectively, but are religiously neutral.

3. On religions practiced in Central Asia, see Menges (1991). On Buddhism in Turpan, see Meng (1982); on Manichaeanism in Turpan, see Legge (1913).

4. On Uyghuristan, see Oda (1978).

5. See Sadri (1984) for more on TIRET.

6. See Chan (1969) on Sheng Shicai's rise to power.

7. For more on the name *Uyghur*, see Clauson (1963).

8. On the influence of the Soviet nationalities model on Chinese minority policies, see Bergere (1979).

9. The dissertation based on this field research (Rudelson 1992) is entitled "Bones in the Sand: The Struggle to Create Uighur Nationalist Ideology and Ethnic Identity in Xinjiang, China."

1. Who Are the Uyghurs?

1. The highest temperatures are above 47°C. Temperatures range from between -2.8°C (January) and 40.0°C (July). The yearly average temperature is 14.7°C. The frost-free period averages 268.6 days (maximum 324, minimum 217). The annual

mean precipitation in Turpan district is a mere 15mm; in Tohsun the annual precipitation is only 3.9mm. Turpan is also affected by strong winds, which are hot and dry, from April to July. The annual mean storm duration is 36.2 days for Turpan (maximum 68 days, 1961) [figures from Hoppe (1987:24–26) and Xia and Hu (1978)]. For Western sources on Turpan geography, see Schomberg (1928 and 1928a) and Stein (1933:236–46). For the distribution of Xinjiang population by country, see Xinjiang Weiwuer Zizhiqu Tongjiju (1992).

2. On the relationship of the Oirats to East Turkestan, see Akimushkin (1974).

3. For a comparison of late Qing policy in Xinjiang, Tibet, and Mongolia, see Fletcher (1978a).

4. For a linguistic study of Turkic languages, see Baskakov (1986).

5. On the Russian national minority of Xinjiang and China, see Svanberg (1988) and Svanberg and Benson (1989).

6. There is also a population of "Säriq" or "Yellow" Uyghurs who are found mainly in Gansu province and who practice Lama Buddhism. This group, officially called "Yugur" by the Chinese, were part of the Uyghur Confederacy (745–840 C.E.). They consider that the Uyghurs of Xinjiang sold out by adopting Islam and giving up Buddhism. For further information on the Yellow Uyghurs, see Malov (1967), Mannerheim (1911), and Li Shangcheng (1983) and (1984). Uyghurs sent to Hunan during the Ming dynasty in the fourteenth century today number 5,000 and live in Taoyuan County, northwest of Changsha in Hunan Province.

7. On the Dolans, see Svanberg (1989) and (1996). For linguistic differences among the Uyghurs, see Hahn (1986:35–54).

8. For a description of the Lopliks, see Lop Lake Comprehensive Scientific Expedition Team (1985), Prejevalsky (1879:104–15), and Svanberg (1987:57–81).

9. See Bruk (1956).

10. For the history of Kashgar, see Bellew (1875). For ethnographic descriptions, see Kuropatkin (1882) and Pevtsov (1982). For a guide to present-day Kashgar, see Li Kai (1988).

11. On the *khojas* of Xinjiang, see Schwarz (1976) and Saguchi (1968).

12. For studies of Yaqub Beg, see Kim (1986) and Yuan (1961).

13. For early British contacts in the initial stages of the Great Game, see Bellew (1875).

14. On British and Russian activities in Xinjiang from 1890 to 1918, see Skrine and Nightingale (1973).

15. See Wiens (1969) and Moseley (1966).

16. For a study of Turks in China under the Mongols, see De Rachewiltz (1983).

17. The geography of the Turpan Depression is described in Schomberg (1928) and (1928a).

18. The origin of the name *Turpan*, variations of which are *Turfan* and *Tu-lu-fan*, is under debate. For one very strong position, see Mair (1990).

19. See Alptekin (1987). On pan-Turkism, see Benson and Svanberg (1988: 79–80).

20. Svanberg (1989c) and (1989a:170–71). For the dissident movement in Turkey from the perspective of Isa Yusup's son, Erkin, see Alptekin (1986).

21. McMillen calls Xinjiang on the eve of Communist takeover "an autonomous appendage of the Chinese state" (1979:25). For a study of regional underdevelopment, see Rhodes (1970).

22. The most informative book on the changes in Xinjiang since Communist takeover of the region is Donald McMillen's *Chinese Communist Power and Policy in Xinjiang 1949–1977* (1979). Much of the information in this section is based on this study. On China's colonization in other regions, see Lattimore (1932).

23. Two excellent studies of core-periphery integration are Allen (1986) and Chase-Dunn and Hall (1991).

24. For more on the incorporation of Xinjiang, see Li Chang (1954).

25. For demographic studies of Xinjiang, see Bruk (1956), Freeberne (1966), and Liao (1989).

26. The industrialization created many urban centers in Xinjiang. Major ones include Hami (trade and manufacturing), Yarkand (trade and textiles), Shihezi (reclamation and manufacturing), Tacheng (trade), Altay (mining, reclamation, and animal husbandry), Khotan (trade and textiles), Aksu (trade and agriculture), Karamay (petroleum), Qitai (agriculture), Turpan (agriculture and fruit), Korla (trade), Wusu (trade and oil refining), and Dushanzi (oil refining) [McMillen 1979:13]. For comparison with the Soviet incorporation of Soviet Central Asia, see Bennigsen (1975).

27. The expansion of industrialization caused an equal expansion in cultivated land, which was centered increasingly more in northern Xinjiang than in the south. In 1885, only 7 percent of the cultivated land was in the north. That had risen to 29.4 percent in the 1944–1949 period, and to 38.4 percent in the 1962–1963 period. The expansion of agriculture was to provide food for the workers extracting Zhungarian oil, coal, iron ore, and other strategic mineral resources in northern Xinjiang (Wiens 1966:84, 88). See also Clubb (1958).

28. The PCC have also participated in road and railway construction and the establishment of light, medium, and heavy industry in Xinjiang.

29. For sources on the PCC, see Esposito (1974) and (1977). Military control from 1949 to 1955 is discussed in Benson and Svanberg (1988:62–66) and the politics of the region is summarized (1988:62–75). See also McMillen (1982) and Reed (1978).

30. The incorporation of Xinjiang into the People's Republic of China is best viewed as a form of internal colonialism as described by Hechter (1977).

2. Oasis Identities and Cross-Border Influence

1. My idea of Xinjiang's geographic template is based on Braudel's (1976) approach to the Mediterranean Sea and the geographic forces of the lands surrounding it that influenced Mediterranean cultures and their interactions.

2. These divisions are similar to those found in Chvyr (1990), who separates the Uyghurs into three types, Northeast, West, and Southeast. She explains the divisions by their contacts with, respectively, Middle Asian, Central Asian, and Far Eastern peoples. She specifically compares dress and shows these three avenues of contact. Hoppe (1987a) makes similar divisions to those I have made except that he limits Turpan's influence eastward and does not include Urumchi within the Turpan sphere.

3. See Zhang Hengde et al. (1983) for further information on Uyghur folk caps.

4. This is similar to the semiotics of yarmulkes among Jews in Israel. Black yarmulkes imply orthodoxy and are usually worn by Hassidic Jews. Knit yarmulkes imply modern orthodoxy, and black knit yarmulkes are worn by modern orthodox Jews sympathetic with Hassidism.

5. These arguments were developed in Rudelson (1992), (1993), and (1994).

6. On Sufism in the Soviet Union, see Bennigsen and Lemercier-Quelquejay (1986).

7. See Aubin (1987). See also Geertz (1973:87–125) and Eikelman (1982).

8. See Waardenburg (1990), Israeli (1981), and Gladney (1991).

9. For studies of the persistence of Islam, see Waardernburg (1990) and Graham (1983).

10. For more on the Abdals, see Svanberg (1989b).

11. For studies of how Islamic identity is reinforced at the local level, see Jarring (1984–1986).

12. On the *hajj* in Islamic law, see Masud (1990).

13. Jarring (1949–1951:102) writes that the Uyghurs who went on the *hajj* went through Rawalpindi.

14. See Benson and Svanberg (1988) and Jackson (1962).

15. This rail link has been projected for a very long time, perhaps even without Chinese knowledge. When Mannerheim traveled through Russian Central Asia, he noticed a map "that showed the principal railway lines of Europe, roughly and often incorrectly indicated. . . . Two dotted lines indicated the future main railways of China, one via Kalgan and Urga up to its junction with the Russian Siberian railway, the other via Lanchow to Hami, where it divided, the northern branch running along the northern foot of the Tianshan to Qulja, while the southern branch extended via Aqsu and Kashgar to Andijan" (1969 [1942]:312).

16. See Nyman (1976) and Karpat (1979).

17. On Japanese interest in Xinjiang in the early 1900s, see Nyman (1977).

18. For information on Soviet Uyghurs today, see Narinbaev (1991:119–29).

19. For a look at how transnational contacts have affected Xinjiang's economy, see Christofferson (1993).

20. For extensive research on the Tungans (Hui) throughout China, see Dreyer (1982), Pillsbury (1984), Lipman (1984) and (1987), and Gladney (1991).

21. For general information on minority education in China, see Lofstedt (1987); for comparisons with education in former Soviet Uzbekistan, see Medlin (1971).

22. For more on the worship of Islamic saints, see Hamada (1978), and Gladney (1987).

23. On grape planting, see Jarring (1949–1951:46–50); Yang Chengshi, Bo Yulin, and Yang Guizhen (1979); Li Zhichao et al. (1988); and Meng Kehuang and Yang Chengshi (1980). For Uyghur folklore on grapes, see Jarring (1986). See also the short story about Grape Valley by Zordun Sabir (1983).

24. For a study of irrigation in Xinjiang, see Golab (1951).

25. On *karez* construction, see Cressey (1958) and Huntington (1907).

26. On shepherds and transhumance, see Jarring (1949–1951:57–62).

27. For a description of cotton growing, wheat cultivation, and melon cultivation in Guma, see Jarring (1949–1951:24–28, 34–36, and 37–45).

3. Local Identities and Turpan Ideologies

1. Owen Lattimore quotes an educated Uyghur in the late 1920s who stated "The people of Turfan really represent the ancient Uyghurs, but have totally forgotten their own origin and written language since the Mohammedan conversion nearly a millennium ago" (1975 [1930]:165).

2. Perhaps the most disconcerting phenomenon I experienced as a Jew while conducting fieldwork in Turpan was the daily "Heil Hitler" salutes and greetings I received.

3. Today Germans still speak of Indo-Germanic culture rather than Indo-European culture. On these Central Asian roots of Indo-European culture, see Gamkredlidze (1990, esp. 13).

4. There is a *Uyghur-Han Dictionary* (Xinjiang University Chinese Language Department 1982); and an *English-Uyghur Dictionary* (Änwär Päyzulla 1988).

5. For Chinese articles on Uyghur names, see Rewäydula (1982) and Du Shaoyuan (1983).

6. Smith mentions visits to a *tekkes*, a convent for dervishes, in Turkey by Xinjiang Sufis, including some from Turpan (1980:132).

7. See Jarring (1949–1951:117–26), who mentions the Islamic education of children and (160–62) a Uyghur account of the Hanfiyah school of Islam.

8. See Basilov (1976); Snesarev (1970–1971:204–25), (1971:329–52), (1972–1973: 219–53); and Jarring (1961).

9. On ghosts, spirits, the evil eye, and bogeymen, see Dankoff (1975:74–76) and Castagné (1930). On *jins* and *alwaste*, see Snesarev (1971:330) and Jarring (1979).

10. Carol Delaney (1988:90) writes that "the first forty days after birth are analogous to the first forty days of gestation. It is a creative and precarious time when life is held in balance."

11. For more on the placenta, see also Roux (1963:87).

12. On the use of lighted fire in a cemetery to cure illnesses such as deafness, sterility, and malaria, see Jarring (1979:3–21). On curing and exorcizing evil spirits, see Jarring (1949–1951:163–67).

13. On Hui marriage customs, see Sharma (1989).

14. Red is a symbol of joy shared by Hans and Uyghurs. Among Hans, brides wear red bridal gowns, neighbors and relatives explode red firecrackers, and red lanterns illuminate the groom's home. During a Han wedding, red is ever present. Among the Uyghurs, red is less flamboyantly displayed. The bride and groom each wear a piece of red fabric, and the car that carries the bride to the groom's home is decorated with red silk.

15. See Jarring (1949–1951:108–16) for a description of a wedding ceremony in southern Xinjiang. For comparison with Uzbek customs see Lobacheva (1967) and (1981–1982), which is also published in Russian (Lobacheva 1981).

16. Mention of this "ransom" performed among the Uzbeks is found in Lobacheva (1967).

17. The use of flat bread and of objects circling over the head of the bride is mentioned in Laude-Cirtautus (1972:44–45).

18. The burning of plants and seeds by the Uzbeks to ward off evil is found in Laude-Cirtautus (1972)

4. Social Group Identity in Turpan

1. Uyghur money changers congregated in all major Chinese cities until 1995, when the government eliminated the Foreign Exchange Certificates (FECs) used by foreigners in China. Many money chnagers attempted to collect U.S. dollars to send relatives to Mecca on the *hajj*. Uyghur money changers were also found in large numbers over a thousand years ago in the Tang dynasty capital Chang'an (today Xi'an).

2. On Uyghur script changes and Uyghur language, see Jarring (1981), Raquette (1927), Hamit Tömür (1987), Zhao Shijie (1981), Ablät Qasim (1989), and Gulam Ghopuri (1986). For a Uyghur translation of a Russian book on Turkic languages, see Baskakov (1986).

3. For an interview with Wang Enmao, see *Minzu Tuanjie* (Sept. 1982:7–9). For nationality policy specific to Xinjiang, see Singer (1984).

4. These undesirables included landlords, rich peasants, counterrevolutionaries, bad elements, rightists, capitalists, and intellectuals.

5. On Islam and birth control in Muslim minority areas of China, see Winters (1985).

6. Birth-control methods are distributed in the village clinic. Five kinds are used: IUDs, condoms, spermicide-covered sponges, birth-control pills, and shots of progesterone administered once a month, five days after the start of menstruation. The shot is the preferred method because it only needs to be administered once and the date of injection is easy to calculate.

7. This is vastly different from villages throughout most of the developing world, where peasants are migrating to the major cities in ever-increasing numbers and do not invest in the improvement of their own villages.

8. See "Shelter Belts" in Xia and Hu (1978:79–85), and Fan Zhiyuan (1963).

9. On trade among the Turkic peoples of China, see Chen Ching Lung (1981).

10. The population of Grape Valley as of 1988 was 20,322, of which 5,060 adult workers were male and 4,650 female. Üzümchilik is divided into sixteen large teams. From the top of the mountain to the bottom of the valley these teams are as follows: 1) Subeshi, 2) Aymula Mechit, 3) Buyluq, 4) Bäshmal, 5) Dapsay, 6) Chilanluq, 7) Baghar, 8) Tashtokhan, 9) Minar, 10) Khanim Jay, 11) Khuyla Karez, 12) Yingsa, 13) Da Qiao, 14) Bulaq, 15) Beilekchi Karez, 16) Tietir.

11. Each brick costs .05 *yuan* or 5 *fen*. A normal home will use about 35,000 bricks. Only the outside of the home is converted to bricks; the inner remains adobe. Many houses face south so they are warmed by the sun. In the summer water is thrown on the brick or mud floor to keep the temperature cool. Water is also tossed onto the dusty streets in the mornings during the hot months to keep down the dust.

12. See Morden (1927) and Hedin (1931).

13. For articles dealing with the question of Uyghur identity, see Helly (1984) and Kanat (1986).

14. On the Ummah, see van Nienwenhuijze (1969).

5. Uyghur Intellectuals: The Path of the Strong

1. Svanberg (1989a:128) mentions the Central Asian custom of giving a child, especially the first born, to the father's parents for adoption out of respect for the father. Kazaks, for example, consider that having a young child in the home will keep the elderly adoptive parents youthful. In this arrangement the child calls his biological father "older brother."

2. See Jin Bingzhe (1990).

3. See Wu (1944). Prior to 1949 there were actually fourteen nationalities, but one of these, the Taranchi who live in the Ili region, has since been reclassified as Uyghur.

4. To compare the double life of Uyghurs, straddling both Chinese and Uyghur cultures, with Uzbeks in Soviet Uzbekistan, see Lubin (1981) and McKenna (1969).

5. This event is also mentioned in Gladney (1990a:62). A similar protest occurred in Beijing a week earlier. See *Huaqiao-Ribao* (1989) and Gladney (1991:2–7).

6. For more on Urkesh, see Gladney (1991:294–296). See also Gladney (1990a:62–63) and Bernstein (1989).

7. See Emerson (1990) in the international edition of *Newsweek*.

8. For Soviet involvement in Xinjiang from 1928–1949, see Hasiotis (1981).

9. See McMillen (1984).

10. McMillen (1979), Dreyer (1976), and Lal (1970).

11. On the first decade of Communist control, see Lo (1961). For the socioeconomic transformation of Xinjiang, see Benson and Svanberg (1988) and Helly (1984).

12. McMillen (1979:42) delineates the following reasons for the Communist Chinese's careful policy in Xinjiang:

1) The existence of strong traditional tendencies among the local nationalities toward autonomy and even separation.

2) The presence of distinct cultures, languages, and religions in the primarily non-Han area.

3) The endurance of a Moscow-oriented communist movement and Soviet influence in the area.

4) The continued resistance by counterrevolutionary and bandit elements in much of Xinjiang during the early postliberation period.

5) The great distances within the province and between Xinjiang and China proper, which were amplified by the inadequate nature of the existing transportation and communications network.

13. See el-Zein (1986) and Piscatori (1986). Similar conclusions are made by Michael Rywkin (1982).

14. This claim has been made by many scholars of this area. See Benson and Svanberg (1988:45), Nyman (1977:19–20), Lattimore (1950:54–55), and Forbes (1986:11–37).

15. In 1985 the only complete history up to the nineteenth century was Liu Zhixiao's *Weiwuer Lishi* (Uyghur History) (1985), which was widely criticized by Uyghur intellectuals. Liu, a Han, wrote the original text in Uyghur, and it was later translated into Mandarin. I was very impressed with Liu's balanced and daring attempt since any book written by a Han about Uyghur history was sure to provoke strong criticisms from Uyghur scholars. His book provided the catalyst for Uyghur intellectuals to contest official government versions of Uyghur history.

16. For articles about the "Fragrant Concubine," see Millward (1994), Mähmutjan Abduqadir (1988), and background material in Terzani (1985).

17. For an excellent study of Soviet revision of a Turkic epic, see Paksoy (1989). The Chinese have enthusiastically sponsored the publication of Uyghur folktales and stories; see Liu Fajun (1980).

18. See Lang Ying (1986). See also Yusuf Khass Hajib Balasagun (1983).

19. See Päkhridin (1979) and Gigliesi and Friend (1982).

20. On the appropriation and official sponsorship of non-Islamic traditional holidays in the Soviet Union, see Rorlich (1983).

6. The Future of the Uyghur Past

1. For the effects of publishing on nationalism in Soviet Central Asia, see Allworth (1965).

2. This is according to Muhammät Shah Niyaz, a Turpan Uyghur who is the author of a three-volume biography of Abdukhaliq.

3. Rudelson (1988) as cited in Gladney (1990:22).

4. For his autobiography, see Burhan Shähidi (1984).

5. Linda Benson (1990a) mentions this in her book *The Ili Rebellion*.

6. See Terzani (1985:228–29).

7. On the background of Mähmud Qäshqäri see Pritsak (1951–1953:243–46), Devereux (1959), and Dankoff (1975).

8. See Svanberg (1989a:173), which shows the front page of the fascist Turkish magazine *Turkeli* with its wolf symbol.

9. The photo of this mummy and a reconstruction of her likeness appear in Allen (1996:50–51). Geng Shimin (1982:109) reports that in 1981 in Lop Nor a mummified girl carbon-dated at 6,500 years old was discovered. Geng writes "She has golden hair and a European nose." The radiocarbon dating was questioned by Japanese scholars because Lop Nor is China's nuclear test site and therefore the dating samples are likely contaminated. Hadingham (1994) and Allen (1996), in articles on the mummies of Xinjiang, provide rarely seen photographs of these "Caucasian" mummies. Rudelson (1996) discusses the mummies in relation to Uyghur nationalism.

10. See Fischer (1970) and Lowenthal (1975).

11. On prominent Uyghur political figures during this period, see Benson (1991).

12. For a firsthand report from Xinjiang in 1948 on the Ili Rebellion, see Barnett (1963). See also Mingulov (1963).

13. For a Uyghur view of the life of Genghis Khan, see Molla Mirsali Qäshqäri (1985).

14. Biographical information on Ähmätjan Qasimi and the manipulation of Ähmätjan as a hero by the Communist Chinese can be found in Benson (1990). A two-volume study of Ähmätjan Qasimi's life has been published in Xinjiang (Abdurakhman Äbäy 1984, 1987).

15. See also Abdurehim Ötkür's study of Yusuf Khass Hajib Balasagun and Uyghur literature (Abdurehim Ötkür 1986a). For information on Abdurehim Ötkür's book *Iz*, see Allworth and Pahta (1988).

16. For a description of pre-Communist Hami, see Zhou (1948).

17. For biographical information on Khoja Niyaz, see Boorman (1967–1979: 58–61).

7. "Hey! Uyghur, it is time to awaken."

1. On ethnic protests against China's religious policies, see Schwartz (1994) on the Tibetan uprising and Gladney (1991) on the Chinese Muslims.

Bibliography

Have you not heard me yet?
—"Uyghur," "Awaken! (*Oyghan*)"

Abdurakhman Äbäy. 1984, 1987. *Ahmetjan Qasimi Haqqida Hikayilar* (*Stories about Ahmetjan Qasimi*). Urumchi: Xinjiang People's Publishing.

Abdurehim Ötkür. 1985. *Iz* (*Traces*). Urumchi: Xinjiang People's Publishing.

———. 1986. *Oyghanghan Zemin I* (*The Awakening Land, Part I*). Urumchi: Xinjiang People's Publishing.

———. 1986a. "Yusufu Hasi-Hajifu yu Weiwuer Wenxue." *Xinjiang Shehui Kexue* 6:73–92.

———. 1994. *Oyghanghan Zemin II* (*The Awakening Land, Part II*). Urumchi: Xinjiang People's Publishing.

Abdurusul Ömär, ed. 1986. *Abdukhaliq Uyghur Sheirliri*. Urumchi: Xinjiang People's Publishing.

Ablät Qasim, ed. 1989. *Uyghur Tili* (*Uyghur Language*). Urumchi: Xinjiang Education Press.

Akimushkin, O. F. 1974. "Le Turkestan Oriental et Les Oirats." *Études Mongoles* 5:157–63.

Allen, James P. 1986. "Core-Periphery Systems as a Framework for Crosscultural Perspectives in World Regional Geography." In Liucija Baskauskas, ed., *Unmasking Culture*, 119–39. Novato, Calif.: Chandler and Sharp.

Allen, Thomas B. 1996. "The Silk Road's Lost World." *National Geographic* 189 (3): 44–51.

———. 1996a. "Xinjiang." *National Geographic* 189 (3): 2–43.

Allsen, Thomas T. 1983. "The Yuan Dynasty and the Uighurs of Turfan in the 13th Century." In Morris Rossabi, ed., *China Among Equals*, 243–80. Berkeley: University of California Press.

Allworth, Edward. 1965. *Central Asian Publishing and the Rise of Nationalism*. New York: New York Public Library.

——. 1990. *The Modern Uzbeks: From the Fourteenth Century to the Present—A Cultural History*. Stanford: Hoover Institution Press.

Allworth, Edward and Gulamettin Pahta. 1988. "A Gentle, New Allegory by an Older Uyghur Author." *Doğu Türkistan'in Sesi* 5 (17): 19–20.

Alptekin, Erkin. 1986. "Eastern Turkistan After 32 Years of Exile." *Central Asian Survey* 1 (4): 149–53.

——. 1987. "The Uygurs." *Journal Institute of Muslim Minority Affairs* 8 (2): 302–10.

Anonymous. 1935. "Chinese Turkestan." *Journal of the Royal Central Asian Society* 22:469–70.

Änwär Päyzulla. 1988. *English-Uyghur Dictionary*. Urumchi: Xinjiang People's Publishing.

Aubin, Françoise. 1987. "Islam and the State in the People's Republic of China." In Olivier Carre, ed., *Islam and the State in the World Today*, 159–78. New Delhi: Manohar.

Barfield, Thomas. 1989. *The Perilous Frontier*. Cambridge, Mass.: Basil Blackwell.

Barnett, A. Doak. 1963. *China on the Eve of Communist Takeover*. New York: Praeger.

Basilov, V. 1976. "Shamanism in Central Asia." In A. Bharata, ed., *The Realm of the Extra-Human Agents and Audiences*, 149–57. The Hague: Mouton.

Baskakov, N. A. 1986. *Turki Tillar (Turkic Languages)*. Beijing: Nationalities Press.

Bellew, H. W. 1875. *Kashmir and Kashgar: A Narrative of the Journey of the Embassy to Kashgar in 1873–74*. London: Trubner.

Bennigsen, Alexandre. 1975. "The Bolshevik Conquest of the Moslem Borderlands." In Thomas Hammond, ed., *The Anatomy of Communist Takeovers*, 61–70. London: Yale.

—— and Chantal Lemercier-Quelquejay. 1986. *Le Soufi et le Commissaire: Le Confreries musulmanes en UrSS*. Paris: Seuil.

Benson, Linda. 1990. "Ahmetjan Kasimi: The Chinese Paradigm of an Uighur Cultural Hero." Paper presented at the Association of Asian Studies Meeting, New Orleans, April, 1990.

——. 1990a. *The Ili Rebellion*. New York: M. E. Sharpe.

——. 1991. "Uygur Politicians of the 1940's: Mehmet Emin Bugra, Isa Yusuf Alptekin and Mesut Sabri." *Central Asian Survey* 10 (4): 87–114.

—— and Ingvar Svanberg. 1988. "The Kazaks in Xinjiang." In Linda Benson and Ingvar Svanberg, eds., *The Kazaks of China: Essays on an Ethnic Minority*, 1–106. Uppsala: Almquist and Wiksell International.

Bergere, Marie-Claude. 1979. "L'influence du Modele Sovietique sur la politique des minorities Nationales en Chine." *Revue Française de Science Politique* 29 (3): 402–25.

Bernstein, Richard. 1989. "To Be Young and in China: A Colloquy." *The New York Times* 7 October, 11.

Bonavia, Judy. 1988. *The Silk Road: Collins Illustrated Guide*. London: Collins.

Boorman, Howard L., ed. 1967–1979. *Biographical Dictionary of Republican China* (3 vols). New York: Columbia University Press.

Braudel, Fernand. 1976. *The Mediterranean and the Mediterranean World in the Age of Philip II*. New York: Harper and Row.

——. 1988 [1986]. *The Identity of France.* New York: Harper and Row.

Bruk, S. I. 1956. "Etnichesky Sostav i rameshcheniya v Sin'czjanskom Uygurskom Avtonomnom Rayone Kitayskoi Narodnoi Respubliki." *Sovetskaia Etnografiya* 2: 89–94.

Burhan Shahidi. 1984. *Xinjiang Wushi Nian (Xinjiang: Fifty Years).* Beijing: Wenzhi Ziliao Chuban She.

Cable, Mildred with Francesca French. 1987 [1942]. *The Gobi Desert.* Boston: Beacon Press.

Castagné, Joseph. 1930. "Étude sur la Demonologie des Kazak Kirghizes." *L'Ethnographie* 21–22:1–22.

Chan, Gilbert F. L. 1969. "The Road to Power: Sheng Shi-tsai's Early Years in Sinkiang 1930–1934." *Journal of Oriental Studies* 7 (2): 224–61.

Chase-Dunn, Christopher and Thomas D. Hall, eds. 1991. *Core/Periphery Relations in Precaptialist Worlds.* Boulder: Westview Press.

Chen Ching Lung. 1981. "Trading Activities of the Turkish Peoples of China." *Central Asiatic Journal* 25:38–53.

Christoffersen, Gaye. 1993. "Xinjiang and the Great Islamic Circle: The Impact of Transnational Forces on Chinese Regional Economic Planning." *The China Quarterly* 133:130–51.

Chvyr, L. A. 1990. *Uiguri Vostochnogo Turkestana i Sosednie Narodi (The Uyghurs of Eastern Turkestan and Their Neighbors in the Late 19th and Early 20th Centuries).* Moscow: Nauka.

Clauson, Sir Gerald. 1963. "The Name Uighur." *Journal of the Royal Asiatic Society* 3–4:140–49.

Clubb, O. Edmund. 1958. "Economic Modernization in Sinkiang." *Far Eastern Survey* 27 (2): 17–23.

Cressey, George B. 1958. "Qanats, Karez, and Fogarras." *Geographical Journal* 48:27–44.

Dankoff, Robert. 1975. "Kashgari on the Beliefs and Superstitions of the Turks." *Journal of the American Oriental Society* 95 (1): 68–80.

Delaney, Carol. 1988. "Mortal Flow: Menstruation in Turkish Village Society." In Thomas Buckley and Alma Gottlieb, eds., *Blood Magic: The Anthropology of Menstruation,* 75–93. Berkeley: University of California Press.

De Rachewiltz, Igor. 1983. "Turks in China under the Mongols: A Preliminary Investigation of Turco-Mongol Relations in the 13th and 14th Centuries." In Morris Rossabi, ed., *China Among Equals,* 281–310. Berkeley: University of California Press.

Devereux, Robert. 1959. "Al-Kashgari and Early Turkish Islam." *The Muslim World* 1959:133–38.

Dreyer, June Teufel. 1976. *China's Forty Million: Minority Nationalities and National Integration in the PRC.* Cambridge: Harvard University Press.

——. 1982. "The Islamic Community in China." *Central Asian Survey* 1 (2–3): 31–60.

Du Shaoyuan. 1983. "Xinjiang Weiwuerzu Renming Chutan" (Introduction of Xinjiang Uyghur Names). *Zhongyang Minzu Xueyuan Xuebao* 3:68–75.

Eikelman, Dale F. 1982. "The Study of Islam in Local Contexts." *Contributions to Asian Studies* 17:1–16.

Emerson, Tony, et al. 1990. "The Other China." *Newsweek* (International Edition). 23 April: 8–12.

Esposito, Bruce J. 1974. "China's West in the Twentieth Century." *Military Review* 54 (1): 64–75.

——. 1977. "The Militiamen of Sinkiang." *Asian Quarterly* 2:163–72.

Fan Zhiyuan. 1963. "Tulufan Pendi De Fenghai Jizi Fanyu." (Mechanical Prevention of Wind Damage in the Turpan Depression). *Xinjing Nongye Kexue* 11:446–49.

Fischer, D. H. 1970. *Historians' Fallacies: Toward the Logic of Historical Thought*. New York: Harper and Row.

Fletcher, Joseph. 1978. "Ch'ing Inner Asia." In John K. Fairbank, ed., *The Cambridge History of China, Vol. 1: Late Ch'ing 1800–1911, Part I*, 35–106. Cambridge: Cambridge University Press.

——. 1978a. "The Heyday of the Ch'ing Order in Mongolia, Sinkiang, and Tibet." In John K. Fairbank, ed., *The Cambridge History of China, Vol. 10: Late Ch'ing 1800–1911, Part I*, 351–408. Cambridge: Cambridge University Press.

Forbes, Andrew D. W. 1986. *Warlords and Muslims in Chinese Central Asia*. Cambridge: Cambridge University Press.

Fox, Richard G. 1989. *Gandhian Utopia: Experiments with Culture*. Boston: Beacon Press.

——. 1990. Introduction to *Nationalist Ideologies and the Production of National Cultures* (American Ethnological Society Monograph Series, No. 2), 1–14. Washington, DC: American Anthropological Association.

Freeberne, Michael. 1966. "Changes in the Sinkiang Uighur Autonomous Region." *Population Studies* 20 (1): 103–24.

Gamkredlidze, Thomas V. 1990. "On the Problem of an Asiatic Original Homeland of the Proto-Indo-Europeans." In T. L. Markey and John A. C. Greppin, eds., *When Worlds Collide: Indo-Europeans and Pre-Indo-Europeans*, 5–14. Ann Arbor, Mich.: Karoma Publishers.

Geertz, Clifford. 1973. *The Interpretation of Cultures*. New York: Basic Books.

Geng Shimin. 1982. "Recent Chinese Research in Turkic Studies." *Central Asian Survey* 1 (1): 109–16.

Gheni Maynam and Keram Tursun, eds. 1988. *Turpan Tarikh Matiriyalliri (Turpan Historical Materials)*. Turpan People's Government. (Internal Circulation).

Gigliesi, Primerose and Robert C. Friend, trans. 1982. *The Effendi and the Pregnant Pot: Uighur Folktales from China*. Beijing: New World Press.

Gladney, Dru C. 1987. "Muslim Tombs and Ethnic Folklore: Charters for Hui Identity." *The Journal of Asian Studies* 46 (3): 495–532.

——. 1990. "The Ethnogenesis of Uighur." *Central Asian Survey* 9 (1): 1–28.

——. 1990a. "The Peoples of the People's Republic: Finally in the Vanguard?" *The Fletcher Forum of World Affairs* 14 (1): 62–76.

——. 1991. *Muslim Chinese: Ethnic Nationalism in the People's Republic*. Cambridge: Harvard University Press.

Golab, L. Wawrzyn. 1951. "A Study of Irrigation in East Turkestan." *Anthropos* 46:187–99.

Goldman, Merle and Timothy Cheek. 1987. "Introduction: Uncertain Change." In Merle Goldman et al., eds., *China's Intellectuals and the State*, 1–20. Cambridge: The Council on East Asian Studies/Harvard University.

Graham, William A. 1983. "Islam in the Mirror of Ritual." In Richard Havannisian and Speros Vryonis Jr., eds., *Islam's Understanding of Itself*, 53–71. Malibu, Calif.: Undena.

Gulam Ghopuri, ed. 1986. *Uyghur Kilassik Adibiyatidin Qisqichä Sözlük (An Abridged Dictionary of Classical Uyghur Literature)*. Beijing: Nationalities Press.

Guojia Tongjiju Renkou Tongjici (National Census Bureau, Population Census Division), ed. 1993. *Zhongguo Renkou Tongji Nianjian (China Population Statistics Yearbook)*. Kexue Jishu Wenxian Chubanshe (Scientific Technology Document Press).

——. 1993. *Zhongguo Renkou Tongji Nianjian 1992 (China Population Statistics Yearbook 1992)*. Zhongguo Tongji Chubanshe [China Census Publishers].

Hadingham, Evan. 1994. "The Mummies of Xinjiang." *Discover* (April): 68–77.

Hahn, Reinhard. 1986. "Modern Uighur Language Research in China: Four Recent Contributions Examined." *Central Asiatic Journal* 30 (1–2): 35–54.

Haji Nurhaji. 1983. *Qarakhanlarning Qisqichä Tarikhi (A Brief History of the Kara-Khanid)*. Urumchi: Xinjiang People's Publishing.

Hamada, Masami. 1978. "Islamic Saints and Their Mausoleums." *Acta Asiatica* 34:79–105.

Hamit Tömür. 1987. *Hazirqi Zaman Uyghur Tili Grammatikisi (Morfologiya) (Modern Uyghur Grammar [Morphology])*. Beijing: People's Publishing.

Haneda, Akira. 1978. "Introduction: The Problems of Turkicization and Islamization of East Turkestan." *Acta Asiatica* 34:1–21.

Hann, C. M. 1987. "Ethnic Games in Xinjiang: Anthropological Approaches." Paper presented at University of London (SOAS), April.

Harris, Lillian Craig. 1993. "Xinjiang, Central Asia and the Implications for China's Policy in the Islamic World." *The China Quarterly* (133):111–29.

Hasiotis Jr., A. C. 1981. "A Study of Soviet Political, Economic, and Military Involvements in Xinjiang 1928–1949." Ph.D. dissertation, New York University.

Hechter, Michael. 1977. *Internal Colonialism: The Celtic Fringe in British National Development*. Berkeley: University of California Press.

Hedin, Sven. 1931. *Across the Gobi Desert*. London: G. Routledge and Sons.

Helly, Denise. 1984. "The Identity and Nationality Problem in Chinese Central Asia." *Central Asian Survey* 3 (3): 99–108.

Hopkirk, Peter. 1980. *Foreign Devils on the Silk Road: The Search for the Lost Cities and Treasures of Chinese Central Asia*. London: Murray.

Hoppe, Thomas. 1987. "An Essay on Reproduction: The Example of the Xinjiang Uighur Autonomous Region." In Bernhard Glaeser, ed., *Learning From China? Environment and Development in Third World Countries*, 54–84. Boston: Allen and Unwin.

——. 1987a. "Observations on Uyghur Land Use in Turpan County, Xinjiang—A Preliminary Report on Fieldwork in Summer, 1985." *Central Asiatic Journal* 31 (3–4): 224–51.

Huaqiao Ribao. 1989. "Sanqian Musilin Xuesheng Beijing Youxing Ti Yaoqiu Yancheng Xingfengsu Zuozhe" (3000 Beijing Muslim Students Protest, Request Severe Punishment of the Author of *Sexual Customs*). 13 May.

Huntington, Elsworth. 1907. "The Depression of Turpan." *Geographical Journal* 30:254–73.

Iminjan Ähmidi and Isma'il Tömüri, eds. 1988. *Abdukhaliq Uyghur wa Uning Ädibiyatimizdiki Orni (Abdukhaliq Uyghur and His Position in Our Literature)*. Urumchi: Xinjiang People's Publishing.

Israeli, Raphael. 1981. "The Muslim Minority in the People's Republic of China." *Asian Survey* 8:901–19.

Jackson, S. A. Douglas. 1962. *Russo-Chinese Borderlands*. New York: D. Van Nostrand.

Jarring, Gunnar. 1949–1951. *Materials to the Knowledge of Eastern Turki: Tales, Poetry, Proverbs, Riddles, Ethnological and Historical Texts from the Southern Parts of Eastern Turkestan*. 4 vols. Lund: C. W. K. Gleerup.

——. 1961. "A Note on Shamanism in Eastern Turkestan." *Ethnos* 26:1–4.

——. 1979. *Matters of Ethnological Interest in Swedish Missionary Reports from Southern Sinkiang*. Lund: Gleerup.

——. 1981. "The New Romanized Alphabet for Uighur and Kazakh and Some Observations on the Uighur Dialect of Kashgar." *Central Asiatic Journal* 25 (3–4): 230–45.

——. 1984–1986. "Ramazan Poetry from Charchan." *Orientalia Suecana* XXXIII–XXXV: 189–94.

——. 1986. *Return to Kashgar: Central Asian Memoirs in the Present*. Durham: Duke University Press.

——. 1987. *Dervish and Qalandar: Texts from Kashgar*. Stockholm: Almqvist and Wiksell.

——. 1991. *Prints From Kashgar: The Printing Office of the Swedish Mission in Eastern Turkestan*. Stockholm: Almqvist and Wiksell.

Jiang an. 1997. "Xinjiang a Danger Zone." *Singapore Straits Times (Financial Times Asia* Intelligence Wire). 29 March.

Jin Bingzhe. 1990. "Jiaqiang Shuangyu Xuexi Zengjia Minzu Tuanjie" (Strengthen Bilingual Education, Increase Unity of the Nationalities). *Xinjiang Shehui Kexue* 1:59–61.

Kanat, Ömer. 1986. "Comments on "The Identity and Nationality Problem in Chinese Central Asia." *Central Asian Survey* 5 (2): 113–19.

Karpat, Kemal H. 1979. "The Turkic Nationalities: Turkish-Soviet and Turkish-Chinese Relations." In William O. McCagg Jr. and Brian D. Silver, eds., *Soviet Asian Ethnic Frontiers*, 117–44. New York: Pergamon Press.

Khewir Tömür. 1987. *Baldur Oyghanghan Adäm*. Xinjiang Yashlar-Ösmürlar Press.

Kim, Ho-dong. 1986. "The Muslim Rebellion and the Kashgar Emirate in Chinese Central Asia, 1864–1877." Ph.D. dissertation, Harvard University, UMI.

Krader, Lawrence. 1971. *Peoples of Central Asia*. Bloomington: Indiana University Press.

Kuropatkin, A. N. 1882. *Kashgaria: Historical and Geological Sketch of the Country, Its Military Strength, Industries, and Trade*. Calcutta: Thacker, Spink and Co.

Lal, Amrit. 1970. "Sinification of Ethnic Minorities in China." *Current Scene* 8 (4): 4–25.

Landau, Jacob M. 1981. *Pan-Turkism in Turkey: A Study in Irredentism*. London: C. Hurst.

Lang Ying. 1986. "Shilun 'Fule Zhihui' Zhong de Fojiao Sixiang" (On the Buddhist Thought in Kutudgu Bilig). *Xinjiang Shehui Kexue* 1:84–88.

Lattimore, Owen. 1932. "Chinese Colonization in Inner Mongolia: Its History and Present Development." In *Pioneer Settlement*, American Geographical Society Special Publication No. 14, New York.

——. 1950. *Pivot of Asia*. Boston: Beacon Press.

——. 1975 [1930]. *High Tartary*. New York: AMS.

Laude-Cirtautus, Ilse. 1972. "On Pre-Islamic Rites Among Uzbeks." *Traditions religeiuse et para-religieuses des peuples Altaiques: Travaux du Centre d'etudes Surperieures specialise d'Histoire de Religions de Strasbourg*, 44–47. Strasbourg.

von Le Coq, Albert. 1985 [1928]. *Buried Treasures of Chinese Turkestan*. Oxford: Oxford University Press.

Legge, F. 1913. "Western Manichaeism and the Turfan Discoveries." *Journal of the Royal Asiatic Society*, 69–94.

Lewis, Bernard. 1975. *History—Remembered, Recovered, Invented*. Princeton: Princeton University Press.

Li Chang. 1954. "The Soviet Grip on Sinkiang." *Foreign Affairs* 32:491–503.

Li Kai. 1988. *Kashegeer Daoyou (Guide to Kashgar)*. Urumchi: Xinjiang People's Publishing.

Li Shangcheng, ed. 1983. *Yuguzu Jianshi (A Short History of the Yugur Nationality)*. Lanzhou: Gansu People's Publishing.

——, ed. 1984. *Gannan Yuguzu Zizhixian Gaikuang (A Survey of the Yugur Autonomous County in Southern Gansu)*. Lanzhou: Gansu People's Publishing.

Li Zhichao, et al. 1988. *Tulufan Putao (Turpan Grapes)*. Urumqi: Xinjiang People's Publishing.

Liao, Hollis S. 1989. "Ethnographic and Demographic Features of the Sinkiang Uighur Autonomous Region." *Issues and Studies* 25 (2): 125–39.

Lipman, Jonathan N. 1984. "Ethnicity and Politics in Republican China: The Ma Family Warlords of Gansu." *Modern China* 10 (3): 285–316.

——. 1987. "Hui-Hui, an Ethnohistory of the Chinese Speaking Muslims." *Journal of South Asian and Middle Eastern Studies* 9 (1–2): 112–30.

Liu Fajun, ed. 1980. *Weiwuer Minjian Gushi Xuan* (Selected Uyghur Folktales). Shanghai: Shanghai Wenyi Chubanshe.

Liu Zhixiao. 1985. *Weiwuer Lishi (Uyghur History Vol. 1)*. Beijing: Nationalities Press.

Lo, J. P. 1961. "Five Years of the Sinkiang Uighur Autonomous Region." *The China Quarterly* 8:92–104.

Lobacheva, N. P. 1967. "Wedding Rites in Uzbek SSR." *Central Asian Review* 15 (4): 290–99.

——. 1981. "Svadebnyi obriad kak istoriko-etnograficheskii istochnik na primere Khorezmskikh Uzbekov." *Sovetskaia Etnografia* 2:36–50.

——. 1981–1982. "Marriage Ritual as an Ethnographic Source for Historical Research (On the example of the Khorezm Uzbeks)." (English translation of "Svadebnyi obriad kak istoriko-etnograficheskii istochnik na primere Khorezmskikh Uzbekov.") *Soviet Anthropology and Archaeology* 20:31–58.

Löfstedt, Jan-Ingvar. 1987. "Education for National Minorities in China: An Overview." *Journal of Negro Education* 56 (3): 326–37.

Lop Nor Comprehensive Scientific Expedition Team (The Xinjiang Branch of the Chinese Academy of Sciences). 1985. *Shenmi de Luobubo (The Mysterious Lop Lake)*. Beijing: Science Press.

Lowenthal, David. 1975. *The Past Is a Foreign Country*. Cambridge: Cambridge University Press.

Lubin, Nancy. 1981. "Assimilation and Retention of Ethnic Identity in Uzbekistan." *Asian Affairs* 68:277–85.

Lukacs, Georg. 1983 [1962]. *The Historical Novel*. Lincoln: University of Nebraska Press.

Macartney, Jane. 1996. "China to build steel Great Wall against separatism." *Reuters News Service*, 4 June.

McKenna Jr., Francis Raymond. 1969. *Education for Elite Development in Soviet Uzbekistan*. Ann Arbor, Mich.: UMI.

Mackerras, Colin. 1969. "Sino-Uighur Diplomatic and Trade Contacts (744 to 840)." *Central Asiatic Journal* 13:215–40.

——. 1972. *The Uighur Empire: According to the T'ang Dynastic Histories*. Columbia: University of South Carolina Press.

——. 1990. "The Uighurs." In Denis Sinor, ed., *The Cambridge History of Early Inner Asia*, 335–42. New York: Cambridge University Press.

McMillen, Donald, H. 1979. *Chinese Communist Power and Policy in Xinjiang, 1949–77*. Boulder: Westview Press.

——. 1982. "The Urumqi Military Region: Defense and Security in China's West." *Asian Survey* 22 (8): 705–31.

——. 1984. "Xinjiang and Wang En Mao: New Directions in Power, Policy and Integration." *China Quarterly* 99:569–93.

Mähmutjan Abduqadir, ed. 1988. *Ipar Khan*. Kashgar: Kashgar Uyghur Publishers.

Mair, Victor. 1990. "Turfan and Tulufan: The Origins of the Old Chinese Names for Tibet and Turfan." *Central and Inner Asian Studies* 4:14–70.

Malov, S. E. 1967. *Yazik Zholtix Uigurov (The Language of the Yellow Uyghurs)*. Moscow: Nauk.

Män Junggoluq (I am a [pan-PRC] Chinese). 1989. Urumchi: Xinjiang Youth Press.

Mannerheim, C. G. E. 1911. "A Visit to the Sarö" and "Shera Yögurs." *Journal de la Societe finna-ougrienne* 27 (2): 3–67.

——. 1969 [1942]. *Across Asia: From West to East in 1906–1908*. The Netherlands: Anthropological Publications.

Masud, Muhammad Khalid. 1990. "The Obligation to Migrate: The Doctrine of Hajira in Islamic Law." In Dale F. Eikelman and James Piscatori, eds., *Muslim Travellers: Pilgrimage, Migration, and the Religious Imagination*, 29–49. Berkeley: University of California Press.

Medlin, William K. 1971. *Education and Development in Central Asia: A Case Study on Social Change in Uzbekistan*. Leiden: E. J. Brill.

Meillassoux, Claude. 1981. *Maidens, Meal and Money*. New York: Cambridge University Press.

Meng Fanren. 1982. "Luelun Gaochang Huihu de Fojiao," (A Brief Discussion of the Buddhism of the Gaochang Uyghurs). *Xinjiang Shehui Kexue* 1:58–74.

Meng Kehuang, Yang Chengshi. 1980. "Tulufan Pendi Zhuzai Putao Jianjie" (A Survey of Grape Varieties Planted in the Turpan Depression). *Xinjiang Nongye Kexue* 1:36–38.

Menges, Karl H. 1991. "Manichaeismus, Christentum und Buddhismus in Zentralasien und ihr gegenseitiges verhältnis." *Central Asiatic Journal* 35 (1–2): 81–95.

Millward, James A. 1994. "A Uyghur Muslim in Qianlong's Court: The Meanings of the Fragrant Concubine." *The Journal of Asian Studies* 53 (2): 427–58.

Mingulov, N. N. 1963. "The Uprising in North-west Sinkiang 1944–1949." *Central Asian Review* 11 (2): 181–95.

Minzu Tuanjie. 1982. "Interview with Wang Enmao." (Sept.): 7–9.

Molla Mirsali Qäshqäri. 1985. *Jingizkhan.* Kashgar: Kashgar Uyghur Language Publishing.

Morden, William. 1927. *Across Asia's Snows and Deserts.* New York: Putnam.

Moseley, George. 1966. *Sino-Soviet Cultural Frontier: The Ili Kazakh Autonomous Zhou.* Cambridge: Harvard.

Naby, Eden. 1987. "Political and Cultural Forces Among the Uighurs: The Struggle for Change—1930's." *The Asian American Review* 5 (2): 98–111.

Narinbaev, Aziz. 1991. *Pod Nebom Kirgizstana (Under the Kyrgyzstan Sky).* Frunze (Bishkek).

Newsweek (International Edition). 1990. "The Other China." 23 April.

van Nienwenhuijze, C. A. O. 1969. "The Umah—An Analytic Approach." *Studia Islamica* 10:5–22.

Nyman, Lars Erik. 1976. "Turkish Influence on the Islamic Republic of Eastern Turkestan (TIRET)." *Materiala Turcica* 2:12–24.

——. 1977. *Great Britain and Japanese Interests in Sinkiang 1918–1934.* (Lund Studies in International History 8). Malmö: Scandinavian University Books.

Oda, Juten. 1978. "Uighuristan." *Acta Asiatica* 34:22–45.

Päkhridin, T. 1979. *Näsridin Äpändi Lätipiliri* (Jokes of Nasruddin Khoja). Urumchi: Xinjiang People's Publishers.

Paksoy, H. B. 1989. *Alpamysh: Central Asian Identity Under Russian Rule.* Hartford, Conn.: Association for the Advancement of Central Asian Research.

Pevtsov, M. V. 1982. "An Ethnographic Sketch of Kashgaria." *Journal of Steward Anthropological Society* 12.

Pillsbury, Barbara. 1984. "Hui." In R. V. Weeks, ed., *Muslim Peoples: A World Ethnographic Survey, Vol. 1,* 332–39. Westport, Conn.: Greenwood Press.

Piscatori, James. 1986. *Islam in a World of Nation States.* Cambridge: Cambridge University Press.

Prejevalsky, N. 1879. *From Kulja Across the Tianshan to Lob-Nor.* London.: S. Low, Marston, Searle, and Rivington.

Pritsak, Omeljan. 1951–53. "Mahmud Kaşgari Kimdir?" *Türkiyat Mecinuasi* 10:243–46.

——. 1959. "Das Neuuigurische." In Jean Deny et al., eds., *Philologiae Turcicae Fundamenta, Vol. 1,* 525–63. Wiesbaden: Franz Steiner Verlag.

Pye, Lucian W. 1975. "China: Ethnic Minorities and National Security." In Nathan Glazer and Daniel P. Moynihan, *Ethnicity: Theory and Experience,* 489–512. Cambridge: Harvard University Press.

Radlov, Vilhelm. 1893. *K voprocu ob uigurax.* St. Petersburg: n.p.

Raquette, Gustav. 1927. *English-Turki Dictionary: Based on the Dialects of Kashgar and Yarkand.* Lund University Papers 23(4).

Reed III, Lawrence C. 1978. "The Role of the People's Liberation Army in the Expansion and Developent of Agriculture in Sinkiang 1949–1965." *China Geographer* 10:13–28.

Renmin Ribao (Haiwai Ban). 1990. "Guanyu 1990 nian renkou pucha zhuyao shuju de gongbao" (Pertaining to the Important Figures from the 1990 Census Report). 14 November: 4.

Rewäydula. 1982. "Mantan Weiwuerzu Renming" (A discussion of Uyghur names). *Zhongyang Minzu Xueyuan Xuebao* 3:121–29.

Rhodes, Robert I., ed. 1970. *Imperialism and Underdevelopment.* New York: Monthly Review Press.

Rorlich, Azande-Ayse. 1983. "Acculturation in Tatarstan: The Case of the Sabantui Festival." *Slavic Review* 41 (2): 316–21.

Rossabi, Morris. 1972. "Ming China and Turfan, 1406–1517." *Central Asiatic Journal* 16:206–25.

Roux, Jean Paul. 1963. *La mort chez les peuples altaiques anciens et medievaux d'apres les documents ecrits.* Paris: Maisonneuve.

Rudelson, Justin Jon. 1988. "Uighur Ethnic Identity Change in the Oases of Chinese Turkestan." Unpublished Master's thesis, Harvard University.

———. 1991. "Uighur Historiography and Uighur Ethnic Identity Change." In Ingvar Svanberg, ed., *Ethnicity, Minorities and Cultural Encounters*, 63–82. Uppsala: Center for Multiethnic Research (Multiethnic Papers 25).

———. 1992. *Bones in the Sand: The Struggle to Create Uighur Nationalist Ideology and Ethnic Identity in Xinjiang, China.* Ph.D. dissertation, Harvard University.

———. 1993. "The Uighurs in the Future of Central Asia." *Central Asia Monitor* 6:16–25.

———. 1994. "Changing Patterns of Ethnic Identity in Xinjiang." In *Xinjiang and the Twentieth Century: Historical, Anthropological, and Geographical Perspectives,* Occasional Paper (65) of The Woodrow Wilson Center, Asia Program, 14–17.

———. 1996. "The Xinjiang Mummies and Foreign Angels: Art, Archaeology, and Uyghur Muslim Nationalism in Chinese Central Asia." *Toronto Studies in Central and Inner Asia* 2:168–83.

Rywkin, Michael. 1982. *Moscow's Muslim Challenge.* New York: M. E. Sharpe.

Sadri, Roostam. 1984. "The Islamic Republic of Eastern Turkestan: A Commerative Review." *Journal of the Institute of Muslim Minority Affairs* 5 (2): 294–319.

Saguchi, Toru. 1968. "The revival of the White Mountain Khwajas 1760–1820." *Acta Asiatica* (Bulletin of the Institute of Eastern Culture) 14:7–20.

———. 1978. "Kashgaria." *Acta Asiatica* 34:61–78.

Samolin, W. 1957–1958. "Ethnographic Aspects of the Archaeology of the Tarim Basin." *Central Asiatic Journal* 3–4:45–67.

Säypidin Äzizi. 1987. *Sutuq Bughra Khan.* Beijing: Nationalities Press.

Schmetzer, Uli. 1990. "China's Ethnic Turks May Wage Holy War." *Chicago Tribune.* 23 April: C7.

Schomberg, R. C. F. 1928. "The Aridity of the Turfan Area." *Geographical Journal* 72:357–59.

———. 1928a. "The Turfan Depression." *Journal of the Royal Central Asian Society* 15:301–4.

Schuyler, Eugene. 1966 [1877]. *Turkistan.* 2 vols. New York: Scribner, Armstrong and Co.

Schwartz, Ronald D. 1994. *Circle of Protest: Political Ritual in the Tibetan Uprising.* New York: Columbia University Press.

Schwarz, Henry G. 1976. "The Khwajas of Eastern Turkestan." *Central Asiatic Journal* 20 (4): 266–96.

Sharma, Triloki Nath. 1989. "Marriage and Marriage Ceremonies Among the Hui Muslims of China." *Nordic Institute of Asian Studies Report*, 139–61.

Singer, Andre. 1984. "Nationality Policy in Xinjiang." *Central Asian Survey* 3 (1): 133–39.

Skrine, C. P. 1926. *Chinese Central Asia*. Boston: Houghton Mifflin.

—— and P. Nightingale. 1973. *Macartney at Kashgar: New Light on British and Russian Activities in Sinkiang, 1890–1918*. London: Metheun.

Smith, Grace Martin. 1980. "The Özbek Tekkes of Istanbul." *Der Islam* 57 (1): 130–39.

Snesarev, G. P. 1970–1973. "Remnants of Pre-Islamic Beliefs and Rituals Among the Khorezm Uzbeks." *Soviet Anthropology and Archaeology* 9 (3) (1970–1971): 204–25; 9 (4) (1971): 29–352; 11 (3) (1972–1973): 219–53.

Spalek, John. 1972. *Lion Feuchtwanger: The Man, His Ideas, His Work*. Los Angeles: Hennessey and Ingalls.

Stein, M. Aurel. 1933. "Note on a Map of the Turfan Basin." *Geographical Journal* 82:236–46.

Svanberg, Ingvar. 1987. "The Loplyks: A Vanishing Fishing and Gathering Culture in Xinjiang." *Svenska Forskningsinstitutet i Istanbul* 12: 57–81.

Svanberg, Ingvar. 1988. "The Russians in China." In Ingvar Svanberg and Matias Tyden, eds., *Multiethnic Studies in Uppsala: Essays Presented in Honour of Sven Gustavson, June 1, 1988*, 97–111. Uppsala: Uppsala Multiethnic Papers 13.

——. 1989. "The Dolans of Xinjiang." Paper presented at the conference "The Legacy of Islam in China," Harvard University, 14–16 April.

——. 1989a. *Kazakh Refugees in Turkey: A Study of Cultural Persistence and Social Change*. Uppsala: Almquist and Wiksell International.

——. 1989b. "Marginal Groups and Itinerants." In Peter Alford Andrews, ed., *Ethnic Groups in the Republic of Turkey*, 602–12. Wiesbaden: Wilhelm Reichert Verlag.

——. 1989c. "Turkistani Refugees." In Peter Alford Andrews, ed., *Ethnic Groups in the Republic of Turkey*, 591–601. Weisbaden: Wilhelm Reichert Verlag.

——. 1996. "Ethnic Categorizations and Cultural Diversity in Xinjiang: The Dolans Along Yarkand River." *Central Asiatic Journal* 40 (2): 260–82.

—— and Linda Benson. 1989. "The Russians in Xinjiang: From Immigrants to National Minority." *Central Asian Survey* 8 (2): 97–129.

Terzani, Tiziano. 1985. *The Forbidden Door*. Hong Kong: Asia 2000 Ltd.

Turghun Almas. 1990. *Uyghurlar* (*The Uyghurs*). Urumchi: Xinjiang Youth Publishers.

Verdery, Katherine. 1990. "The Production and Defense of the Romanian Nation, 1900 to World War II." In Richard G. Fox, ed., *Nationalist Ideologies and the Production of National Cultures* (American Ethnological Society Monograph Series, No. 2), 1–14. Washington, D.C.: American Anthropological Association.

——. 1991. *National Ideology Under Socialism: Identity and Cultural Politics in Ceauşescu's Romania*. Berkeley: University of California Press.

Vilkuna, Kustaa. 1969. "Mannerheim's Collection of Sart Specimens." In C. G. Mannerheim, ed., *Across Asia*, vol. 2, 116–50. The Netherlands: Anthropological Publishers.

Waardenburg, Jacques. 1990. "The Persistence of Islam in Central Asia." *Temesos* 26:139–57.

Wiens, Harold J. 1963. "The Historical and Geographical Role of Urumchi, Capital of Chinese Central Asia," *Annals of the Association of American Geographers* 53 (4): 441–64.

——. 1966. "Cultivation Development and Expansion in China's Colonial Realm in Central Asia." *Journal of Asian Studies* 26 (1): 67–88.

——. 1969. "The Ili Valley as a Geographic Region of Hsin-chiang (Xinjiang)." *Current Scene* 7 (15): 1–19.

Winters, Clyde Ahmad. 1985. "Islam and Birth Control in Muslim Minority Areas of China." *Asian Thought and Society* 10 (30): 179–85.

Wu, Aitchen K. 1944. "The Fourteen Peoples of Chinese Turkistan." *Journal of the West China Border Research Society* 15 (4): 83–93.

Xia Xuncheng and Hu Wenkang. 1978. *Tulufan Pendi.* Urumchi: Xinjiang People's Publishing.

Xinjiang Shengchan Jianshe Bingtuan and Tongji Nianjian Bianji Weiyuanhui, eds. 1993. *Xinjiang Shengchan Jianshe Bingtuan Tongji Nianjian (Statistical Yearbook of the Xinjiang Production and Construction Corps).* Urumchi: Zhongguo Tongji Chubanshe.

Xinjiang University Chinese Language Department. 1982. *Uyghurchä-Khanzuchä Lughät (Uyghur-Han Dictionary).* Urumchi: Xinjiang People's Publishing.

Xinjiang Weiwuer Zizhiqu Tongjiju, ed. 1992. *Xinjiang Tongji Nianjian (Statistical Yearbook of Xinjiang).* Urumchi: Zhongguo Tongji Chubanshe.

Yang Chengshi, Bo Yulin, and Yang Guizhen. 1979. "Putao Zhiguan Youliang Pinzhong Jieshao" (An Introduction to Superior Varieties of Grapes). *Xinjiang Nongye Kexue* 4:20–23.

Yuan, Tsing. 1961. "Yakub Beg (1820–1877) and the Moslem Rebellion in Chinese Turkestan." *Central Asiatic Journal* 6 (2): 134–67.

Yuan, Qing-Li. 1990. "Population Changes in the Xinjiang Uighur Autonomous Region (1949–1984)." *Central Asian Survey* 9 (1): 49–73.

Yusuf Khass Hajib Balasagun. 1983. *Wisdom of Royal Glory (Kutudgu Bilig): A Turko-Islamic Mirror for Princes.* Trans. Robert Dankoff. Chicago: University of Chicago Press.

el-Zein, Abdul Hamid. 1977. "Beyond Ideology and Theology: The Search for an Anthropology of Islam." *Annual Review of Anthropology* 6:227–54.

Zhang Hengde, ed. 1983. *Xinjiang Weiwuer Minjian Huamao Tuanji (A Collection of the Xinjiang Uighur Folk Cap Designs).* Urumchi: Xinjiang People's Publishing.

Zhao Shijie. 1981. *Weiyu Goucifa (Uyghur Sentence Construction).* Urumchi: Xinjiang People's Publishing.

Zhongguo Minzu Renkou Ziliao: Renkou Pucha Shujiao. 1990. Beijing: Statistical Publishing.

Zhou, Lisan. 1948. "Hami: A Typical Oasis." *Dili* 6(1).

Zordun Sabir. 1983. "Putaogou Jishi" (An Incident in Grape Valley). *Xinjiang Minzu Wenxue* 3:4–38.

Index

If you don't rescue *yourselves*
From this death,
Your situation will become very grave.
—"Uyghur," "Awaken! (*Oyghan*)" (emphasis mine)